Sally Butcher

*The New*
# Middle Eastern
# Vegetarian

*Modern Recipes from Veggiestan*

INTERLINK BOOKS
an imprint of Interlink Publishing Group, Inc.

# contents

introduction

Veggiestan, or "land of the vegetables"—there is, of course, no such word, and no such country, but to my mind the Middle East more than merits the name. The region's constituent nations are simmering, bubbling, and bursting with sumptuous vegetarian traditions and recipes.

When I was writing my previous book, *Persia in Peckham*, the temptation to stray and explore other parts of the Middle East was pretty compelling. You see, I am an omnivore, but I don't like meat very much. In fact, I have a better relationship with vegetables than I do with a lot of people. This book is born of that passion.

It is also born of an awareness that our markets and delis are filling up with strange-but-delightful foods that we often avoid and that sometimes scare us. Alien squash, sour cherries, okra, taro, any number of strange herbs and spices; this is the stuff that goes into the dishes that feed our changing population. And I'm not just talking changing demographics; the indigenous population is shifting towards a more enlightened and healthier diet.

Even vegetables that we thought we knew pretty well—Mr. Bean, Mrs. Turnip, Miss Beet—will, with a twist of Middle Eastern expertise, change before our very eyes, like a neighbor finding her naughty, inner floozy. OK, so we've all tried ratatouille and moussaka, but the eggplant (and its sidekick the zucchini) is bursting with more potential than an American Idol finalist; pumpkin is far too much fun to be the preserve of October ghouls; and most of us have little knowledge of other squashes.

Fragrant spices, aromatic herbs, beans, and grains beckon. When I was knee-high to a soybean, being a vegetarian meant tofu and always having to say you're sorry. But in the capable hands of a Middle Eastern cook, stalwarts such as the trusty but much maligned lentil reach new pinnacles of tastebud titillation. Or what about barley: slow-cooked, risotto-style, dotted with fresh cilantro, crunchy pine nuts, saffrony raisins? This is not the same humble grain that we bury in soups, surely?

I would like to think that, armed with this tome, you will be able to boldly go to the aisles and stores that you have never been to before and seek out new vegetables, weird ingredients, and strange fruits. And cook them.

What have I personally discovered? I already knew that hummus is not the only career option for a self-respecting chickpea. And I already had a few winning Persian ways with vegetables in my repertoire. But I have learned what a sensible, backseat place meat occupies in Middle Eastern cuisine: it is not the main event, but rather a luxury, and in many cases an optional extra.

VEGETABLES IN THE MIDDLE EAST
I have begun to embrace simplicity. Vegetables in the West have had to endure centuries of over-complication and over-cooking. The day that my Iranian mother-in-law took me to task over broccoli stems remains stuck in my mind: I was about to lob them in the trash, as you do, when she pointed out that I was actually jettisoning the best bits. She peeled the broccoli so that the white core was revealed, sprinkled it with some salt, and offered it to me to, um, prove her point.

My first time with *ful medames* (p.115) was similarly revelatory. A bitterly cold Ramadan day a number of years ago saw us trying to assemble a pallet of pickles in a windswept cul-de-sac somewhere exotic like Hayes (a suburb of London). The storekeeper to whom we were delivering was a man of few words and little inclination to pay, but he had the natural courtesy of the Arab nations, and as his staff were about to break fast, he indicated that we should join them. Upturned olive cans became improvised seats, and out came sweet tea, dates, bread, cheese, and a huge vat of unprepossessing sludgy brown beans. No sauce, no nothing. Just a pot of salt and some lemon wedges by way of accompaniment. A nervous first prod with a broken plastic spoon took me straight to bean heaven. Me and fava beans have been intimate ever since.

You see, Middle Easterners seem to have a clearer idea of what is best for a vegetable, and the tastiest way to prepare it while retaining its innate goodness.

NEW FOODS BROUGHT BY TRADERS
The climate of the fertile crescent and the "-istans" stretching across towards India is famously suited to the cultivation of just about anything, even when the terrain is unfriendly. The position of Mesopotamia (now mostly Iraq) as the "cradle of civilization," and the fact that the region is at the crossroads of the routes of a myriad of traders between the East and West, has meant that the Middle East has always been in the "middle" of stuff, perfectly placed to grasp new foods, methods, and cultural elements from passers-through. So ingredients there are aplenty.

This mingling of traders and blurring of borders has meant that, in terms of food, it is at times irrelevant to differentiate between some of the Arab nations. Many of the recipes I have featured are for generic Middle Eastern dishes, the precise origins of which have long been buried in the shifting sands that comprise the region.

THE GEOGRAPHY OF THE MIDDLE EAST
The Middle East is something of a geographic amoeba, shape-shifting with the tides of history and indeed in the eye of the beholder. Does it include Turkey, which is also part of Europe? What to do about Morocco, which is mostly populated by Arabs, but is no more easterly than Doncaster, England?

The Iranians use the loose term "Arabistan" to denote any of the Arab countries; it's a nice word and one that I will happily use here. The term "Arab" refers to the people whose spoken language is Arabic. When Islam came along, it spread its culture and the word of Allah far beyond the Arab world. The Indo-Iranian tribes, which ranged from India through to Kurdistan, and Turkic-speaking people, from Turkey through Azerbaijan to Uzbekistan, had strong cultural identities of their own, and so although most of them embraced Islam, they resisted total conquest and retained their own languages and social structures. This means that you shouldn't call them Arabs, or they will be upset.

Regardless of their origins, Middle Eastern people are generally "in touch with their roots" (the worst clichés are often used in the culinary sphere), and so the real properties of food, its medicinal values, and foodie anecdotes are kept alive around the dinner table and passed from mother to daughter. Middle Easterners live their food: it is part of their day-to-day existence, not a function of it. And the family meal is non-negotiable. As such, it is a pleasurable and relatively easy task to capture the region on paper.

## A VEG-SPECTIVE

OK, so I am not a card-carrying, full-time vegetarian. I have a terrible weakness for chorizo. And I eat my (very occasional) steaks blue. But I truly prefer vegetables. And I am not alone; there are hordes of "new (part-time) vegetarians" out there.

I first realized this on my annual girlie vacation. I am lucky enough still to be buddies with a number of former school friends, and we go away together for one weekend a year. While discussing catering arrangements, it became clear that none of us wanted meat. This has little to do with girlie-ness, and everything to do with a gradual national shift towards a healthier lifestyle.

It is easier to lead a meat-free existence than ever before: more and more food manufacturers are telling us exactly what is in their food; more and more vegetarian and vegan options appear on grocery store shelves each year. And we have more time to dwell on gastronomy. Creating a veggie dish is easy, but to a veggie lover who still has a learner's permit, creating a complete vegetarian meal can be challenging. It's a bit like a room with no windows, or without a fireplace (or a TV): the focus of the meal shifts, and rather than the emphasis being on one component, each ingredient becomes something

to savor. When you realize that you are no longer slave to one focal foodstuff, a degree of liberation sets in, which I can only compare to going out for the day without my handbag. (Gents, you'll just have to take my word for this.)

## MUSLIMS AND DIET

By the way, I empathize with the needs of the real vegetarian more than you might realize: not only did I cook food for a living before starting to import it and write about it, but I still cater in various ways for a number of practicing Muslims. The connection between Muslim and veggie is not obvious; let me explain.

Muslims, to summarize what is a very complex set of dietary guidelines, eat only food that is regarded as "*halal*." Mostly this refers to animal products, and the method of slaughter and preparation. Animals that are deemed fit for consumption are given a drink of water, made to face Mecca, and then have their throats cut: this is considered to be the most painless and humane method of slaughter. There are many foods that are simply "*haram*" (which translates as "forbidden" and can refer to behavior as well as food): pork and alcohol are the obvious ones, but lots of types of seafood are also regarded as unclean, and, for some, food that is prepared by a non-believer is automatically *haram*.

But the fact is, Muslims now living where *halal* meat/food is not always readily available face the same shopping dilemmas as vegetarians. If it doesn't say "vegetarian," every set of ingredients needs to be scanned; if it's got cheese, the cheese must be free of animal rennet;

if it contains fats, they must be non-animal fats; it must not contain any strange fish-derived extracts. And even if it has vegetarian accreditation, the Muslim has to beware of any alcohol or its derivatives that have crept into the recipe. Eating out presents similar predicaments.

THE MIDDLE EASTERN DINING EXPERIENCE
Middle Easterners generally enjoy their food and the daily rituals of its preparation and consumption.

Of course, the region has its share of stressed executives and working parents. Microwaves and fast food outlets abound. Not everything is tinted with the rosy glow of yester-millennia, nor is every homemaker a squeaky clean parragon of efficiency and domesticity.

But mealtimes are important, and the business of sharing food is, I believe, one of the pillars of "Veggiestan" society (as well as one of the Five Pillars of Islam). In *Shi'ia* countries, food is even used as a way of commemorating the dead: when food is prepared or purchased and shared out in the name of a departed loved one, it is believed you are promoting the interests of that person in the afterlife. Not only is sharing food with one's family a sacrosanct part of the day, it is also regarded as a matter of civic and personal duty to ensure that no one else goes without. In times of yore, beggars and wandering dervishes would gather at the door of wealthier households to collect any donated scraps: this practice may have died out, but on high days and holidays the wealthy will still host parties for the less well-off in their neighborhood, or send food out for them.

Food constitutes one of the main allegories in Middle Eastern literature, and the theme of sharing is mentioned repeatedly in the Koran. Thus: *"The perfect Muslim is not a perfect Muslim, who eats 'til he is full and leaves his neighbors hungry."*

The main meal of the day in the Middle East would traditionally have been at lunchtime, and this remains the case in many outlying areas. This reflects a different, slower way of life, and a different, warmer climate: what better than a post-prandial siesta when the overhead sun renders it too hot outside to work? But in practice now, most Middle Easterners lead a more modern existence: they work all day, take a light lunch, and eat a bigger meal in the evening. That is not to say that any less thought or love goes into making food: it is not unusual for the women of the house to spend hours preparing dinner, and my mother-in-law often dedicates a whole day to cooking "fridge food," dishes that are just there, ready for unexpected guests or super-hungry offspring.

What sets "Veggiestanis," or Middle Easterners, apart is the manner of eating. The business of a quick bite in front of the TV, or the family eating in shifts as suits their respective routines, would simply not be acceptable (although the TV, per se, can be a part of the evening meal, turned up so that it can be heard above the chatter). The family always eats together, and while that wonder of Roman engineering, the dining table, has reached the shores of Arabistan, dinner is often spread out on a cloth on the floor in some households. This induces an intimacy that is hard to achieve around a table, and of course, floor-dining is a great leveler. Banter, laughter, gossip, scandal, debate, teasing, reminiscing: all of these are to be found in the course of one dinner time. This is how youngsters learn: how to behave, how to discourse, the history of their own family, and the verbal lore of their land (and this is also how I learned to speak Persian). And it is over dinner that the stresses of the day are diffused, differences resolved, and future challenges set.

In most of Veggiestan, men and women eat together but in the further corners thereof— Yemen, parts of Saudi Arabia—women still eat apart from and after their menfolk. (Visiting Western women are customarily given honorary male status so that they may join in as guests at dinner parties.) The most disconcerting dinner habit I have found during my bumbling encounters with Veggiestan culture is that of watching guests eat: one arrives and is served a sumptuous array of the resident cook's house specialties while the entire family looks on. More often than not they will join in once you are well and truly digging in, but sometimes the repast is just for you, and you know that refusal is not an option. It is not for the shy or those naturally prone to drooling when they get excited.

Traditionally, meals were eaten with the hands (always the right hand after the advent of Islam), using bread to mop up. In practice now, most people use silverware. Platters of food are invariably brought to the cloth to be shared, and there will always be more than enough to go around. Typically there will be rice, bread, and some sort of sauce or casserole. And there will be salad, yogurt, and pickles. There may in addition be a range of *mezze* items: dips, eggy dishes, stuff wrapped in pastry, or *dolmeh*. It is, you will note, perfectly suited to vegetarian dining. There will be lots of carbonated drinks (which in Iran at least are rather tellingly known by their color—yellow, black, or white are the norms), and maybe some sherbets or diluted fruit syrup. If the weather is hot, you may be offered *ayran* (see p.64), or non-alcholic beer.

If you are a guest in a Middle Eastern house, it is hard to get the balance right between eating enough, so as not to offend, and eating so much that they think you're a (*halal* alternative to a) pig. A sense of humor will help.

At the end of a meal, women withdraw to the kitchen to wash up and gossip (oh-my-goodness, do they like to gossip, no punches pulled), quite often to smoke (which they won't always readily do in front of their husbands or elder relatives), and generally to be girls. The men are left to carry on watching the television, smoke, play *tavoli/tahkteh* (backgammon), and, well, to be boys.

Desserts are rarely eaten, but fruit and tea are popular closers to a meal.

A word of warning: it is a common hospitable gesture for a host to insist that his guests stay the night, so either take your toothbrush or be ready with a good excuse …

bread and pastry

*Mullah Nasruddin had been accused of heresy by the king's advisers, and was thus dragged to court to learn his fate.*

*The king asked the Mullah if he had anything to say in his defense. Nasruddin took a step towards his accusers, and addressed them. "O wise ones, what is bread?"*

*Bemused and amused, the first one answered, "Why, it is a foodstuff, the basis of a meal."*

*The second replied, "Well, to be pedantic about this, it is a compound of yeast and flour and water … "*

*"Oh no," cried the third, "It should in the first place be regarded as a gift, the provenance of God."*

*Allowing himself only the smallest smile, the Mullah turned to the king. "So these men are the wisest in your kingdom? You see—they cannot even agree on something as simple as the definition of bread. How is it that they can be unanimous that I am a heretic?"*

The unwise men are right in some ways, though; there are many definitions of bread in the Middle East.

Bread is quite the carbohydrate of choice across the region, the first element of any meal. We are, of course, not talking sliced, packaged stuff to slather with butter; we're talking flat or slightly leavened bread to rip and dip and dunk.

It is impossible to underestimate its significance either as a food or as a symbol: pick pretty much any religion, and you will find that bread is regarded as a gift from God. Muslims regard it as *haram* (forbidden) to throw bread away, and go to great lengths to ensure that it is treated and enjoyed with reverence. If I get my store ordering all wrong (it happens)—well, suffice it to say that the local starlings are very fond of me; this business of "waste not, want not" rubs off.

There are, in fact, an admirable number of ways of using "mature" bread in Middle Eastern cuisine—try baking more or less anything on top of some stale bread, or using crumbled, soaked bread to thicken sauces and dips. Or make it into croûtons for soups and salads, with or without spice: flatbread is especially good for this purpose, as it crisps quickly without absorbing too much oil. Pita bread nachos are useful as well: just toast some unloved looking pita, chop it into nacho shapes and then fry it. Or … you can use it to keep the tigers out (see p.33).

Traditionally, throughout the Middle East housewives would take their loaves along to be baked in a communal village oven. In practice now, at least in the cities, bread is instead bought on a daily (sometimes hourly) basis from the corner bakery.

I've included pastry in this chapter because the Turkish and Arabic take on pastry is really rather bread-like.

As baking is my culinary Achilles Heel (actually, I am just lazy), I am in this context extremely thankful that I am a storekeeper: we have six bakers supplying my store, Persepolis, and I have been able to pick their brains and lift their oh-so-secret recipes.

## PERSIAN BREAD

The most common form of Persian bread is *lavash*, which is wafer-thin. You may have tried it in Iranian restaurants—it is cooked on the walls of a *tanoor* oven, and comes in enormous sheets. It is available in Middle Eastern supermarkets, where you can quite often buy it slightly undercooked (which means it will keep a bit longer). Sometimes it is made a bit thicker and dotted with sesame or nigella seeds—it is then known as *taftoon*.

I have to confess that after 15 years of eating Persian food I still cannot embrace *lavash* as my daily loaf—it's rather like cardboard. So I have omitted the recipe for it, offering instead a recipe for *naan–e–sangak* (stone-baked bread).

# *Naan–e–Sangak*
## STONE-BAKED WHOLE-WHEAT BREAD

This is really the showpiece of the Iranian bread world; it has a strong nutty flavor and a chewy texture. It is not too difficult to recreate the stone-baked thing at home; you just need to find a selection of fairly evenly sized, smooth pebbles. These will need washing thoroughly, and then oiling before use. You will also need the mother of all baking trays (strong enough to bear half a beach, at least).

**MAKES 3 SHEETS**

1 teaspoon active dry yeast
scant ½ cup/3½fl oz/100ml lukewarm water
2 ⅔ cups/12oz/350g whole-wheat flour
generous ⅔ cup/4oz/110g white bread flour
1 level teaspoon salt
some cold water

Sprinkle the yeast on to the warm water and allow it to sit for about 15 minutes. After this time, pour it into a big basin. Sift together the flours and salt, then add to the yeast, mixing all the while, and blend in enough cold water to make it all hang together. Knead with vigor—the mixture should start to come away from your mixing bowl and feel quite rubbery. Cover the bowl with a clean damp cloth and leave it to stand for 3 hours; then knead it again and let it sit for 1 hour more.

Preheat the oven and your tray of pebbles to 475°F/240°C. Divide the dough mixture in two and stretch and pummel it into submission as two flattish, squareish sheets. Oiling or flouring your hands before working with the dough should make it easier.

Cook the sheets one at a time, resting each sheet over the pebbles; after 3½ minutes, turn each one over, and bake for a further 3½ minutes. When the bread is cooked, it should be a rich brown color and lift easily from the pebbles. This bread is best consumed warm. Reheat by sprinkling it with water and then pop it in a really hot oven for 30 seconds.

# Piroshki

## PERSIAN PIROSHKI

OK, I know what you are thinking. *Piroshki* are Russian pie things. And you're right. But like a lot of things across that vastness that is Asia, they traveled, and thus Iranians came to love them. With a childlike passion. They are up there with *poofak* (sinisterly yellow chips) and PK (chewing gum) on the nostalgia charts. Yes, it is rather funny that they get homesick for a foodstuff that is actually foreign, but no stranger than an American college freshman who misses his mother's lasagna, for instance. In Iran *Piroshki* are either filled with ground lamb, cheese, or custard.

They are a great snack hot or cold, and for that reason make a good lunch-box/picnic filler.

SERVES 6–8

1 x ¼oz/7g envelope active dry yeast

1 teaspoon sugar

scant ½ cup/3½fl oz/100ml warm water

3 ⅓ cups/1lb 2oz/500g all-purpose flour

1 teaspoon salt

3 eggs

generous ¾ cup/7fl oz/200ml milk

generous 1 cup/2 sticks/125g melted butter

FOR THE FILLING:

3–4 sticks celery

1¼ cups/10½oz/300g cottage cheese

1 cup/3½oz/100g walnuts, chopped

generous ⅔ cup/3½oz/100g green olives,
    preferably stuffed with sliced
    pimento (optional)

1 egg yolk

salt and black pepper

Sprinkle the yeast and the sugar on to the water in a bowl, swirl to mix and set aside for 15 minutes, or until you get a reaction.

Sift the flour and salt into a bowl and make a well in the middle. Beat the eggs, milk, and butter together and trickle the mixture into the flour along with the yeast. Mix with a wooden spoon, and then with your hands—it should all come together into one large ball. Cover the mixing bowl with a damp cloth, and let the dough proof for 2 hours.

In the meantime, make the filling: wash and chop the celery, and mix it with the cheese, walnuts, olives, egg yolk, and a little salt and pepper.

Once the dough has doubled in size, knead it some more, and then break off a walnut-sized lump. Roll this out into a 3½in (9cm) disc, and then spoon a little of the filling on to each. Fold the disc across so that you end with a half-moon shape, pinch and crimp the edges so that the filling is sealed within a pocket, and then repeat with the rest of the dough. Alternatively, roll out all the dough and use a pastry cutter. Place the uncooked *piroshki* on a lightly floured board, and cover with a cloth to rise for 20–30 minutes more.

You can bake them—35 minutes at 375°F/190°C but they are much nicer deep-fried. Fry a few at a time until golden brown, and set to cool on paper towels. *Piroshki* keep for around three days in the fridge, and freeze beautifully.

# Khobez

## ARABIC BREAD

*Khobez*, or *khubz*, is the most common Arabic word for bread. It is also known as *aish* (in Egypt), and *samoon* (in Iraq). It comes in different shapes and thicknesses (make it small and ovoid and you've got pita bread), but it is fundamentally the same recipe/principle: soft dough, which, when toasted, puffs up to form a really neat pocket. It is readily available, but I have included the recipe because it is such an important part of Arabic daily life.

I incorporate *za'atar* (see p.98) into the dough, which is not authentic but is very tasty. In the Arab lands *za'atar* and olive oil are either sprinkled on top of the bread before baking to make *mana'eesh*, or the bread is dipped in oil and *za'atar* as it is eaten.

FEEDS A FAMILY FOR A DAY
¼oz/7g active dry yeast
scant ½ cup/3½fl oz/100ml tepid water
½ teaspoon sugar
1 teaspoon salt

4 cups/1lb 5oz/600g all-purpose flour
    (or generous 3¾ cups/1lb 5oz/600g
    whole-wheat flour)
2 tablespoons oil, plus a bit
2 tablespoons *za'atar* (see p.98), optional

Sprinkle the yeast on to the water, add the sugar, stir a little and leave for 10 minutes, or until it becomes frothy and primeval looking.

Sift the flour and the salt into a pre-warmed mixing bowl, and make a well in the middle. Pour the yeast mixture into the well, and start to mix and work the gloop, adding more tepid water as required, into a soft, malleable dough. Drizzle the oil in, add the *za'atar*, and keep pounding. Once it comes together, you can take it out of the bowl and knead it on a floured board if you find it easier: you are aiming to pummel it for around 15 minutes.

Once you feel you can knead no more, put a little oil in the base of the mixing bowl, and roll your ball of dough in it—this will keep the dough supple and keep it from drying out. Then cover the bowl with plastic wrap or a clean damp dish towel, and leave the dough to rise for a couple of hours: it should double in size.

After this time has elapsed, flour up your work surface or a large board and knead the dough again. Divide the ball into about 10 fist-sized pieces (for large bread), or 12–14 smaller lumps, and roll them or flatten them until they are in rounds ¼-in (5-mm) thick. Lay them between two flour-sprinkled cloths, and leave them to rise a bit more.

Time to heat your oven—it needs to be really hot, so set it to maximum.* Place a baking sheet (or 2 or 3) in the oven to heat up. After 30 minutes, carefully oil the baking sheet(s) with a piece of paper towel, and slide the first dough round on to it. Bake for around 6 minutes (resisting the urge to open the oven before then): the *khobez* should puff up and become a gentle golden color. Remove the cooked flatbread and repeat with the remaining dough. Like all flatbreads, *khobez* keeps well as long as you keep it wrapped up: a plastic bag works. Eat within two to three days, either cold or warm. Or freeze it.

\*
If you don't have a very efficient oven, you can do all of this under a broiler as long as you watch it carefully: when the bread starts to puff up, turn it over and broil the other side for a minute or so.

## TURKISH BREAD

The Turks field an impressive array of bread. Unsurprising if you study a map of the country. It extends in all directions: south to the Mediterranean, north to the Black Sea, permeating ever easterly. Its cuisine reveals a huge number of influences.

I have included recipes for the two most intriguing and versatile breads: *yufka* and *pide*.

# TURKISH PIZZA BREAD

*Pide* is an exciting bread: soft and chewy, made with yogurt, and traditionally shaped with a slight hollow that can accommodate any number of fillings.

FOR 2 MEDIUM LOAVES:
¼oz/7g active dry yeast, or ½oz/15g fresh
½ teaspoon sugar
generous ¾ cup/7fl oz/200ml tepid water
3 ⅓ cups/1lb 2oz/500g unbleached flour
1 teaspoon salt

2 tablespoons Greek yogurt
2 tablespoons olive oil
1 egg, lightly whisked
1 tablespoon seeds of choice (mustard, nigella, sesame, caraway), optional
extra flour and oil, for dusting and greasing

Sprinkle the yeast and the sugar into half the water in a small bowl and leave somewhere warm to interact for 10–15 minutes. Sift the flour and salt into a big bowl, make a well in the middle, and trickle in the yeast mixture together with the yogurt, oil, and the rest of the water. Beat it with a wooden spoon until it all comes together, and then pop the dough on to a floured board and use your hands to knead and knead and knead—it will need about 10 minutes of your most enthusiastic pounding.

Pour a little oil into the mixing bowl, tipping it so the bottom area is well covered. Roll the dough ball in the oil (to stop it from drying out), cover the basin with a damp dish towel or some plastic wrap, and leave to proof (as real bakers say) in a warm place for a couple of hours.

Once the dough has doubled in size (more or less), flatten it vigorously with the palms of your hands, and then knead it some more. Divide it into two balls, and form each one into a pointed oval shape, pinching the edges to form a fat rim—they should look like badly built kayaks. Actually, you can make it any shape you like, but this torpedo shape is the most fun/traditional. Cover the loaves and set aside for another 20 minutes to rise a little more.

Heat the oven to 450°F/230°C. Grease a couple of baking trays and pop them into the oven to heat up. Brush the loaves with the egg and sprinkle them with seeds (if using). Slide each one on to one of the piping hot baking sheets and cook for 15 minutes, or until golden brown. This bread is best enjoyed fresh—if you want to eat it later in the day, wrap it in foil or a clean dish towel.

\*
Use this bread like a pizza base—fill with grilled vegetables, halloumi, eggs, *biber salçasi* (p.226) ... You can even fill it with fruit and crème patisserie and serve it as cake. This stuff rocks.

# TURKISH WAFER BREAD

Ah, now this is a challenge. Wafer-thin unleavened bread, rolled into huge circles, cooked over a dome shaped griddle called a *sadj*. Apparently even paragons of Turkish domestic virtue find this hard to make properly. But it is surely a contender as one of the world's most useful foodstuffs: it keeps for up to six months (making it a winter staple for more remote villages), and as it is somewhere between pastry and bread it is able to fulfill the functions of both.

It is used as a wrap (often known as *durum*), fried to make *boregi*, or just used as regular bread. It can even be used in place of filo pastry, but it takes a special kind of baker to get it that thin and crisp.

The *sadj* is usually about 5 ft (1.5 m) in diameter, and supported convex-side up on stones (or suspended over a pit on the ground). A fire is lit underneath it, and another small one on top to make it red hot: as the fire on top dies down, the ashes are swept clear and an *oklava* (a long rolling pin) is used to stretch the rolled dough over it to cook. As all of this would make an awful mess of your kitchen, I propose that we make much, much smaller rounds of bread using your biggest, most spotless frying pan.

ENOUGH FOR 15 SHEETS
⅔ cup/3½oz/100g white bread flour
⅓ cup/1¾oz/50g whole-wheat flour

pinch of salt
2 tablespoons melted butter
about scant ½ cup/3½fl oz/100ml tepid water

Sift the flours into a bowl together with the salt. Make a well in the middle, and add the butter, followed by the water, beating with a wooden spoon and then your hands until it all comes together. Knead for a few minutes, and then lift it on to a floured board, divide the dough into 15 even lumps, and cover with a damp dish towel for about 30 minutes.

Flatten the dough balls with your hand, and then, making sure that the board is still well covered with flour, roll each one out. You are aiming for paper-thin circles, 8in (20cm) in diameter (or to fit your frying pan).

Heat your frying pan until it is hissing, spitting hot, and then cook each *yufka* for about 30 seconds a side.

Leave to cool, and then store stacked in a sealed container. To use, moisten slightly, and then fill with cheese, or herbs, or spinach, or what you will. Roll up and fry. Or just heat through and then wrap around your favorite ingredients for a delicious Turkish sandwich.

# Peynirli Boregi
## CHEESE AND WILD GREEN PIE

*Boregi* really just means "pie." The word—and indeed, the concept—came from those opulent Ottomans, who spread their cuisine and customs far and wide: Tunisian *brik* to Greek *galatoboureko* are both derived from it. Anyway, the Turks have got them down to a fine art, and there are hundreds of variations in terms of filling and shape. Some are boiled. Some are fried. Ours are baked. You can use filo—but the pastry of choice here is *Yufka* (see opposite).

I have used mostly nettle in this, as it is authentic. Turkey seems to produce a vast amount of healthy green stuff—a lot of it unknown to us—and impressively very little of it gets wasted. (Unlike us: we ought to be ashamed about how much of our herbal lore we have lost. When did you last go and engage with a hedgerow?)

Nettles are incredibly good for you: they're great for flushing out the system and fighting allergies (yes, including urticaria, or nettle rash). And since I have been attached to an Iranian family I have learned to look again at vegetables: the tops of root vegetables are mostly edible, and I know that most of us throw them away. You can, of course, easily substitute spinach: this dish is, in fact, very similar to the Greek *spanakopita*, or spinach pie.

Anyway, pruning shears at the ready? You can buy nettles at the funkier farmers' markets, but it is more satisfying to acquire them—there are enough growing wild, after all. If you are picking your own, avoid those which may have been sprayed or are situated by a busy road—you don't want to be detoxing and retoxing at the same time. Nettle tops are best picked when very young, and it goes without saying that you should wear gloves when you do it.

Supplement (or replace) the nettles with radish tops, beet greens, watercress, and spinach if you have to; I tend to use a mixture.

SERVES 6
OR BUFFET NIBBLES FOR 40
2lb 4oz/1kg nettle tops
1 large onion
7oz/200g feta cheese, crumbled
3 eggs

a little pinch of salt and a much bigger pinch of
    black pepper
2 tablespoons plain yogurt
2 tablespoons olive oil
10 sheets of ready-made *yufka* (see opposite),
    or 1 package of frozen filo, defrosted

OK, rubber gloves on first. Wash the nettles well: wild green stuff should always be sloshed around in a bowl of cold water and then squeezed out—running water over them in a colander just doesn't get the mud off, and merely serves to provide any resident creepy crawlies with a nice shower. Blanch the nettle tops in boiling water for around 15 minutes—this removes the sting and means you can take off your gloves. If you are using any other vegetables, 5–10 minutes will do. (In theory, you should retain the blanching water and use

When working with *yufka* or filo, always make sure that you keep the pastry covered with a damp towel or wrapped up in plastic wrap: filo especially dries out really quickly, and this renders it useless.

it as a tea—but I won't tell if you don't.) Once the nettles are softened, drain them and plunge them into cold water: this helps them to retain their pretty green-ness. Drain once again, and then chop roughly.

Chop the onion finely, and put it in a bowl with the feta, chopped nettles, and one of the eggs. Add the salt and pepper, and mix well—using your hands will ensure homogeneity.

Beat the remaining two eggs gently with the yogurt and olive oil—it will probably curdle, but there you go.

Now you can make this two ways: small individual ones (fiddly but fun) or one big pie (much easier, though difficult to cut).

If you opt for the former (which are known as *sigara boregi*, or cigarette pies), you will need to cut each sheet of pastry into four. Work on a very clean, very dry board. If you are using round *yufka*, just divide them into quadrants.

Meanwhile, preheat the oven to 350°F/180°C.

Brush each portion of pastry with some of the yogurt "glaze." Place a teaspoon of the green mixture near the pointy end (which should be pointing towards you), and roll the pastry up around it away from you, tucking in the pastry flaps as you go. Arrange the finished *boregi* on an oiled baking sheet and brush the exposed pastry with the remaining glaze, then bake in the oven for about 35 minutes.

If you are making the chunkier, family version, grease an oven dish of an appropriate shape/size (slightly smaller than the size of your pastry sheets), and layer half the pastry in, brushing in between each sheet with the yogurt mixture as you go (but not on the top layer). It may be easier to shred the *yufka* to make it fit your dish. Spoon the cheese mixture evenly over the pastry, and then layer the second half of the pastry on top, again brushing with the glaze in between each layer. If you are using filo, you will need to trim the overhanging bits when you reach the top (otherwise they will burn): use a sharp knife, and the task is an easy one. *Yufka* is usually thicker and more malleable, so just tuck the ends in. Brush the top with the rest of the glaze, score through lightly (I usually cut the pie into six or eight portions), and then bake at 350°F/180°C for about 40 minutes, or until the *boregi* is golden brown and pleasingly puffy.

Enjoy with salad and *çaçik* (see p.61). (Unless, that is, you are preparing it for a finger buffet, in which case a glass of champagne would be a more appropriate accompaniment.)

# Fatayer
## MRS. HADDAD'S SPINACH *FATAYER*

Mrs. Haddad is my Lebanese bread supplier. Her company, Dina Foods, is the biggest of its kind in London. We buy from them because of the quality. Oh, and also because they are very nice people. I have to say that lest they put our prices up—but really, they are fun. Mr. and Mrs. Haddad have lived in the UK for more than 20 years now, but make regular trips back home. Like all Lebanese, they find it hard to remember a past without conflict and violence: the knowledge of it is a constant background noise. But in the kitchen at least little has changed: as with so many cultures, the baking of the daily bread provides continuity when nothing else seems to make much sense. This is her family recipe.

MAKES AROUND 40 PIECES
½oz/12g fresh yeast, or ¼oz/7g active dry yeast
1 teaspoon sugar
⅔ cup/5fl oz/150ml warm water
3⅓ cups/1lb 2oz/500g all-purpose flour
1 teaspoon salt
2 tablespoons oil, preferably olive

FOR THE FILLING:
2lb 4oz/1kg fresh spinach (or frozen)
pure olive oil for frying
1 large onion, chopped
1 tablespoon sumac
scant 1 cup/4½oz/125g chopped walnuts
    (or pine nuts), optional
1 tablespoon pomegranate paste
1 tablespoon lemon juice
salt and pepper, to taste

**\* A few tips**
*these freeze really well, so don't let the idea of making 40 pieces put you off.
*spinach is the most traditional filling for *fatayer*, but I have made really nice ones with cheese, or with hummus and celery. Playtime in the kitchen.
*use pure olive oil for frying, not extra-virgin, which has a low smoke point.
*if you don't have any pomegranate paste, simply use 2 tablespoons of lemon juice instead.

Sprinkle the yeast and the sugar over the warm water, and leave it to sit for about 10 minutes. Sift the flour and salt together, and then add the yeasty mix and the oil slowly, mixing well, until the resulting gloop comes together in a ball. Either wrap it in plastic wrap or cover with a damp cloth, and leave it somewhere warm and secluded for at least 1 hour to rise.

In the meantime, prepare the filling. Wash and drain the spinach well: you really don't want this to be watery. Heat a little oil in a pan, and fry the onion. As it softens, add the spinach, sumac, and nuts and cook for a couple of minutes. Stir the pomegranate paste and lemon juice through the mixture, season to taste and set aside.

Roll out the dough and cut into 2½–3¼in/6–8cm circles with a pastry cutter or upturned glass. Or if you have a less than happy relationship with your rolling pin, you can just make little balls of dough and flatten them with your palm.

Preheat the oven to 375°F/190°C.

Meanwhile, place a teaspoonful of the spinach mixture in the middle of each round, and fold up the sides so they meet at the top like a pastry pyramid (it doesn't matter if some of the filling is left coquettishly peeping out). Place on a non-stick or greased baking tray and bake them in the oven for around 20 minutes, or until lightly browned.

This is great buffet food, or you could sneak it into your progeny's lunchbox.

# Eliopitta

## OLIVE BREAD

OK, so this is a slightly fatter bread. It is enjoyed in Greece, parts of Turkey, and Armenia, and it is just one of the nicest (and easiest) breads to bake at home. There is something very Mother Earthy about it: the olives, the flour, the simple rustic shape ... *A jug of wine, a loaf of bread and thou*, was Khayyam's recipe for bucolic bliss—I reckon this was the loaf he was talking about. Pictured overleaf.

MAKES 2 LOAVES

3⅓ cups/1lb 2oz/500g white bread flour (preferably unbleached)

1 tablespoon superfine sugar

2 teaspoons salt

1 x ¼oz (7g) envelope active dry yeast

3 tablespoons olive oil

1¼ cups/10fl oz/300ml or so tepid water

3½oz/100g pitted sliced olives (you choose the color)

1 tablespoon rosemary (or mixed herbs), optional

Sift the flour, sugar and salt into a mixing bowl, sprinkle in the yeast, and add the olive oil and water. Mix well with a wooden spoon, and then your hands—when it all comes together, knead it on a board for around 10 minutes. Pop the dough back in the bowl, cover with a damp cloth or plastic wrap and leave it to double in size. After about 30 minutes, punch it down, knead some more, add the olives and the rosemary, and then re-cover in the bowl to proof for a further 30 minutes.

Now shape the dough into two rounds (about 6in/15cm diameter) on a floured board. Cover with a damp cloth, and leave to rise for a final 30 minutes. Grease a large baking tray, and put it in the oven on 475°F/240°C to heat up. Just before you are ready to cook the bread, pop a baking pan of water in the bottom of the oven—it helps keep the bread soft and elastic while cooking. Slide the loaves on to the tray and bake for around 10 minutes, then turn the oven down to 375°F/190°C and cook for a further 20–25 minutes. The bread should be golden brown and sound hollowish when you tap its bottom. Cool and gobble; although this is so tasty it may not get the chance to cool down ...

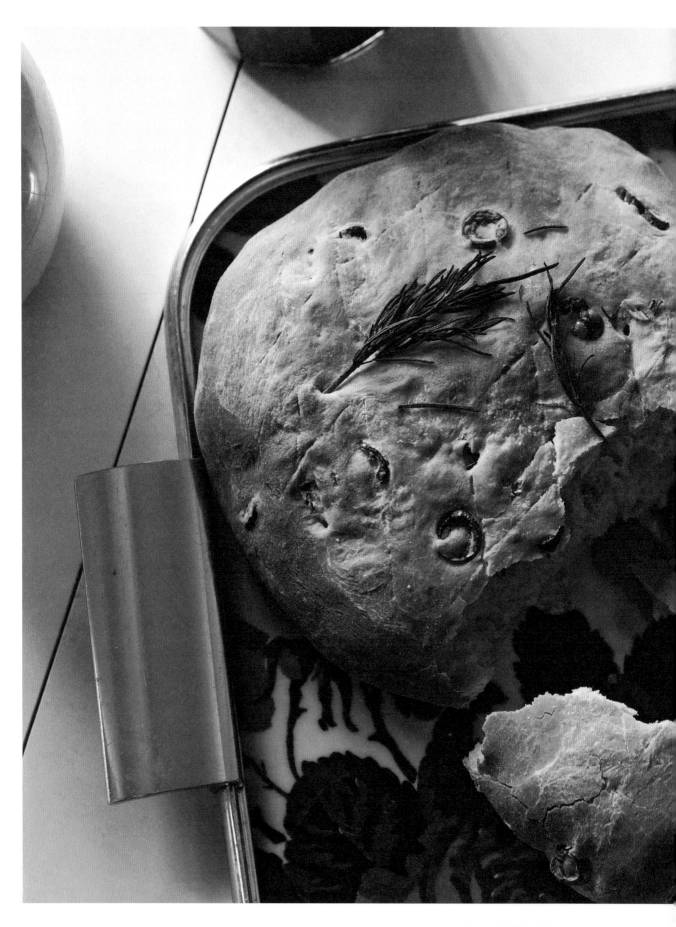

# Boulanee

## AFGHAN LEEK PIES

These are lovely, and so simple. Similar to the *piroshki*, but quicker to make and crisper to bite. This recipe is drawn from a collection of my many lovely Afghan lady customers, but although they do make them at home, this is really regarded as street food in Afghanistan.

MAKES ABOUT 20
3 ⅓ cups/1lb 2oz/500g all-purpose flour
1 teaspoon salt
1 cup/9fl oz/250ml water
oil, for frying

FOR THE FILLING:
2 leeks, thoroughly washed and finely chopped
2–3 scallions, washed and chopped
12oz/350g cooked potatoes (left over mash is cool too)
½ teaspoon ground turmeric
½ teaspoon chili powder
2 teaspoons salt

Sift the flour and the salt, and then add the water a little at a time until it all comes together and starts to look dough-like. Knead well on a floured board, and then cover and set aside for 30 minutes to rest.

Now make the filling: just mix all the ingredients together really well …

When the dough is rested, either roll it out into two big sheets and use a pastry cutter, or break off little lumps and roll them into discs of the right size (3½–4in/9–10cm diameter). Spoon a little of the mixture into each disc, fold the dough over, and press the edges firmly to make a pocket. Fry them in about 1in (2cm) of oil until they are golden brown on each side, and then settle on some paper towels to drain.

One of the coolest things about *boulanee* is the range of sauces you get offered: the most authentic is *Kashk* (see p.85), but try with *Gashneetch* (p.225)—or just with plain yogurt. These keep for a few days in the fridge, and freeze well.

# VEGGIESTAN STREET FOOD

In Afghanistan, *boulanee* would normally be bought from a *tabang wala*, a street vendor who carries his market stall on a yoke around his neck—a round table that he can set up with a minute's notice on a street corner (would that all corner trading was as simple). The *tabang wala* sells anything and everything, from hot winter treats such as *halim* (porridge) to twists of candy, salted and sugared chickpeas (*nokhod*), or roasted *jalouz* (pine nuts in their shells). My Afghan contacts are happy to report a resurgence of these resourceful traders in recent years: street business is once again booming in downtown Kabul.

Street food is a prominent and fun part of the Veggiestan diet, and every country therein has its specialties. Of course, the climate helps: nations with warmer weather are naturally inclined to spend more time perambulating and socializing, and street vendors are an essential part of the whole outdoor scene. It is doubtful whether any foodie vista anywhere in the world touches the awesome Jemaa el Fna in Marrakech (when I went, it reduced me to doing that silly, girlie, hand-flappy thing that silly girlies do when we get over-excited). The night market there with its dozens of food stalls, the buzz of the street entertainers, the beguiling wail of the *ghita* (a Moroccan cornet-like instrument), the sizzle of a hundred griddles, and the aroma of every spice under the sun is a sensory experience not easily forgotten. But if it is the ultimate in street fare, it has to be said that a lot of it is quite elaborate and the antithesis of vegetarian.

Iranian street food is simple by comparison, comprising, for the most part, grilled or steamed vegetables cooked just so and seasoned to perfection. My in-laws often cook such treats at home, and thanks to them I have learned to embrace the full-on flavor of seasonally fresh veggies. In the bazaars and towns of Iran, people wait in line for cooked corn on the cob rolled in

salty water, or fresh boiled turnips, or al dente steamed beets, or spiced baked potatoes. And fresh nuts—pistachios, hazelnuts, and almonds—still green and fully dressed: these are sold washed and ready to be dipped in a paper twist of salt.

Arabic countries from Egypt all the way round to Iraq offer the classics: little pots of *ful* with can-never-get-enough-of-it garlic sauce, or falafel pockets with chili and yogurt and tahina. And, of course, the regional equivalent of the range of pies and pastries featured in this chapter. These are enjoyed not only in the bazaars and souks but along broad shady promenades, where families stroll in the evening or picnic in the summer.

In the Levant and the Arabian Peninsula, bread such as *kaak* (sesame rolls) and *ma'anoushe* (pizza type bread) are hawked with twists of *za'atar*, alongside fruits and nuts of the season: peeled and chilled prickly pears, slices of watermelon, roasted chestnuts, tubs of ready-strimmed pomegranate seeds. My favorite of all has to be *kushari* (see p.126), a mix-it-all-up bowl of rice and pasta and lentils and spicy tomato: I've never been lucky enough to have it in its hometown of Alexandria, but I was once given a very welcome bowl of it by the owner of an Egyptian grocery store we supply just off the Edgware Road, and I just love the concept.

The best-known Turkish street food is, of course, the *doner kebab* (similar to the Greek *gyro*), which has become popular in the West. But the fact is that Turkey offers the outward bound a beguiling range of street snackettes. *Pide* topped with cheese, olives, tomato, and fresh herbs, or *lahmacun* (like pizzas) spread with spinach and feta or *biber salçasi* (p.226), are both hugely popular, as are *kumpir* (baked potatoes filled with salad and veggies).

All of which means that it really is sad that the American vegetarian-about-town can still face a struggle to get anything other than a very dreary pizza. Perhaps we should all move East …

*Tahinopitta*

# ALKI'S MOTHER'S *TAHINOPITTA*

Alki is my adopted Cypriot cousin and runs a Cypriot taverna in the suburbs of London. Versions of this are enjoyed in Armenia and Turkey, and if you like *tahini* this is about as good as it gets. The recipe for *tahinopitta* is a bit of a trade secret in Cyprus, and not at all like the Lenten cake of the same name, found on the Greek mainland—so don't tell too many people about it now, will you …

MAKES ABOUT 15
FOR THE PASTRY:

1 envelope/¼oz/7g active dry yeast

¼ cup/1¾oz/50g sugar

scant ½ cup/3½fl oz/100ml warm water

3 cups/1lb 2oz/500g flour

pinch of salt

2 eggs, separated

generous ¾ cup/7fl oz/200ml heavy cream

½ cup/1¾oz/50g sesame seeds

zest of 1 orange (reserve for juice)

1 cup/2 sticks/225g chilled unsalted butter

FOR THE FILLING:

1 cup/9fl oz/250ml *tahina* paste

1 cup/7oz/200g sugar

¼ cup/2fl oz/50ml cold, strong black coffee

2 tablespoons orange juice

1 teaspoon ground cinnamon

½ teaspoon ground cardamom

1 teaspoon allspice

Sprinkle the yeast and sugar into the water, and set aside for 10 minutes to do frothy things. Sift the flour and the salt into a big bowl, making a well in the middle. Whisk the egg yolks, cream, and the yeast mix into the flour, beating well with a wooden spoon. Add the sesame seeds and the orange zest, and roll the dough into a ball. Cover the bowl with a damp cloth and leave the mixture to rise for about 1 hour.

Beat the *tahina* paste with the sugar (a blender will really help here), and trickle in the coffee and the orange juice to make it more workable. Mix in the spices, and pop the paste in the fridge until you need it.

Knead the dough on a floured board, and then roll it out into a rectangular sheet about ½in (1cm) thick. Dot the butter into the pastry in ½in (1cm) knoblets, and then fold the pastry over on itself. Roll it again, and fold it again, turning the dough through 90°—this is just to ensure that the butter is properly incorporated across the dough.

Let the pastry rest for about 30 minutes, and then roll it out into a 14in (35cm) square about ¼in (5mm) thick. Spread the *tahina* mixture across the dough to within ¼in (5mm) of the edges, and then roll up Swiss-roll style. Cut the resulting sausage into about 15 even rounds, and flatten each one slightly with the palm of your hand.

Heat the oven to 350°F/180°C. Pop the discs on to a greased baking tray, and brush the tops with beaten egg white. Bake them for 20 minutes, or until golden brown.

These make great breakfast treats, and can be enjoyed warm or chilled. They are good for a couple of days, and are best kept wrapped up somewhere cool, but not in the fridge.

# Houmous Sambousic

## HUMMUS-FILLED PIES

Here's a confusing etymological puzzle; the word *sambousic* exists in some format across most of the Middle East, and yet has come to mean different, but mostly pie-shaped, things. *Sanbusaj* are mentioned in the fascinating *Baghdad Cookery Book*, Charles Perry's translation of parts of the *Kitab al Tabikh*, a thirteenth-century cooking manual—in that context, they are triangular pies filled with lamb or ground almonds. Clearly they are related to Indian samosas. In Yemen and Somalia, they are known as *samboosa* and seem uniquely to be sweet.

As they are usually triangular, it is suggested that the word comes from middle Persia: *se* is the Persian word for three, and *ambos* is an ancient type of bread. But this is odd, because no Iranians of my acquaintance seem familiar with them.

Anyway, ours are savory and filled with hummus and totally yummy.

*Tip*

To clarify butter, melt gently and then strain through a paper towel.

MAKES 24

FOR THE PASTRY:

scant ½ cup/3½fl oz/100ml clarified butter
scant ½ cup/3½fl oz/100ml vegetable oil
scant ½ cup/3½fl oz/100ml water
3 ⅓ cups/1lb 2oz/500g all-purpose flour, sifted
pinch of salt
1 tablespoon sesame or caraway or nigella
   seeds (optional)

FOR THE FILLING:

splash of oil, for cooking
1 teaspoon cumin seeds
1 teaspoon fennel seeds
2–3 garlic cloves, minced
1 large onion, finely diced
1 red or yellow pepper, finely diced
1 green pepper, finely diced
1 large zucchini, finely chopped
2 sticks celery, finely chopped
1 can (14oz/400g) cooked chickpeas, drained
7oz/200g hummus (see p.122)
generous handful of chopped cilantro
salt and pepper, to taste

beaten egg or milk for glazing

Pour the liquid parts for the pastry into a bowl, and then gently sprinkle the flour and salt in, followed by the seeds if using, mixing thoroughly as you go with a wooden spoon. It should all come together fairly easily: you will end up with a soft sticky dough. This is one that does not brook too much fondling, so no kneading is needed. Set aside somewhere cool while you make the filling.

Heat the oil in a frying pan and add the spices and garlic, followed by the onion, peppers, zucchini, celery, and chickpeas. Fry gently until the onion and the celery are soft and just starting to brown. Take off the heat and allow to cool a little.

Back to the pastry. Divide the dough into two, and on a floured board, roll each part out into an oblong. Cut each section into 12 smaller oblongs.

Now stir the hummus and cilantro through the vegetable mixture, and season to taste. Put a teaspoonful of the mixture at the base of each dough oblong, and then take the

*Psst:*

A lot of my East African customers cheat and make this with filo pastry, so you could always do the same.

right-hand corner nearest you and fold it diagonally left across the mixture to a point one-third of the way up the pastry. Then take the pastry corner that is now nearest you, and flop it over to reach a point two-thirds of the way up the oblong. Finally bring the top right-hand corner of the pastry over on top of the triangle, so that you have a neat triangular pie. Trust me, it is easier than I have made it sound.

You can fry *sambousic*, but I think baked works better. Put the *sambousic* on a non-stick oven tray and brush the top with a little milk or beaten egg. Bake at 350°F/180°C for 30–35 minutes—they should end up a pretty golden color.

You can eat these hot or cold—but they are probably at their most enticing served warm with a crisp salad. They will keep for 2–3 days in the fridge.

## FINALLY, ON STALE BREAD…

*One of Mullah Nasruddin's friends caught him throwing pieces of stale bread all around the perimeter of his property.*

*"What on earth are you doing, Mullah?" he enquired.*

*"Trying to keep the tigers away," came back the answer.*

*"But there aren't any tigers around here," protested the friend.*

*"Exactly," said Nasruddin, happily. "It works."*

herbs and salads

Westerners are wusses when it comes to herbs. By way of example: one of our leading supermarkets prides itself on its fresh fish, and its packages offer temptations such as "trout fillet with parsley," or "tuna loin with parsley," as if the very act of the inclusion of a sprig of the green stuff is in some way avant-garde or a contributing factor to the cost of the pack. We should take a green leaf out of the cookbooks of the Arab and Indo-Iranian nations: herbs are used in profusion, perhaps nowhere more so than in Iran, where four of the national favorite dishes positively glow with greenness.

In fact, in Iran herbs (or *sabzi*) are eaten as an appetizer or accompaniment to most meals: an Iranian housewife will keep a colander of fresh washed herbs in the fridge ready to dish out with food or wrap into sandwiches, and it's a practice I recommend. Good herbs to start with are the practically ubiquitous flat-leaf parsley and cilantro, together with fresh mint, basil, and tarragon. Add in things like watercress, radish tops, chives, and arugula. Just pluck away the woodier bits of the stalks, and dunk your herbs all jumbled up together into a bowl of cold water for 10 minutes or so: this allows any dirt or sediment to settle to the bottom. Then scoop the herbs out and drain them, change the water and do it all over again. This time, when you have drained the herbs thoroughly, invert a plate or saucer on top of the colander: you can store it

in the fridge just like that, or if space is at a premium, tip the herbs into a plastic bag. They will keep for 5–6 days with the former storage method, slightly less in a bag. It does seem a bit weird at first, chomping on clumps of raw greenery—"How now, brown cow," and all that—but add in a little white cheese, some top-notch shelled walnuts, and some warm bread, and you've got the basis of an Iranian *mezze.* And eating herbs like this is the perfect aid to digestion: they variously act to stimulate the appetite (cilantro), help the food go down (mint and tarragon), remove any bad odors from the breath (parsley), and conquer flatulence (mint again).

I can't actually imagine working without fresh parsley, cilantro, and mint: I am lucky in that in South London every grocery store sells big cheap bunches of the stuff. If you're less well supplied, I strongly recommend that you start growing your own.

Of course, this chapter is not only about herbs, but is celebrating leaves and salads generally. The region seems to have a more natural affinity with salad leaves: lettuce is not used merely to make up a tired threesome with tomato and cucumber, but is rather honored with sauces and dips uniquely its own. And if herbs are used with greater understanding and to greater effect, the essence of the Veggiestan salad is, by contrast, simplicity.

# BEET AND ORANGE SALAD

This is quite simply a stunning salad. But then beet is a stunning vegetable.

I think this dish is sort of where Morocco meets London. At any rate, the Moroccans make much of orange in their salads.

SERVES 4 AS A SIDE DISH

2 medium-large beets

2 sweet potatoes (the orange-fleshed variety)

1 large grated carrot

1 big handful fresh parsley

1 big handful fresh mint

juice and zest of 1 orange

knob of peeled ginger, minced

¼ teaspoon ground cumin

¼ teaspoon ground cinnamon

4 tablespoons olive oil

1 teaspoon orange blossom water

2 teaspoons balsamic vinegar

pinch of salt and pepper

Peel and cube the beets (aim for ¼in/1.5cm squares) and cook them in a minimal amount of water, keeping an eye on the water levels so they don't actually dry out. Peel and cube the sweet potato, keeping it in water until you are ready for it. The beets will take about 35 minutes to cook and the sweet potato about 15 minutes, so add the sweet potato to the pan after about 20 minutes and things should work out just dandy.

Drain, then allow them to cool before mixing them with the carrot and fresh herbs. Whisk all the rest of the ingredients together as a dressing and spoon it over the vegetables.

## Potato Salada
# WARM TARRAGON AND POTATO SALAD

The Middle Eastern take on this recipe is refreshingly free of mayonnaise. Like so many traditional *mezze* dishes, simplicity is the key.

SERVES 4

4 large waxy potatoes

handful each of fresh tarragon and parsley, washed and roughly chopped

1 medium onion, finely sliced

4 tablespoons olive oil

juice of 1 lemon

salt and black pepper

Scrub the potatoes (or peel them if they have thick skins), and cut them into ¾in (2cm) cubes. Bring to a boil and simmer in salted water until they are cooked: about 10 minutes should suffice. Drain and place in a bowl with the onion and herbs. Whisk the oil, lemon, and seasoning together and toss through the salad. Enjoy while still warm. You can tart it up with chopped boiled eggs and olives—but really this is practically perfect the way it is.

# Jeleh-ye-Sabzi va Limoo
## GELLED LEMON AND HERB SALAD

Is it possible to cook facetiously? Well, this recipe was born from facetiousness, at any rate. Middle Easterners love jello, and at one stage my family-in-law seemed to be having rather a lot of the stuff. So I made them a gelled salad. And it worked. No, really.

It is of course nothing new: chefs have been setting anything and everything in aspic and with gelatin since the gastronomic year dot. My grandmother used to be a dab hand with it too, but as she was an averred witch, I usually refrained from asking her what was "under the jelly." Anyway, let's think of this as being in the great spirit of the Ottoman or Safavid empires: ostentatious, but fun.

### SERVES 4 AS A SIDE DISH
lemon and lime vegetarian gelatin crystals—
   enough to make generous 2 cups/
   17fl oz/500ml
juice and zest of 1 lemon
few sprigs lemon thyme

either 2 baby cucumbers, or about 3¼in/8cm
   of a regular cucumber, scrubbed
1 small onion
big handful flat-leaf parsley, chopped
small handful fresh basil, chopped
salt and pepper

\*

Lemon thyme is hard to find in stores, but is easy enough to grow!

Make up the gelatin as per the instructions on the package, but use only about three-quarters of the liquid content that they recommend—vegetarian gelatin never seems to set properly otherwise. Include the lemon juice in this measurement. Add the lemon zest and the lemon thyme to the gelatin, and pour it either into a fancy mold or a pliable plastic tub, and pop it in the fridge (or freezer if you are in a hurry) to set.

Grate the cucumber and the onion. When the gelatin is half set, add the vegetables and herbs to it, mixing thoroughly with a fork. Season to taste, and return it to the fridge to finish gellifying.

You can either turn the gelled salad out on to a platter of lettuce leaves, or serve it in individual scoops. It makes a great accompaniment to spicy food, and is a real hit on a cheese board.

# ON HOME AND HERBAL REMEDIES

Doctors were kind of invented in the Middle East, both the regular and the herbal varieties. Of course, the former grew out of the latter. And it is also true that the Chinese developed their own practice of medicine simultaneously. Anyway, suffice it to say that the first systems of formalized medication and understanding of anatomy came out of the region.

There is evidence of medical practices going back thousands of years both in Mesopotamia and Egypt, but the exciting stuff started happening when Hippocrates got hold of ancient Persian Zoroastrian tenets on balance in the diet and added it to his own considerable empiric observations. The theories that he laid down on the human constitution were not bettered until over a thousand years later, when Islamic physicians including Rhazes, Averrois, and most notably Avicenna started experimenting and producing vast treatises on every aspect of human health and disease. A lot of it may seem quaint (or completely bonkers) in view of what we now know, but their advances were in truth quite astonishing.

A school of medicine known as *Unani* was set up to continue their works, and the school (in the loosest sense of the word) is still going strong today. Not only are there thriving clinics in the US among other places, but most interestingly the healing arts are still passed by word of mouth among the *hakims* or healers of Afghanistan, Uzbekistan, and Kashmir. (During periods of unrest in that region, the *hakims* have enjoyed a huge surge in business as many of the inhabitants had no access to conventional doctors.) In fact, herbal lore and pantry medicine is passed down verbally across the region in a way that we are losing in the West.

*Unani* practitioners believe that most of our ills are caused by an imbalance in our four basic bodily humors (if you studied history this will ring bells: remember sanguine, phlegmatic, choleric, and melancholic?), and they work with the idea that they need to trigger the body to heal itself. This involves a range of herbs and spices, abstention and actions, and as this is a (light-hearted, fun) cookbook I am not going into too much further detail. But here's a small selection of Middle Eastern home remedies/herb lore (see www.veggiestan.com for more). Most of them are from my store customers, but I should also like to acknowledge the wonderful Dr. Khoshbin, a prolific Iranian herbal practitioner.

AJWAIN, ANISE, and CARAWAY: All three are used extensively and (seemingly) interchangeably among Afghans, Uzbeks, Kashmiris, and Pakistanis as a remedy for digestive problems, especially for colic in babies and infants. Grind the seeds to a powder and drink with a little warm water twice a day. For adults pound a little fresh ginger into the mix.

ARGAN OIL: If you've been to Morocco you've probably had some of this flogged to you: if you're wise, you'll have snapped it up and more besides. Argan oil is produced from the nuts of the very rare argan tree: Tradition has it that it is ingested by tree-climbing goats and then harvested from their, um, poo. But don't let this put you off: the stuff is one of those legendary panaceas, credited with the ability to heal all sorts of things. It is also rated at a culinary level for salads. But it is in the beauty sector that it is most prized: it is full of vitamin E and apparently works wonders on one's saggy bits. Bring it on…

CARDAMOM/CINNAMON: Neither is indigenous to the region, but in all likelihood arrived with traders via the Silk Road. Both are good for coughs and colds, especially mixed with ginger. Add ½ tsp of each to a cup of boiling water, add some honey, and drink twice a day. Cinnamon especially is known as a relaxant and an anti-inflammatory, which makes it a soothing brew for asthmatics. Keep a jar of cinnamon quills or bark in your cupboard and lob them into your night-night tea to aid sleep. Barbers (who were the original dispensaries, after all) in Turkey and the Levant traditionally gave their customers cups of cinnamon tea to keep them calm while they got busy with razor and scissors.

NABAT (crystallized sugar): is dished out as a remedy for almost anything in Iran and Kurdistan. It is the ultimate "warm" food (see p.106), and thus counteracts the effects of too many "cold" foods or general over-indulgence. It is the best hangover cure ever. Dissolve a knob in some boiling water or tea and sip gently while you stop trying to feel so sorry for yourself.

TAMARIND: is now widely available. Look out for the pods at Caribbean and Asian grocery stores. This most exotic-sounding and alien-looking of fruits is known to be a terrific laxative. In Southern Iran and Saudi Arabia, tamarind is boiled in water with a little sugar, strained, and chilled for use as a drink to combat fever. In times of old (really old, not "olden times" as construed by the average twelve year old these days, wherein they usually mean ten years ago) tamarind was regarded as a good friend to the desert traveler: it quenches thirst, cools, and nourishes simultaneously. It is a very "cold" food (see p.106), and will thus generally sooth the febrile constitution.

TURMERIC: is incredibly bad for your wardrobe—it seems to be the one stain that nothing will bust. But apart from that it is really good for you—Iranians reckon it is an aid to the liver, and it (originally) found its way into Persian cuisine owing to its strong antibacterial qualities (it has now quite simply been incorporated into the flavor of many dishes). It is good as a sore-throat buster too: mix ½ tsp with 1 tsp of honey in a small amount of warm milk and sip as required.

# Sahan Mezet Khas

## LETTUCE *MEZZE* PLATTER

The poor lettuce leaf grinds away in the background of catering, the binding force of a squillion salads, the forgotten hero of food presentation. This gives it an opportunity to star for once.

You will need to gather about 4 varieties of lettuce. Romaine is knockout for sweetness and crispness, frisée (or curly endive) for general flashiness, and lambs leaf, spinach, or arugula for a bit of darker greenness. But oakleaf and radicchio are also good with their hint of redness, and the dear old Boston bibb or iceberg deserve a chance too. Pull the leaves apart and arrange in sectors on a large plate—the idea is to offer four different leaves with four different sauces. Try *zhug* (see p.218) or *tahini* (see p.56). Or either of the below:

### SPICED HOLLANDAISE:

Mix 2 tablespoons of *dukkah* (p.101) with scant ½ cup/3½fl oz/100ml of hollandaise. What do you mean, you don't remember how to make hollandaise? It's a cinch. Throw an egg yolk, 1 teaspoon mustard, and the juice of 1 lemon into a blender, switch on and trickle in melted butter (about 6 tablespoons/2¾oz/75g) until you get a lovely, shiny yellow emulsion. Two second job.

### GREEK GUACAMOLE

Avocado. Tomato. Feta. Fresh mint. Olive oil. Black pepper. And 1 teaspoon dried oregano. Whizz whizz whizz in the blender. A sort of puréed Greek salad, but it makes a great dip. Garnish with olives.

# VEGGIESTAN WALDORF SALAD

This is the classic American dish with a Middle Eastern twist.

Mix 3 sticks of chopped celery with two cored and diced eating apples and a scant ½ cup/1½oz/40g roughly chopped walnuts. Add in some chunked cucumber; ½ onion, diced; a handful of raisins; and a chopped green pepper. Throw in a big handful each of freshly chopped mint and cilantro. Whisk 2 tablespoons plain yogurt into 4 tablespoons olive oil, 1 tablespoon apple cider vinegar and 1 teaspoon honey. Add salt and pepper to taste. Steep a little ground saffron in some boiling water to diffuse, and when it has cooled sufficiently, stir it into the dressing. Line a bowl with some crispy lettuce leaves, pile the salad in, and drizzle the dressing over the top.

# CUCUMBER AND POMEGRANATE SALSA

This is just a knockout as accompaniments go. A really lovely salad, appetizer, or relish, depending on your requirements. It's a real looker and it takes nanoseconds to make.

If available, you can use redcurrants instead of the pomegranate.

SERVES 6

1 luscious, large pomegranate
1 medium cucumber, finely diced
2–3 tomatoes, finely diced
1 green pepper, finely diced
1 hot chili, chopped

½ bunch each of mint and cilantro, washed and chopped
1 bunch scallions, finely diced
salt and pepper
a drizzle of olive oil
1 lime, juiced

Firstly, make sure that you are wearing pomegranate-colored clothes (or perhaps put an apron on). Cut the pomegranate in half with a sharp knife, and with your fingers gently prise free the seeds, pulling off any pith as you go. Mix them together with all the other ingredients, stir well, then cover and chill.

## On Mezze

*"We are the flowers in the gardens of heaven, the* mezze *and wine at God's gathering."* Rumi

This pomegranate recipe, in my opinion, captures the essence of *mezze*: simple dishes that showcase one or two ingredients with the minimum of fuss. Anissa Helou, the UK's most authoritative Lebanese chef, defines the *mezze* experience as "the leisurely savoring (of) a tremendous selection of small dishes."

The word *mezze* originates from the Persian word *mazeh*, meaning "taste," and it is likely the principle of eating thus also originated in Iran: little tasters of food offered alongside (and to soak up) *arak*, or alcohol, as part of the Persian equivalent of a night on the town. But the extent and potential of *mezze* goes a lot further than a bag of peanuts.

It is true that the simplest *mezze* dishes are often nuts and legumes, freshly roasted and salted. Or marinated olives, or pickles.

But then there is a terrific range of dips: *tsatsiki, hummus, baba ghanouj, tahina,* finished with sumac or paprika. And a myriad of salads, fresh-sprinkled with herbs, platters of *al dente* vegetables drizzled with garlic sauce. And pies and patties served with a twist of lemon. Mouth-watering stuff.

The concept of *mezze* has changed over the years, and moved West. In Iran, while restaurant appetizers are often eaten in *mezze* format, the vanquishing of alcohol put the kibosh on its culinary evolution, but in the Levant, Turkey, and Cyprus it has been raised to an art form. And, of course, it appeals to our newly adventurous tastebuds, together with our increasing preference for grazing on food—hence the success of not only *mezze* but also its cousins, *tapas* and the *smorgasbord.*

I love it, as it is taking food back to its essence and allows us to savor individual flavors: modern food is so often over-complicated, and, in the case of vegetables, often disguised. You could serve any number of the dishes in this book in *mezze* form, but why not experiment with the idea: instead of stir-frying veggies or making a salad, why not take each ingredient and honor it with its own little platter? Coat sautéed broccoli in sesame sauce, or fry cauliflower in batter and serve with spiced mayo. Or use the potato salad dressing (p.36) for any number of vegetables, from roasted peppers to baked zucchini. Flash raw nuts in the microwave with a teaspoon of salt and a squeeze of lemon and you have tasty home roasted nibbles in seconds. Go on—take the evening off, open a bottle of something nice, and linger over each dish for once...

# Salad-e-Makhlout va Saus-e-Chiveed
## MIXED LEAF SALAD WITH
## A DILLY DRESSING

This recipe is all about the dressing: the mixed leaves are going to depend on the season, your preferences, what the kids will eat, what's in your garden, your farmers' market or your corner store or (as a final resort) your supermarket. But try to be inventive: use radish tops, purslane, dandelion greens, baby beet greens and whole sprigs of fresh herbs in addition to your regular radicchio, arugula, and romaine.

Salad leaves are best pulled apart with the hands: cutting them just bruises them, especially if your knife is anything other than scalpel-sharp. I once worked with a chef who used to go off the culinary deep-end if he saw anyone taking a knife to a lettuce leaf. (The same guy also once accused me of murdering his Brie by putting it in the fridge, and refused to speak to me for a week. Colorful occupation, catering.)

So get yourself a bucket of pretty and seasonal leaves. Add wafer-thin sliced onion and shavings of radish (white or pink). And toss with the following dressing:

\* Sekanjabin:

This is actually one of my secret ingredients for all sorts of things. It is a mint-based Persian syrup, which is traditionally either diluted with water and served over ice in hot weather, or used as a dip for crisp lettuce leaves. But it has so much more potential than that: try sneaking it into cocktails, or into marinades, or any number of salad dressings, or even as a glaze for hot veggies. It is a cinch to make: boil 1 cup/ 9fl oz/250ml water with 1¾ cups/12oz/350g sugar to form a syrup. Add 4 tablespoons of white wine vinegar to it as it cools, and then when it is nearly cold shred in about half a bunch of fresh mint. Bottle, seal, and chill.

SERVES 6
FOR THE DRESSING:
6 tablespoons olive oil
1 tablespoon *sekanjabin,* \* or substitute
　　1 teaspoon honey
2 teaspoons mustard

2 teaspoons dill (dried or fresh)
1 teaspoon tarragon (dried or fresh)
1 tablespoon apple cider vinegar
1 tablespoon runny plain yogurt
3 baby pickled cucumbers, chopped real fine
salt and cracked black pepper

Just whisk it all together. And pour it over your selected leaves. This is a cool and cooling accompaniment to hot spicy foods and to fried dishes.

# Fatoush

## A FAT *FATOUSH*

*Stolen water is sweet, and hidden bread delicious...* (Hebrew saying)

More useless etymology for you. *Fatoush* is actually one of a range of dishes collectively known as *fatta* (which means "crushed bread," or "crumbs"), the common culinary denominator being the inclusion of stale bread.

    This is probably the most common salad in the Levant. It is eminently tweakable (i.e. you can throw all kinds of ingredients into it depending on the season and the contents of your fridge), and a terrific way to use up stale bread.

SERVES 4 AS A SIDE SALAD

1 plus ½ piece whole-wheat pita bread

a little non-virgin olive oil, for frying

2 teaspoons sumac

4 tasty tomatoes

2 baby cucumbers, scraped, or ½ regular
    cucumber, peeled

4 scallions

1 green pepper

1 Boston bibb (butter) lettuce

about 20 black olives

1 handful fresh mint, chopped

1 handful fresh parsley, chopped

1 handful cilantro, chopped

6 tablespoons olive oil

juice of 1½ lemons

2 garlic cloves, minced (optional)

salt and black pepper

Toast the pita bread until it puffs up, split it, and then cut it into 1¼in (3cm) chunks. Heat a little oil in a frying pan, and tip in the bread; cook for a couple of minutes, turning it over halfway through, then lift out on to a piece of paper towel to drain. (Don't worry if the bread still seems soft—it will become crunchier as it cools.) Put the sumac in a paper bag, add the croûtons, and shake the bag to coat evenly before setting to one side.

    Cube the tomatoes and cucumbers: about ¾in (2cm) chunks are good. This should be a salad with texture, not a salsa. Chop the scallions, green pepper, and lettuce to match, and then add the olives and herbs. Whisk the olive oil with the lemon juice, garlic, and seasoning, and pour it over the salad ingredients. Toss in the croutons, and there you have it.

Note:

If, as per the quotation, hidden bread is delicious, snuck-in cheese is divine. I often add *labneh* (see p.76) or feta to this dish, and it is pretty cool with Boursin too.

Handy housekeeping hint:

When you have squeezed lemons, don't throw them away. They are great sink aids. Just toss your used wedges/halves in the sink … and leave them there. As hot water hits them, not only will they reward you with a lovely burst of lemony zing, the oils and remaining juice from the skin will help cut through life's greasier challenges. Used lemon wedges are also great for rubbing into the hands to shift stubborn odors such as onion and garlic.

Kookoo Sabzi

# HERBY OMELET THINGIES

This is another of the great green dishes of Iran—an omelet so stiff with herbs that it is practically viridescent. The word *kookoo* actually applies to a range of eggy dishes, which can be made with ingredients as diverse as eggplant and sugar. This recipe can be prepared in the form of baby patties, or you can make it as one large omelet and cut it into wedges (I nearly always opt for the latter, as I am very clumsy). They are great as a lunch or light supper option with some bread and salad or you can tart them up into a dinner party appetizer—but in Iran *kookoo* are most often used as a sandwich filling together with fresh herbs and spicy pickled cucumbers.

You can replace the cilantro, parsley, and fenugreek with a bag of *sabzi kookoo* dried herb mix, available from Middle Eastern supermarkets.

SERVES 6 AS A SNACK

1 bunch cilantro
1 bunch flat-leaf parsley
few sprigs fenugreek
1 small bunch scallions
6 eggs
2 teaspoons flour
½ teaspoon baking powder

salt and pepper
olive oil, for frying

OPTIONAL EXTRAS:
1 cup/3½oz/100g lightly broken walnuts, or
1⅓ cups/3½oz/100g soaked barberries, or
scant ⅔ cup/3½oz/100g soaked raisins, or
⅔ cup/3½oz/100g toasted pine nuts

Trim and soak your herbs and leave to drain a while. Wash and chop the scallions, and then chop the herbs. (If using dried herbs, soak them for 15 minutes and then squeeze as much of the moisture out as possible.)

Beat the eggs well, and then blend in the flour, baking powder, seasoning and any of your chosen "optional extras." Fry the herbs and scallions in hot oil for around 5 minutes, turning constantly, and then pour the egg mixture on top. Cook on a lowish heat for around 15 minutes, and then either toss the omelet or pop the pan under a broiler for about 3 minutes. Slide on to a plate, and then cut into wedges. Enjoy hot or cold.

# Khoresht-e-Carafs

## HERBY CELERY CASSEROLE

This is a super blend of flavors and textures: there's the sharpness of the sour grapes, the crunchiness of the celery, the curiousness of walnuts floating around therein, the surprise of the odd taste of apple, the freshness and verdancy of the herb combination ... Yes, it is one of my favorite Iranian dishes. It is traditionally prepared with chicken or lamb (and without the apple or walnuts), but the meat is really quite irrelevant to the flavor and in my opinion this vegetarian version is much nicer.

SERVES 4

1 plump head of celery, well washed
a slosh of sunflower oil
1 large onion, chopped
1 teaspoon ground turmeric
¼ bottle sour grape juice (or 1 tablespoon lemon juice)
4 teaspoons fresh or pickled sour grapes (optional)

salt and pepper
1 small bunch mint, or generous ½ cup/1½oz/40g dried mint
1 small bunch parsley, or generous ¾ cup/2¼oz/60g dried
1 small bunch cilantro, or generous ½ cup/1½oz/40g dried
2 medium cooking apples
¾ cup/2¾oz/75g shelled walnut pieces

Cut the celery into 1½–2in (4–5cm) strips, splitting the fatter chunks from the base in half, and then fry it in some sunflower oil. Once the celery has softened, toss in the onion and turmeric. After another 5 minutes, add the sour grape juice, sour grapes, salt and pepper, and enough water to cover; bring to a boil and set to simmer.

In the meantime, sort, wash, drain, and chop your herbs, or *sabzi*. (If using dried herbs, soak them first for 15 minutes.) Pour a little oil in a frying pan, and fry the herbs, stirring constantly so that they do not "catch." Cook for around 8 minutes, and then add to the casserole.

Peel, core, and chunk the apples and add them to the *khoresht* together with the walnuts. Let it all bubble away gently for another 15 minutes, or until the apple is cooked. Check the seasoning: this dish benefits from extra freshly milled black pepper.

Serve with plain or smoked basmati rice, yogurt, and fresh raw garlic. And because I'm into themed meals, I often serve a matching Waldorf-style salad, with celery, apple, and walnuts (see p.42). Twee, I know.

### Variations on the theme...

*Khoresht-e-Carafs* is but one of several casseroles based on the mint and parsley theme. Other veggies to get the same treatment in Iran include rhubarb (in which case, you just drop it in at the end, and leave out the apple) and cardoons. The latter are perhaps not something you find easily at the produce section of your nearest supermarket, but can easily be grown in the garden. The plant is a wild cousin of the artichoke; it is the stalks which are eaten: just sauté them as you would the celery above.

# Khudruwat Magliya bi Salsat a'Shab

# FRIED VEGETABLES WITH HERB SAUCE (*TARATOR*)

*Tarator* is another one of those foodie words that exists in different countries and means entirely different things. The word is often applied to *tahini* (see p.56), but in the context of this recipe (based on the Turkish dish of the same name) it is more like a sort of emulsified pesto. And it is really, really useful.

Savory is used extensively in the Middle East. By contrast, we have largely forgotten what to do with it and it is quite hard to find in stores. So, once again you either need to be very nice to your neighbor, get busy in the garden yourself, or scour the farmers' markets. It is kind of thyme-like, so you could substitute a bit of thyme or marjoram in its place. Or use dried savory. Oh, and be careful with whom you enjoy it: it has a reputation for stirring up all manner of saucy acts...*

SERVES 4 AS AN APPETIZER
FOR THE *TARATOR*:
2 slices stale bread, crusts off
1 cup/3½oz/100g shelled walnuts
2 garlic cloves, minced (optional)
2 tablespoons wine vinegar
½ bunch cilantro, woody
    stalks removed
handful of summer savory (or winter, but use
    less; it has a more pungent flavor)
generous ¾ cup/7fl oz/200ml olive oil
salt and pepper, to taste

FOR THE FRIED VEG:
8 small florets of cauliflower
8 x ½in (1cm) slices of zucchini
4 small florets of broccoli
8 mushrooms
2 tablespoons flour, seasoned
2 eggs, beaten
scant 1¼ cups/5½oz/about 150g
    breadcrumbs (or polenta)

Soak the bread in water, and then squeeze the liquid out. Put it in the blender together with the walnuts and the garlic, and give it a quick whizz. Add the vinegar and the herbs and blend it a bit more before trickling in the olive oil. You should end up with a smooth green paste.

Roll the veggies in flour (if they have been washed and are still slightly wet, this will help the flour to stick), dunk them in the egg wash, and then roll them in the breadcrumbs. Putting them in the fridge for 1 hour will give you a better result when you fry them, although it is not essential.

When you are ready, shallow- or deep-fry the vegetables until they are crispy and golden. Arrange them on a platter with a bowl of the *tarator* in the middle.

*
It is believed that the word "satyr" is derived from the Latin name for summer savory: *Satureja hortensis*. They reputedly roamed and grazed on the savory-strewn slopes of Rome's Seven Hills, getting friskier and friskier, generally being naughty little half-humans. Fortunately, winter savory is deemed to be whatever the opposite of an aphrodisiac is, soothing the libido. The power of herbs, eh?

# Sabzi Pulao

## HERBY RICE WITH SAFFRON VEGETABLES

This is one of the four great green dishes of Iran, stiff with so many herbs that they really do look green. *Sabzi* is the generic word for herbs in Farsi, and adding its name to the dish you are to prepare (in this case rice, or *pulao*) denotes a particular mix and proportion of herbs—in this case, parsley, cilantro, dill, and chives. You can buy bags of pre-washed, chopped, and dried herbs in Middle Eastern supermarkets, but the fresh herbs for this dish are pretty easy to find.

    *Sabzi pulao* is traditionally served with smoked fish, and is a great favorite at the Persian New Year, *Nowrooz*. When you are making this, don't forget that it is the rice that is the star here—the saffron veggies are just the garnish.

    You can substitute the herbs and chives for 1 bag of dried *sabzi pulao* mix.

SERVES 4
FOR THE RICE:

4 measures (¾ cup/5½oz/150g per measure) basmati rice
4 cloves garlic, finely chopped
1 bunch each parsley, cilantro, and dill
either 2 bunches chives, or 2 leeks
(or substitute the herbs and chives for 1 bag of dried *sabzi pulao* mix)
1–2 teaspoons turmeric
oil or vegetable ghee
salt

FOR THE SAFFRON VEGGIES:

knob of butter (3½ tablespoons/1¾oz/50g)
1 onion, peeled and chopped
2 zucchini, scrubbed and chunked
1½ tablespoons capers, chopped
4 tomatoes, chunked
1 bag/bunch watercress, washed and roughly chopped
1 can (14oz/400g) butter beans
¼ teaspoon ground saffron
juice and zest of 1 unwaxed lemon
salt and black pepper

Trim, soak, drain, and chop the herbs (or, if using the dried variety, just soak and then squeeze out the excess moisture). Heat some oil in a frying pan and fry the garlic without allowing it to turn brown. Toss in the herbs, a handful at a time, and the turmeric, stirring constantly. Fry the mixture for around 7 minutes to make sure that all the particles are coated and cooked.

    Wash the rice and boil it for about 15 minutes; then drain and rinse it. Sizzle some oil in the bottom of the pan. Add a layer of rice, and let it fry until it starts to catch (stick and burn) and then layer the rest of the rice and fried herb mixture alternately on top. Make four or five "fumaroles" through the rice with the handle of a wooden spoon. Fit a cloth-covered lid on top, cook for 5 minutes on high, and then reduce the heat and allow to cook through for about 30 minutes. (If you are using a rice cooker, wash your rice as usual and then add the garlic with the butter right at the beginning.) Stir the herbs through the rice just at the end of the cooking process—the rice should end up looking quite green.

*(continues overleaf)*

Melt some butter in a pan and when sizzling throw in the onion, zucchini, and capers. Fry them gently for around 5 minutes, then add the tomatoes. After a further 5 minutes add the watercress and butter beans. Steep the saffron in a very small amount of boiling water, and then add the lemon juice and zest. Pour this fragrant mixture over the vegetables, cover the pan, and leave to simmer for a few minutes more. Season to taste.

Take your rice off the heat, run ¾in (2cm) of cold water into the sink and stand the pan in it for a few minutes—this will make the sticky "*tahdik*" (see p.131) unstick a little and come out looking just so. Even if you are using a rice cooker, turning it off a few minutes before you turn it out aids the process. Turn the rice on to a large serving dish, and then crack the crust in one line through the middle. Pour the saffron vegetable mixture in a stripe along the length of the crack. Eat with fresh herbs, lots of posh and piquant Persian pickles, and some plain yogurt.

*

Saffron: some
mellow yellow facts

Saffron is the costliest spice on earth, and never more so than at the time of writing. This is hardly surprising when you learn that it takes around 15,000 crocus flowers to produce just 3½oz/100g of the stuff. But its unique aroma and sunny, smiley disposition is invaluable in the kitchen, and it is one of the most distinctive characters in Middle Eastern cuisine. The best comes from Iran, where it is used in everything from sweets, to rice, to ice cream. There is even an ancient urban myth suggesting that putting it in your tea will make you laugh. But all sorts of other countries produce it, from Spain to India. There is even a burgeoning saffron industry in Wales! Always buy real stamen saffron and grind it yourself: you never know what has gone into the powdered variety. To get the best out of it, steep a little in a saucer of boiling water: the flavor and color will thus get evenly distributed throughout the dish. If you have any of the saffron liquid left, just store it in an airtight jar in the fridge.

# Salat Basal wa a'Shab
## ONION AND HERB SALAD

This is such a useful accompaniment to just about any savory dish. You can make it into a more substantial salad by adding tomato and olives and even feta, but in this format you can use it as a base for fried veggies, a side dish for dishes as diverse as pizza and curry, a garnish, or a *mezze* dish in its own right.

If you find raw onions too strong, you can make a very good alternative using baked onions. And if you are in a hurry, just skip the dressing: the onions and the herbs have a synergistic, mollifying effect on each other, and are a great combination without anything added.

SERVES 4

2 teaspoons brown sugar

3 tablespoons olive oil

1 tablespoon apple cider vinegar

2 large onions, peeled

1 big handful fresh mint, chopped

1 big handful cilantro, chopped

1 big handful fresh parsley, chopped

salt and pepper

Dissolve the brown sugar in a tiny splosh of boiling water, and then whisk it into the olive oil together with the vinegar.

Cut the onions in half from top to bottom, and then slice them very finely so they fall in semi-circles. Mix the herbs through the onion, and then stir the dressing over everything. Season to taste.

This salad benefits from being made a little in advance, say 1 hour, although it doesn't keep well through to the next day: leftover sliced onions sweat and sag, and ooze a horrible aroma if you leave them too long.

# *TAHINI* CROSTINI

Most folks don't know the difference between *tahina/eh* and *tahini*. It is left to us sesame geeks to explain. The thick, cement-like sesame paste that you ladle into hummus is *tahina/eh*, while the word *tahini* is applied to products made from *tahina*, most notably a dip/sauce.

It is of great nutritional value to the dedicated vegetarian/vegan, as it is strong on trace minerals and high-ish in protein. And it is also a firm friend of the Middle Eastern chef, as it is so versatile. (See opposite.)

There are two types of *tahina*—the dark one, which is made from whole sesame seeds, and the lighter one, which is a blend of hulled sesame seeds. You can use either here, although the latter is more authentic and more commonplace.

*Tahini crostini* are a great party option: you can make the dip well beforehand and they are quick to assemble.

FOR A BUFFET FOR 20
FOR THE *TAHINI*:
about 6 tablespoons *tahina*
6 garlic cloves, peeled
1 bunch flat-leaf parsley, washed
4 tablespoons nice olive oil
4 tablespoons lemon juice
about 3 cups/24fl oz/700ml cold water
salt and pepper

TO FINISH:
3 sheets *taftoon* bread, or 1 baguette
some more nice olive oil
1 grated carrot
2 sticks celery, shredded
20 sliced green olives

Mixers at the ready? (Yes, you can do it by hand, but this is much easier with a blender.) Spoon half the *tahina* into the blender along with half the garlic. Pull away the woodier bits of the parsley, but you can leave most of the stalk on; add about half of it to the *tahina* along with 2 tablespoons of the olive oil. Turn the blender on and immediately add half the lemon juice. Slowly trickle in half of the water to make an emulsion. Season to tase. You should end up with a pale khaki, creamy paste: if it looks a bit runny don't worry, as this stuff sets when it is chilled. Repeat with the other half of the ingredients, and then cover and put it in the fridge for about 1 hour.

Ready to assemble your crostini? If you are using chunky flatbread such as *taftoon* or *barberi*, cut it into rounds or squares or hexagons, about 1½in (4cm) wide. If you are using baguette, just slice it into rounds about ½in (1.5cm) thick. Toast the bread lightly under the broiler or in the oven, and then brush it with olive oil. Spread a little of the *tahini* on to each bread round, and top with a pinch of the grated veggies and some slices of olive.

*Tahini* is also great as a dip to serve with fancy chips and crudités, and is a great *mezze* dish. I confess to enjoying it with a spoon straight out of the bowl when no one's looking.

\*  *Jahina — the lowdown*

*Tahina* is really thick and
unprepossessing just as it is: hardly
surprising, as it is mostly oil. In order
to get the best out of it, you need to
dilute it, either as opposite, or with
hot liquid for cooking. It is practically
indestructible in the fridge once you
have opened it—but here are a few
ideas to help you use up that big jar
you bought:

\* Mix it with *pekmez*, or Turkish fruit
paste, as a spread to eat with bread for
breakfast or supper. Or use date or
carob syrup. (See p.213.)
\* Use it to thicken soups and sauces.
Take a little of your hot cooking stock
and add it to a spoonful of *tahina*:
mix well and stir the whole lot back
into the pan.
\* It is great in dips other than *tahini*
or hummus: try blending some with
ripe avocado, roasted eggplants, or
baked squash.
\* Add it to salad dressings for a lovely
nutty flavor: try tossing some toasted
sesame seeds into the salad to boot.
\* You can pretty much use it in the same
way as you would peanut butter—just
blend it with a little water until it is
workable, and then smooth it into
sandwiches, add it to stir-fries, or use
it as a dressing on steamed veggies.

dairy and eggs

Long long ago in Egypt, when the pyramids were still shiny new, there lived a young peasant lad. He was a dreamer, this one: he felt he could do better than the life of a second-rank sarcophagus builder. So he borrowed some money and bought some eggs. Lots of eggs. To take to market and sell.

With his goodies all packed up, he wandered down to the Nile and waited for the next felucca to ferry him north, towards the big city. It was a hot afternoon, so he put his basket of eggs down, settled in some shade by the jetty and lazily contemplated his "prosperous" future.

He would get a good price for the eggs and use the profit to buy some beautiful fabric to sell to the womenfolk back home: they would be sure to fall upon it, and with the money he raised therein he could buy a ewe. He could sell the ewe's milk while he waited for her to bear lambs, and he would then trade these for a water-buffalo. With the buffalo he could tender his services to local farmers, and when the water-buffalo came to calf, he would sell both of them and put down a deposit on his own land. And with the earnings he reaped from farming his plot, he would finally be able to afford his own servant. Someone he could boss around, or even KICK as a punishment for laziness.

And in his excitement that is exactly what he did: he kicked out, sending the basket flying and all of his eggs rolling down the bank splish-splosh-splosh into the murky waters.

Which is why you should never put all of your eggs in one basket. And never count your chickens before they have hatched.

In ancient Veggiestan, eggs and dairy products were an important part of the food chain, offering protein at a time when meat was perhaps not so widely available. And this is still the case.

Without a doubt, Middle Easterners eat a lot of eggs. Health worries seem largely to have passed them by. The region seems blissfully immune to food fads and scares. All the nations involved seem to have variations of the same dishes: thick omelet, egg scrambled randomly with spice, tomato paste, or vegetables, and little fried patty things. This chapter comprises my selection of the most interesting.

Eggs also have a place at the finest feasts: eggs were regarded as the ultimate garnish for many classic dishes. Spiced hard-boiled eggs, served hot and thus impossible to eat, remain a popular street-food treat in parts of the Levant.

While the Middle East does not share the West's fixation with fresh milk (milk is generally understood to be something that comes in cans, and is often evaporated or condensed), it does boast a complexity of offerings from the dairy: from yogurt through to cheese and a confusing array of hybrids. Many of these were discovered by accident by nomads trying to find the best way of traveling with and preserving food.

## THE YOGURT AISLE

It is the Turks who gave us the word yogurt, although the earliest evidence of its production seems to come out of Bulgaria (which is why its chief, active, friendly bacteria is called *bulgaris*). Like so many dairy products (and many of the best things in life), it was almost certainly discovered by accident.

Yogurt is undoubtedly one of the linchpins of Veggiestan cuisine. It gets everywhere: in marinades, soups, sauces, appetizers, mains, and desserts. And it is a favorite accompaniment for other dishes, as its bacterial content is a great digestive soother.

So firstly let's learn how to make our own: there's nothing much to it and we should all be doing it more often. Certainly, across the Middle East the average housewife would consider it a very odd (decadent, lazy) notion to buy yogurt.

Then we'll have a look at some ways to tart it up a bit.

# BASIC RECIPE FOR YOGURT

Equipment first. Assemble one large bowl, one large saucepan, and a bit of old blanket. Ideally you also need some muslin to strain the finished product, but any bit of clean cotton will do. Old pillowcases are ideal.

Instead of using whole milk, you can make vegan yogurt with soy milk and bacteria culture—it works on exactly the same principle—but the results may not be as thick as the dairy version.

This is my mother-in-law's recipe, and she always makes a lot!

MAKES 8½ CUPS/2 LITERS
8½ cups/68fl oz/2 liters whole milk

generous 1 cup/7oz/200g cheap plain yogurt
(ideally live, but not essential)

Bring the milk to a boil in the pan, and then take it off the heat. Allow it to cool to the point that you can stick your finger in it without yelling, then take a ladleful and whisk it into the yogurt in the bowl. Pour in the rest of the milk, mix well, cover the bowl with a plate, and wrap it in the blanket. You need to find it somewhere warm and draft-free to sit for around 8 hours (or overnight); a warm linen cupboard is ideal if you have such a luxury.

After this period your yogurt is effectively ready: it should be thick and gloopy. But you can make it even thicker by straining it: just spoon the yogurt into the pillowcase (or the middle of your cloth), and then suspend it over the sink (hanging it from the faucet works well) for 1 hour, or until all the excess liquid drains away.

Obviously after this you need to keep it in the fridge. If you're pleased with the results, one trick of the trade is to use the last spoonful of the first batch as a culture to start a second.

*Tip*
Burned yourself in the kitchen? Smear some yogurt on to the burn straight away: it soothes instantly and is just as good as the swankiest burn creams.

# Çaçik, Tsatsiki, Jajik, Must-o-Khiar
## YOGURT WITH CUCUMBER

Call it what you will, this recipe is the cornerstone of *mezze* spreads and a rival to hummus and falafel as the most well-known Middle Eastern dish of all. It probably came from Turkey, where it is often enjoyed as a watery, iced accompaniment to other dishes. The Greek, Arabic, and Persian versions are thicker and consumed as an appetizer with bread. In Armenia and the Northern -istans, the dish is found in soup form, sometimes made with *kefir* (see p.88) in place of yogurt.

SERVES 6–8 AS A DIP/SIDE DISH
½ regular cucumber (or about 5 baby ones)
2½ cups/1lb 2oz/500g plain yogurt
3–4 garlic cloves, crushed

a handful of fresh mint, chopped
   (or 1½ teaspoons dried mint)
2 tablespoons olive oil
salt and pepper

Most of the cuisines mentioned above would have you peel your cucumber first. I don't: the skin is such a pretty color. They also suggest that you grate it. Which I also don't do: grating bruises a vegetable (which means that the end-product will become watery or "go bad" much more quickly). Instead, dice the cucumber very finely, and then stir it into the yogurt. Add the garlic and the mint, beat in the olive oil (which helps to thicken the yogurt and gives it a lovely sheen), and season to taste.

*Regional variations*
In Iran walnuts and raisins are often added. This is because yogurt is a "cold" food, and the walnuts and fruit are "warm" and help to balance it out. (See p. 106.) In Georgia and parts of Turkey, the mint is replaced by dill. In Syria and parts of Turkey, sumac is used as a garnish.

# Must-e-Laboo
## PERSIAN YOGURT WITH BEET

Worth making for its looks alone, this is a lovely dip/*mezze* dish. It also makes for a stunning centerpiece to a salad—instead of using a conventional dressing, just spoon a good dollop of this lovely pinky lilac-y stuff into the middle of a bowl of green salad leaves and let folks help themselves.

SERVES 6–8 AS AN APPETIZER
1lb 2oz/500g cooked beet
2½ cups/1lb 2oz/500g thick plain yogurt

2 tablespoons olive oil
salt and pepper

Dice the beet really finely and stir into the yogurt. Whisk in the olive oil, and season to taste. Best enjoyed with warm flatbread and fresh *sabzi* (see p.53).

# Burani Bonjon

# AFGHAN YOGURT WITH EGGPLANTS

The origin of the word *burani* is lost in the swirls of gastro-time, but it is popularly believed that it is named after one Pourandokht, the queen of Ctesiphon, in Mesopotamia. She was partial to yogurt, and so her chefs created a range of dishes comprising yogurt.

In Iran the ingredients of *borani* are well blended and served cold: in Afghanistan, they are layered while still warm, turning *burani* into a textured, creamy platter of delight. This is the most famous version.

SUPPER FOR 4

3 large eggplants, washed
salt
canola oil, for frying*
1 large onion, chopped
4 green chilies, chopped
1 teaspoon ground turmeric
4 tomatoes, chopped (or use 1 large can)
1 small bunch cilantro, chopped

FOR THE YOGURT:

scant 2 cups/16fl oz/450ml thick strained
    yogurt
2 tablespoons lemon juice
4–6 garlic cloves, minced (not pulling any
    punches here)
handful of fresh chopped mint (or 2 teaspoons
    dried mint)
salt and pepper

\*
    I suggest using canola oil, though sunflower oil is more authentic, because canola (or rapeseed) oil is one of the good guys in a world of general oleaginous badness: it's got Omega 3 and 6, and the right proportion of saturated and unsaturated fats. As eggplants gobble up so much oil, it makes sense to use a good one.

## Variations on the theme

Just substitute the eggplant with zucchini or marrow. And no need to salt the vegetables in advance. I especially favor the marrow option, as it is such a maligned and under-used squash.

Purists would have you peel the eggplants. Not me. Simply remove the calyx and slice the vegetables into slices about ¼in (6–7mm) thick. Sprinkle salt over them, and leave to draw for at least 30 minutes, then rinse and wipe dry. Heat a slosh of oil in a deep frying pan (one with a lid is good) and sizzle the onion and chilies until the former is soft. Remove with a slotted spoon and set to one side. Now add a bit more oil to the pan and fry the eggplant slices so that they are gently browned on both sides. Sprinkle them with the turmeric, and add the tomatoes and cilantro (retaining about a quarter of it for garnish), together with the cooked onion/chili. Add a little water to the pan (so that the ingredients are more or less covered), place the lid on it (or improvise one), turn the heat right down, and leave to simmer for around 30 minutes (but keep an eye on the liquid level).

In the meantime rustle up the "sauce." Blend the yogurt and the lemon juice in a bowl, stir in the garlic and the mint, and season to taste. Chill well.

Time to assemble the dish. Check the seasoning of the eggplant concoction—you may need to add salt. Spoon half of the yogurt across a decent-sized platter, spreading it to get good coverage. Then layer the eggplants on top, and follow that with the rest of the yogurt. Scatter the remaining cilantro over the top and serve immediately—even as you are arranging the hot and the cold elements, they will start to leach into each other. This is a treat best mopped up with warm naan bread, although you could eat it with rice. There won't be any left over.

*Ayran, Laban Rayeb, Doogh*

# THE STRANGE PHENOMENON
# OF SALTED DRINKING YOGURT

This is one of the stranger things I have been persuaded to sample since I hooked up with an Iranian. If you haven't tried it before, it is a real shock to the taste buds: how can drinking something that is really quite salty possibly slake the thirst?

The West is perhaps most familiar with the Turkish word *ayran*; the Arabs call drinking yogurt *laban* or *laban rayeb*, while the Iranians and Afghans call it *doogh*. (The Iranian version enjoys the additional weirdness of being sparkling.) All three words refer to a basic blend of thinned yogurt with salt, ice, and mint, which is enjoyed across the region as an accompaniment to heavy meals and a tonic for hot weather. If you think about it, it does make sense: the yogurt is cooling and aids the digestion, the added water quenches the thirst, and the salt replaces what is lost through sweating/perspiring (delete as applicable, unless you are a real lady, in which case you may prefer merely to "glow"). The drink also has a reputation for being somewhat soporific.

While *ayran* at least is readily available in Middle Eastern stores, it is very easy to make at home.

MAKES 4½ CUPS/1 LITER
generous 2 cups/17fl oz/500ml plain yogurt
generous 2 cups/17fl oz/500ml cold water

2 teaspoons salt
2 teaspoons dried mint or pennyroyal*

Whisk (and I do mean whisk) the yogurt and the water together, add the salt and the mint, and chill well. Serve over ice.

To make the fizzy version, *doogh*, follow the same method, but use about twice as much soda or sparkling mineral water as yogurt.

If you are using soy yogurt, use less water, as the yogurt is thinner in the first place. Or you can try thickening it with agar agar flakes.

**\* Pennyroyal**
While pennyroyal is not dangerous in small quantities, it should not be consumed by pregnant women.

# Sabzi Jaht to Khamir Mayeh
# CRISPY FRIED VEGGIES IN
# *DOOGH* BATTER

A sort of Persian tempura, this makes for a quick and easy appetizer or party platter. The fried vegetables obviously beg for a sauce, and I cannot think of any better than the garlicky *laban mutboukh* (see p.74). *Tahini* (see p.56) would also work well.

To make the *doogh*, follow the recipe opposite, but use half yogurt and half sparkling water; the batter needs to be thick.

SERVES 4

5 tablespoons flour

1¼ cups/10fl oz/300ml *doogh* (see opposite)

1 teaspoon turmeric

1 teaspoon chili flakes

½ teaspoon salt

4 bite-sized chunks each of 3 of the following:
  eggplant, zucchini, mushroom,
  broccoli, onion, peppers

peanut (or sunflower) oil, for frying

Beat 2 tablespoons of the flour into the *doogh*, add the turmeric, and set aside for around 20 minutes.

Sift the rest of the flour on to a plate, combining it with the chili flakes and the salt. Rinse and drain the veggie chunks, then roll them in the spiced flour. Give the batter another quick whisk, then dunk the vegetables into it. Suspend each piece briefly over the batter to drain off any surplus, and then deep-fry (in batches) until crispy golden and floating on the surface of the oil. Scoop out and drain on paper towels and keep warm until you are ready to serve. Present on a warmed plate with your choice of dipping sauce(s) in a bowl on the side.

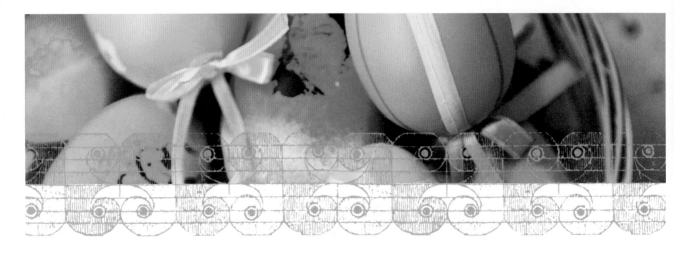

# WESTERN INTERNATIONAL BREAKFAST

We were import rookies. It was all new to Jamshid and I. *Going to market.* The very words made us feel like big boys, players in the nationwide early morning throng of the fruit and vegetable trade. Shame about the painfully early start...

We were off to Western International Market to meet a "contact," Hamid, an expert in the market trade, who was going to help us shift our first container of Bam dates. There are three wholesale fruit and vegetable markets in London: New Spitalfields Market, New Covent Garden Market, and Western International. WIM is the cocky young upstart of the trio—the other two each have 400–500 year pedigrees, whereas WIM is really only in its fourth decade. It has become known for perishable goods that need to come in by air: it is, in effect, a market for the produce of Veggiestan.

Anyway, back to our first visit. 4am we got there. Mid-winter (dates being a winter fruit), in a rundown transit van with very little heating. After a lot of hassle we were allowed in… only to find most of the units locked up. A chill wind blew through, leeching from us what little warmth we had left. Brush wood and prairie dogs would not have been out of place: even the café was closed.

After about two hours, our man turned up, clutching some still-warm twists of sesame bread. A cheery, bristling chap, he found it very funny that we'd turned up at the arranged time (we didn't laugh), but he soon had the doors of his unit swung open, a choking oil heater started up in his musty, smoky office, and the kettle on for chai. While Jamshid and he talked in grown-up, manly, business-like fashion about fruit and pallets and brokers and potential customers and after-shave, I went a-noseying… only to find that the warehouse was full of secondhand shoes. And books. Hamid is from Iraq you see, and at the time was engaged in all sorts of totally-above-board-but-very-strange schemes to help his fellow countrymen. You wouldn't find that at the other two markets, that's for sure. By the time I got back to the office they'd gotten a real fug up in there—a grease-caked Baby Belling in the corner had been brought into play, and our host was cooking us breakfast, Iraqi style. I'm ashamed to admit that by that time I was so cold and tired and hungry that I started drooling.

Anyway, here's the recipe: *Beid bil Tamriya*—Fried Eggs with Dates. Because the best food in the world is often the simplest.

# Beid bil Jamriya
## FRIED EGGS WITH DATES

SERVES 4
knob of butter (3½ tablespoons/1¾oz/50g)
1lb 2oz/500g pitted dates (fresh are best)

4 eggs
1 level teaspoon ground cardamom (optional fancy extra)

Melt the butter in a frying pan. Toss in the dates and mash them up a bit with a wooden spoon, stirring all the while. After a couple of minutes, break the eggs in, continuing to stir. Cook for a couple of minutes more, or until the eggs are cooked, then take off the heat and sprinkle with ground cardamom.

Serve immediately with fresh warm bread, and alongside hot black tea.

# Beid Hamine
## EGYPTIAN BOILED EGGS

*Beid Hamine* was a favorite with Egypt's ancient Jewish community, and was probably devised to fit with the rules of the Sabbath, which prohibit cooking thereon. The eggs are traditionally cooked very slowly overnight, and then enjoyed as a gourmet breakfast or reserved to garnish soups and casseroles.

The recipe appeals not least because it is using two ingredients that you would usually throw away. And since you are bound to ask, the onions add a really creamy flavor and the grounds lend a delicate beige color to the eggs. The oil is to slow the evaporation of water.

SABBATH BREAKFAST FOR 4
8 eggs
water

the skins of 3–4 onions
2 tablespoons coffee grounds
1 tablespoon oil

Put the eggs in a pan and cover them with water. Add the onion skins and the coffee grounds, followed by the oil. Set on a very, very low heat and let it do its thing for 6–8 hours.

Slice or quarter and use to top hot beans (see *Ful Medames*, p.115) or spicy veggie dishes. Or use them as part of a breakfast *mezze*.

Jahcheen Esfanaji

# PERSIAN RICE CAKE

This is a great dinner favorite in our household. Seems we're not alone in liking it: even the great Shah Abbas was partial to it. It is the sort of food that you just keep eating until you feel near ready to explode. You know, a bit like pistachios, or *halva*—you just keep finding room for a little bit more until you have to be carried from the table. Well, it is made from some healthy stuff, especially if you use brown basmati.

Another brilliant thing about it is that although we eat it as a weekday supper, you can dress it up in fancy ramekins (reducing the quantities accordingly) and serve as an appetizer at a dinner party. You can even serve it as an accompaniment to another dish.

SERVES 4

2 cups/14oz/400g basmati rice

about 7 tablespoons/3½oz/100g butter or
    veggie ghee

salt

¼ teaspoon ground saffron steeped in
    boiling water

1 large onion, chopped

2 lb 4oz/1kg spinach, washed and chopped

2 eggs, beaten

generous 2 cups/17fl oz/500ml thick whole-
    milk yogurt

generous 2 cups/17fl oz/500ml vegetable stock

½ teaspoon ground black pepper

Cook the rice with butter and salt in the normal manner (see pp.130–132), but using a bit more butter than usual—i.e. most of that 3½oz (100g)'s worth —and taking the rice off the heat just as soon as it is cooked. Stir the saffron through it, and set it all to one side.

Fry the onion in a little oil, and when it has softened add in the spinach: stir well until the spinach has wilted.

Beat the eggs into the yogurt, and then trickle in ⅔ cup/5fl oz/150ml of the stock, stirring all the while, followed by the pepper. Pour the resulting slurry over the cooked rice, and mix well.

Now grease a glass oven dish (which should be at least 2in/5cm in depth) using the remaining butter and pack half of the eggy rice mixture into it. Spread the spinach over the top, and cap with the rest of the rice. Cover the dish with a piece of well-greased foil, and cook on 375°F/190°C for about 30 minutes; then turn the oven down to 350°F/180°C and let it cook for another 1 hour. The dish should be visibly golden brown all over—you are aiming for a lovely sticky brown crust (see *tahdik*, p.131). Heat the rest of the veggie stock through to serve on the side.

Serve with plenty of pickles and relishes and a big bowl of salad.

# Avgolemono me Kukia
## *AVGOLEMONO* WITH FAVA BEANS

This much-loved Greek soup is usually made with chicken, but its name just means "egg and lemon" soup, and the dish is just as tasty in this vegetarian version. If not more so. If I may be so bold.

Things you should know about *avgolemono*: you can use the same recipe/principle to make/thicken a sauce for *kufte* or braised vegetables. The combination of fresh vegetable stock, soft rice, and lemon also means that it is ideal invalid food.

The only drawback with it is that because the making thereof is quite a delicate matter, it is really best just to make it in small batches, for you and a friend. It does not reheat well either. This is why you will rarely see it on restaurant menus.

SOUP FOR 3–4

butter, for frying (add a dash of oil to stop it from burning)

1 large leek, chopped

2 sticks celery, chopped

2 medium carrots, diced

1 small bunch fresh dill (or 2 tablespoons dried)

juice and zest of 1 lemon

scant 5 cups/40½fl oz/1.2 liters veggie stock or water

½ cup/3½oz/100g long-grain rice

1 cup/10½oz/300g fresh baby fava (broad) beans, shucked

2 large eggs, beaten

salt and pepper, to taste

handful of fresh basil and/or parsley, shredded, for garnish

Melt the butter in a saucepan and stir in the leek, celery, and carrot. Fry on a low heat until the vegetables become quite soft, and then add the dill and the lemon zest (but not the juice). After another minute, pour in the stock or water and bring to a boil. Add the rice and the fava beans, and set to simmer for about 15 minutes: the rice should then be more or less cooked.

Whisk the eggs with the lemon juice. Then take a ladleful of stock and pour it on top of the eggs, stirring all the time. Remove the soup from the heat, and pour the egg/lemon/stock mixture into the pan, stirring all the while. Season to taste, garnish, and serve immediately with fresh warm bread for dunking.

# *SHAITANY* FRIED EGG PITA POCKETS

*Shaitan* is the Arabic word for the devil. And these are his egg sandwiches. Not only are they naughty on the waistline front, but they are spiked with spices. Do we care? Do we heck. They really are the business. Great brunch or supper fare. Cholesterol be damned.

SERVES 2

2 slices whole-wheat pita bread

4 tablespoons olive oil

2 large tomatoes, finely sliced

4 free range eggs

1 teaspoon chili flakes

½ teaspoon turmeric

1 teaspoon *za'atar* (see p.98)

pinch salt

fresh *sabzi* (optional healthy extra—see p. 53)

Toast the pita until it puffs up a bit, cut the pieces in half, and split the pockets open. Wrap in a cloth to keep warm.

Heat the oil in a frying pan and slide the tomato slices in: cook for 30 seconds on either side, and remove to a small plate. Next the eggs: crack them into the pan and cook them for 30 seconds, then sprinkle the spices evenly over them. Once they are cooked the way you like them, take them off the heat. Using a spatula, fill each pita pocket with some sliced tomato, an egg, and *sabzi* if using, and enjoy straight away, right there, standing in the kitchen, egg running down your chin, giggling like naughty children.

I have a theory that the release of serotonin caused by this indulgence far outweighs any dietary trespasses.

# Eggeh wa Laban Mutboukh
# FAVA BEAN *EGGEH* WITH GARLIC YOGURT SAUCE

*Eggeh* is an Arabic omelet. Kind of. Not the light, thin fluffy type that a French chef would whisk up for you, but rather a thick, pan-baked Spanish-style omelet job that can be sliced and diced, eaten hot or cold, tarted up or dressed down.

This particular recipe is unusual in that the sauce (called *laban mutboukh*) carries the dish. It's an incredibly useful sauce, and will go with practically any hot vegetable dish (see Crispy Fried Veggies in *Doogh* Batter, p.65).

LUNCH FOR 4–6
FOR THE *EGGEH*:

1lb 2oz/500g fresh fava (broad) beans (or frozen)

7 eggs plus 1 yolk (see below)

1 tablespoon milk

1 teaspoon salt

ground black pepper

generous handful of fresh parsley or dill, chopped

knob of butter (3½ tablespoons/1¾oz/50g)

FOR THE *LABAN MUTBOUKH* SAUCE:

tiny splosh of oil

8 garlic cloves, finely chopped

1¾ cups/14fl oz/400ml plain yogurt

1 whisked egg white

½ teaspoon cornstarch

pinch of salt

Shuck the fava beans and cook them in boiling water for 10 minutes, or until tender. Then whisk the eggs together with the milk, salt, and pepper, and stir in the parsley/dill and the drained beans. Melt a generous knob of butter in a heavy-bottomed frying pan and, when it is sizzling, tip in the egg mix. Turn the heat right down and leave it to cook through (about 20 minutes).

In the meantime make the sauce. As it is to be served hot, the yogurt needs to be stabilized, hence the egg white and cornstarch. Heat the oil in a heavy-bottomed saucepan and sauté the garlic. Remove the garlic, set it to one side, turn the heat way down, and tip the yogurt in. Now add in the egg white, cornstarch, and salt, stirring constantly in the same direction. Stirring the yogurt randomly will cause it to curdle—trust me on this. Bring the pan's contents slowly to a boil, then simmer for a few minutes. Take it off the heat and stir the garlic back in.

Once the *eggeh* is looking firm all over, pop it under a broiler for a few moments to seal/brown the top, and then slide it out on to a serving plate. Stripe some of the sauce across the top, and offer the rest in a bowl on the side. Serve cut into wedges, with warm bread and a pretty bowl of salad.

Alternatively, you can bake *eggeh* in the oven: just pour the mixture into a well-greased oven dish, and cook it at 325°F/160°C for about 45 minutes.

# TURKISH EGGS WITH A KICK

We're basically talking fancy scrambled eggs. Every nation has a version of this: *piperade* springs to mind; the Tunisians have a similar thing called *chakchouka*. But this dish is a strong contender for the position of Turkey's favorite breakfast.

SERVES 4

1 green and 1 red pepper

1–2 small hot green chilies

2 scallions

1 medium onion

2 large tomatoes

olive oil, for frying

about 12 black olives, pitted

8 eggs

3½oz/100g feta cheese or equivalent white
    *peyniri* (optional)

a handful of fresh, chopped flat-leaf parsley

salt, to taste

1 level teaspoon sumac

Roughly chop the peppers, chilies, onion, scallions, and tomato. Heat a sploosh of oil in a frying pan. Fry the vegetables for about 5 minutes or until they soften a little, and then add the olives. Whisk the eggs together, stir them through the veggie mix, and then add the cheese (if using) and the parsley. Season to taste. Cook for a couple of minutes, stirring gently, and serve sprinkled with the sumac. This is probably at its tastiest straight out of the pan.

# CHEESY COTTELETTES

Possibly Iran's favorite snack. You will find these at Iranian events, filling school lunchboxes, piled high at *iftar* (the fast-breaking meal during Ramadan), and in all likelihood, hidden away in every Iranian fridge. My mother-in-law turns them out by the truck load, and hordes of relatives ensure that they are despatched swiftly.

    They are eaten hot or cold with *lavash* bread and plenty of *sabzi*.

BRUNCH FOR 6–8

7–8 floury red potatoes

a little butter

2 medium onions, grated

1 teaspoon turmeric

salt and pepper

3½oz/100g crumbled white cheese

1½ tablespoons roasted chickpea flour

3 eggs, lightly beaten

oil, for frying

Boil the potatoes in their skins and then drain, peel, and mash them with a little butter. When the mash is cool-ish, mix in all the other ingredients (except for the oil). With wet hands, form the potato mixture into flat oval patties; heat the oil in a frying pan and slide them in. Fry until golden brown, then turn them over and cook the other sides.

# VEGGIESTAN CHEESES

One of my greatest pleasures when discovering the cuisine of somewhere is the sampling of that region's cheeses. This makes Veggiestan a somewhat disappointing destination. I'll pardon Greece—it is the home of two of the world's favorite cheeses (feta and halloumi, of course).

The curious thing is, the inhabitants of Veggiestan eat cheese, and quite possibly "invented" (discovered) it. It is believed that the business of carrying milk in flagons made from sheep stomachs (which probably contained residual rennet) caused the formation of curds— and the rest of it, as they say, is turophilia history.

There are undeniably some outstanding Arabic cheeses. But for most of the area's inhabitants, the words *jibbneh* (Arabic) or *peynir/panir* (Turkish/Persian) imply a simple village cheese made from goat's or sheep's (or camel's or horse's) milk and along the lines of feta: white, crumbly, salted. Salt is one of the main characteristics of the region's cheesy offerings—this is mostly to do with the climate and the need to preserve dairy products against excessive fermentation. The good news for the real vegetarians among you is that because of the laws governing the preparation of *halal* food, most of the cheeses in the Middle East are prepared without animal rennet.

Anyway, here's a few of the more interesting, lesser known cheeses:

JIBBNEH MASHALLALE: String cheese (literally "ladies' hair cheese"). Great fun. The curds are dried in strips and twisted together to form a firm, if rather salty, cheese. Available in Egyptian and Levantine stores—worth buying for its quirky appearance alone.

BALADI: Arabic cream cheese. To spread on Arabic crackers.

ACKAWI: White cheese, but just hard enough to cut. Again, very salty—usually arrives packed in brine. It is useful for cooking because it does not crack (and become all oily) at high temperatures.

NABLUSI: is from Nablus, in Palestine. This cheese is very popular in Jordan as well. Like *ackawi*, it is made from ewe's milk

LABNEH: mmmm. Just the best. It is basically thick, strained yogurt that behaves as cheese. Usually sheep's or goat's yogurt. It is salted and often blended with olive oil and *za'atar* to have with bread as a snack. I could live on it or its exotic friend *shanklish*. You can make your own *labneh* by buying the thickest, nicest yogurt you can find (or make your own—p.60) and then salting it to taste.

SHANKLISH: *labneh* that has been dried and rolled into balls. It is then usually preserved in olive oil and flavored spices or herbs. It is the ambrosia of the cheese world. Crumble a couple of balls into *fatoush*, or even a regular salad, and mix well—it takes food to another level. You can (apparently) make your own by rubbing some olive oil over your hands and then forming *labneh* into balls: these are traditionally sun-dried, but you can improvise by leaving them in a warm, dry cupboard for a few hours. At the end of this time the *shanklish* should be rolled in thyme, mint, or red pepper, and then stored in a jar under olive oil.

Other cheeses of note include Iraqi *meira* (made with sheep's milk and then fermented), *kadchgall* (made in Afghanistan with camel's milk and yogurt) and *serat* (a waxed, smoky Afghan cheese). Iran stands alone as being undistinguished in the field of cheese (although Iranians that I know get nostalgic for an incredibly strong white cheese from Tabriz).

# Salat wa Shanklish

## *SHANKLISH* AND CARAWAY SALAD

This recipe makes a substantial salad that is more than capable of being the main event rather than a mere supporting act. It is lent extra versatility by the fact that you can serve it at any temperature: I usually opt for a rather trendy "warm."

If you can't source *shanklish* and don't want to mess around making your own, softish goat's cheese is an almost-acceptable substitute.

SERVES 4

3 carrots, peeled

10½oz/300g pumpkin, peeled

1 apple, cored and thinly sliced

about 5 tablespoons extra-virgin olive oil

2 teaspoons caraway seeds

2 tablespoons apple cider vinegar

1 teaspoon Dijon mustard

salt and black pepper

½ cup/2¾oz/75g pumpkin seed kernels (or sunflower)

1 bunch (1¾oz/50g) watercress

3½oz/100g *shanklish* (see opposite page)

Quarter the carrots lengthwise and cut the pumpkin into 1¼in (3cm) cubes. Preheat the oven to 400°F/200°C.

Put the vegetables in a pan with water, bring to a boil, add salt, and cook for about 5 minutes (they should still be firm). Drain them, and arrange them on an oven tray with the apple slices. Drizzle with 2 tablespoons of the olive oil and sprinkle with the caraway seeds. Bake in the oven for 25 minutes, or until the veggies are cooked and just starting to brown. Scoop them into a serving bowl.

Whisk the rest of the olive oil together with the vinegar, mustard, and seasoning and pour it over the vegetables. Just before serving, sprinkle the salad with the pumpkin seeds, strew it with watercress, and crumble the *shanklish* on top.

\* Handy housekeeping hint:
To preserve the life of your pans, never add salt to cold water, as it will abrade the metal once the water starts to move. Add it once the water has boiled, wherein the salt will dissolve straight away. (So says our mole in the kitchen department of a large department store.)

# A TRIO OF HALLOUMI STACKS

There probably isn't much that we can say about halloumi that die-hard vegetarians don't already know. It is a godsend of flavorsome and versatile protein. I have to confess that since I discovered it as a sous-sous-sous-chef, I have never gotten over the novelty of it: a cheese that you can grill! Whoop! Best thing about it is that it is one of the few remaining acceptable faces of saltiness. Don't get me wrong—I loathe over-seasoned food and avoid fast food outlets for this very reason. My husband calls me a salt-fascist. But halloumi, like soy sauce or olives, is salty by definition and offers an injection of mouth-watering savoriness into all sorts of dishes. The other best thing about halloumi is that it is the vegetarian's best friend at barbecues: since it reached the great foodie West, gone are the days when a veggie had to make do with a "kebab" of rather revolting, over-cooked mushrooms and zucchini.

The concept of hard cheese preserved in brine was almost certainly not devised by the Cypriots, but they have made it very much their own. The Bedouins of North Africa are believed to have "invented" it, as it travels so well. Similar products are to be found in Turkey and Egypt.

Some other halloumi facts: it is strangely squeaky on the teeth if you eat it cold—although it is quite nice cold-cubed into salads. It can be fried, grilled, baked, or even microwaved. Some brands of halloumi are saltier than others: you can counteract this to some extent by rinsing the cheese before cooking it. The good news is that halloumi is towards the lower end of the cheese naughtiness scale—it is relatively low in calories and fat.

If you're not already sufficiently convinced, how about Sidqui Effendi's much quoted words on the subject:

*Put a portion of cheese in silver paper. Wrap it up and put it over a fire. When the paper starts to glow the cheese is ready to eat and deliciously creamy ... This is good food that enhances sex for married men.*

Er, right.

# FIGS AND HALLOUMI

Possibly one for dinner à deux, this—it is incredibly sensual and exotic. Figs are a known aphrodisiac, as is ginger...

TO SERVE 2 YOU WILL NEED:
an old CD of Fairuz or Googoosh

FOR THE DRESSING:
3 tablespoons olive oil
small knob fresh ginger, peeled and minced
1½ tablespoons raspberry vinegar
1 teaspoon honey
black pepper and a pinch of salt

FOR THE STACKS:
6 slices halloumi
6 fresh figs, halved
⅓ cup/1¾oz/50g raw shelled pistachios

TO ASSEMBLE:
1 small bag arugula leaves
⅓ cup/1¾oz/50g raw pistachios
1 candle

Put the CD in your sound system and hit play. Whisk the dressing together. Heat the grill. Check your lipstick/tie in the mirror. Grill the halloumi on both sides until golden, and the figs for a couple of minutes with the cut side up. Take two plates and pile a handful of arugula on each, followed by a piece of halloumi, a piece of fig, etc. They won't exactly stack, but you can layer them like toppled dominos. Sprinkle the pistachios on top. Give the dressing another quick beating, and trickle it over the halloumi. Light the candle. Oh my.

# HALLOUMI PIZZA STACKS

This needs some good dunky bread for mopping up the sauce.

FOR 4 STACKS
2 green chilies, chopped
good splosh of olive oil for cooking
1¾oz/50g pickled cucumbers, diced
1½ tablespoons/1½oz/40g capers, chopped
scant ⅓ cup/1¾oz/50g black olives, sliced
handful of chopped parsley, plus a few sprigs

1 teaspoon oregano
scant ⅓ cup/1¾oz/50g raisins, soaked in cold water for 10 minutes
scant ⅓ cup/1¾oz/50g pine nuts (or pumpkin seed or sunflower seed kernels)
1 pack of halloumi, cut into ¼in (5mm) slices
4 medium tomatoes, sliced

Fry the chilies in a little olive oil, and then stir in the cucumbers, capers, olives, parsley, and oregano. Cook for a few minutes and then scrape into a bowl and keep warm.

Next fry the raisins for a couple of minutes, and then add the pine nuts; cook for another 1–2 minutes, stirring constantly so that the kernels don't burn. Again, spoon this into a bowl and set aside.

Finally fry the halloumi slices, turning them so that both sides brown nicely, and add the sliced tomato.

Take four small plates and layer the stacks, starting with a slice of halloumi. Follow with a sprinkle of raisins and pine nuts, then more halloumi, and then the spiced caper sauce. After that you need another cheese slice and a piece of tomato. Wedge a final slice of halloumi on top. If you are aiming to impress, use a wooden skewer to keep your stack upright. Garnish with the remaining fried tomato and the sprigs of parsley.

This is best served with a crisp green salad and some chunky warm bread.

# GRILLED VEGETABLE HALLOUMI STACKS

Really easy on the barbecue or in the kitchen.

MAKES 6 STACKS
FOR THE DRESSING:
4 tablespoons olive oil
generous 2 tablespoons balsamic vinegar
handful of fresh mint, chopped
2 garlic cloves, minced
freshly milled black pepper

FOR THE STACKS:
1 red pepper
1 green pepper

1 large, beheaded zucchini, sliced lengthwise
1 beheaded eggplant, sliced horizontally
olive oil for basting—use non-virgin as it has a
   higher smoke point
8oz/225g halloumi

TO SERVE:
2 slices whole-wheat pita
cherry tomatoes
baby cucumbers

Whisk the dressing ingredients together and set aside to mingle.

Either scorch the peppers on the barbecue, or bake them in a hot oven for 10 minutes. Pop them in a plastic bag for a few minutes while still hot, and then flake the skin off and quarter them, discarding the calices/seeds.

Season the zucchini and the eggplant and brush them with olive oil, then grill until they are appropriately browned on both sides. Put them in a barely hot oven along with the peppers to keep warm.

Slice the halloumi at ¼in (5mm) intervals—the average block yields about 16 slices. Place on or under a hot grill and cook until golden and griddled looking before flipping them over and doing the other side.

To assemble, grill the pita bread and cut in half. Put one of the pita halves on each plate, then top with a piece of halloumi, a slice of pepper, a chunk of zucchini, and a slither of eggplant. Repeat. Realistically two layers of veggies between three pieces of cheese is enough—anything else and the stacks wobble over.

Decorate the plates with slices of cucumber and cherry tomatoes, and then at the last minute drizzle some dressing over each stack.

# Baid bi Tamaten

## CHEESE-BAKED EGG-STUFFED TOMATOES

This Iraqi-inspired recipe is the stuff of Sunday evening suppers—nourishing, full of the taste of years gone by, but with a hint of the exotic propelling you into the week ahead. Oh, and most importantly it's real easy.

The eggs are settled onto bread for two reasons: it stops them from falling over, and it also serves to absorb some of the tomato-y goodness. Dishes served this way are known as *tashreeb* (which kind of means "drinking bread"), and it is a great way to cook—the bread somehow feels quite sinful, oozing with vegetable "dripping," and what may be a simple vegetable concoction is rendered something more substantial and filling. It's also a good way to use up not-quite-freshly-baked bread.

SERVES 4

8 big tomatoes

olive oil

2 onions, chopped

4 garlic cloves, minced (optional)

1 teaspoon marjoram

½ teaspoon turmeric

salt and pepper

1 sheet *khobez* (see p.15) or 3 pita

8 eggs

3½oz/100g grated cheese

1 teaspoon *za'atar* (see p.98)

Cut the tops from the tomatoes, and scoop out the flesh inside using a pointy teaspoon (or a melon-baller, if anyone has such a thing any more). Put the tomato shells to one side, and chop the inside bits, retaining as much of the juice as possible. Heat a little oil in a pan and cook the onion; when it becomes translucent add the garlic, marjoram, and turmeric. After a few minutes, add the chopped tomato.

Toast the bread and lay it in the bottom of a greased oven dish. Preheat the oven to 350°F/180°C.

Spoon a little of the oniony mix into each of the tomato shells, and smear the rest across the bread. Nestle the tomatoes into the dish, and then crack an egg inside each one. Top with cheese and a sprinkling of *za'atar*.

Bake in the oven for 15 minutes, or until the eggs have set. Serve with additional warm bread.

# Lahmacun

## TURKISH PIZZA SNACKS

*Lahmacun* is possibly evidence that the pizza was invented in the Middle East before the Italians reinvented it: it has been around for centuries. A soft and oh-so-thin round of just-baked dough encases just a smithering of cheese or chopped vegetables, and is then wrapped into a cone and twisted in paper for perfect picnic fare or food on the go. My customers wax lyrical about the joys of wandering the markets of Istanbul chomping on one of these. The original ones were made with meat, but we'll ignore that.

### FOR THE DOUGH:

2 teaspoons active dry yeast

⅔ cup/5fl oz/150ml warm water

½ teaspoon sugar

2⅓ cups/12oz/350g all-purpose flour

½ teaspoon salt

2 tablespoons olive oil

### FOR THE TOPPING*:

3 tablespoons tomato paste

1 can (14oz/400g) tomatoes, drained
    and squidged

7oz/200g feta cheese, crumbled

7oz/200g grated Turkish *peynir*, or mozzarella

2 beaten eggs

black pepper

handful of fresh chopped parsley

7oz/200g soft *labneh* (see p.76)

## *
### Alternative Vegan Topping:

Very finely dice 2 onions and fry them in a little olive oil together with 3 garlic cloves. Add in 1 diced green pepper and 4–5 chopped tomatoes, and fry until the onion is just beginning to brown. Mix around 7oz/200g black olive paste (tapenade) with 1 teaspoon oregano, ½ teaspoon chili flakes, and 2 tablespoons olive oil, and smear very thinly across the *lahmacun*. Top it with the fried vegetables, and sprinkle the whole lot with fresh chopped parsley. Roll, wrap, and away.

Sprinkle the yeast on to the water together with the sugar and set to one side for about 15 minutes. Then sift the flour and the salt into a bowl, make a well in the middle, and tip the yeast water in. Add the olive oil and work it into a dough with your hands, before covering and setting to one side to prove.

After about 1 hour, the dough should have doubled in size: punch it down on a floured work surface, and then divide the dough into six equal balls. Roll them out until they are really thin and pizza shaped, and cover them with a cloth. This is a good time to put the oven on as well—set it to 450°F/230°C—and pop in a couple of baking sheets to heat (or even your pizza stone if you're a kitchen gadget supremo).

Mix the tomato paste with the drained tomatoes. In a separate bowl, mix the feta, *peynir*, and eggs with some black pepper and the parsley.

Spread the tomato mix evenly over the six *lahmacun*, taking it right to the edges. Follow it with the *labneh*, and then spoon the cheese mix over the top. Slide the "pizzas" on to the heated baking trays and cook for 8 minutes, or until the base is cooked (but still soft) and the cheese bubbling. Remove from the oven and roll each one up while it is still hot—if you are serving it to go, roll them with greaseproof paper. If not, arrange them on a warm serving platter, with a bowl of tomato and onion salsa on the side, which your guests can then spoon into the middle of their pizza cones. As with all pizza, coleslaw also provides a good contrast …

# INTRODUCING *KASHK* AND *QUROOT*

*Umami.* Thank goodness someone discovered it. *Umami* is the "fifth taste," after salty, sour, bitter, and sweet. The Japanese cottoned on to it first of all: soy sauce and seaweed are prime examples of the *umami* experience. Mushrooms are *umami* too. And so are *kashk* and *quroot.*

These are, respectively, Iranian and Afghan dairy products, which are often confused and used interchangeably. *Kashk* is liquid whey—you know, the stuff that Miss Muffet drank along with her curds. The liquid is dried out and then reconstituted into a strong sauce, which is used most notably with *ashe* (soup) and fried eggplant (to make a famous dish called *kashk-e-bademjan*). It is scarce in the West (you may find it glorying in the wonderful name of Iranian Sauce), but if you do find some, take a tip from Iranian housewives and boil it for 20 minutes first. As Alan Davidson points out in *The Oxford Companion to Food*, the world is awash with unwanted whey, for it is of course a bi-product of the cheese industry; a clever dairyman could make a killing by marketing *kashk* over here. (Someone naturally inclined to pun would instantly suggest that it is the whey forward.)

*Quroot* is sun-dried yogurt, and its discovery on the shelves of our shop seems singlehandedly to generate more homesickness among Afghans than any number of phone calls home. It is pretty hard to find, but its distinctive flavor is core to many favorite Afghan dishes. It is easy enough to make it at home, if home happens to be somewhere hot and sunny: strained yogurt is salted, rolled into small spheres, and baked in the sun until it is quite hard. Many Afghans seem to enjoy it just as it is as a snack, but it is more often seen reconstituted and drizzled into dishes such as *maushawa*, a mung bean soup. *Gara quroot* is *quroot* that has been boiled until it scalds and evaporates into a thick, black paste: this is a favorite "confection" for adults and young squiddlywinks alike.

soup

*A poor man was walking past the open windows of a restaurant when he saw a steaming bowl of soup on the table. He had but a crust of bread in his pocket and was hungry, so he held the bread over the bowl so that it absorbed some flavor from the steam, and ate it quickly. The restaurateur, being a mean old so and so, took exception to this and hauled the pauper off to the local judge. Who happened to be our friend Mullah Nasruddin.*

*The Mullah listened to the businessman's claims for recompense, and after a little hemming and hawing took some coins from his pocket, which he then proceeded to shake next to the man's ear.*

*"Case settled! Next!" he cried.*

*"What are you talking about? Where's the money for my soup?" asked the restaurateur.*

*"Don't you think that the sound of those coins was more than enough payment for the smell of your soup?" replied the Mullah...*

It is hardly surprising that this was the first chapter that got written. Quite apart from the fact that I love the stuff, I find the process of making it therapeutic, even ritualistic, and the business of sharing homemade soup with loved ones, or donating it to the needy, or spoon-feeding it to the sick, is about as fluffy and rewarding as it gets with food.

Soup is the beginning of food, of culture: the very word *restaurant* (which is, of course, fairly recent) was derived from the idea of a fancy soup kitchen offering restorative foods. It is a source of great glee to me that so many soup recipes come with legends attached, like the tale of Ezo Gelin on p.96. To view a nation's most typical soups is to understand a lot about where they've come from, what the people are all about, the nature of their economy. What spices do they use? Can they afford to use spices? Are they a land of sheep farmers, or rice growers? Is the country cold, demanding fortifying broth, or so hot that they like their soups chilled? The Middle East has such a diversity of soups that it was really really hard to choose which to include.

Soup-making is, of course, the quickest way to squeeze flavor, nutrition, and maximum value out of a handful of the most modest ingredients. That's why there are so many different textures to be found in the recipes in this chapter: some just seem like glorified stock, while others seem to have half a vegetable patch in them. In the wonderful world of one-pot cooking, what started off as soup in the morning was often allowed to cook down to solids to enjoy with bread in the evening.

The Arabic word for soup is *shorba*, a word with Farsi roots (*shor*, meaning salty, and *ba* meaning cooked in water). *Shorba* has been in use at least since the appearance of the excellent, fascinating *Kitab al-Tabikh* (Medieval Arab Cookbook) in the thirteenth century, and its derivatives have spread into Turkish (*çorbasi*) and out East (*sherwa* in Pashtun).

Perversely, the soups that excite Westerners the most are the more authentic, peasant recipes, while the ones that are most esteemed by Middle Easterners are quite often derived from Western or Russian recipes.

# Katyk Shurva va Zafaran
## CHILLED YOGURT AND SAFFRON SOUP

Strange one, this. I reckon it was Russian originally, as it is very similar to *Okroshka*, but one of my Uzbek customers makes it regularly and claims it as her (great-great-grandmother's) own. Research shows that it is more usually and traditionally made with *kefir*\* in Uzbekistan: I tried making it with Iranian *doogh* to give that slightly fermented effect, and it was horrid. So I will stand by this easy-peasy, westernized version.

It is rather addictive. I've actually made it as an exotic sauce to go with grilled vegetables before—but really it's a summer soup. Makes a pleasant change from the delicious-but-rather-more-commonplace yogurt and cucumber soup.

### FOR 4 GOOD BOWLFULS

3 cups/25fl oz/750ml plain yogurt

¼ teaspoon ground saffron, steeped in a splash of boiling water

4 hard-boiled egg yolks

2 teaspoons grainy mustard

1 teaspoon balsamic vinegar

1 bunch of radishes, washed and diced real small

½ cucumber, washed and diced real small

2–3 scallions, sliced

1 large cooked potato (waxy is best), peeled and finely diced

2 tablespoons fresh (or dried) dill (or use other fresh herbs of choice—mint, parsley, cilantro)

salt and pepper

The yogurt should be of a fairly runny pouring consistency: you will need to dilute it with cold water, whisking vigorously, until it is, well, soup-like.

Add the saffron, and mix well. Next mash the egg yolks with the mustard and vinegar, and beat this mixture into the yogurt.

Put all the other ingredients in a bowl, and pour the yogurt on top, mixing thoroughly. Season to taste, and then cover and chill well. Serve over ice cubes (optional—but great on a hot summer night) garnished with a sprig of fresh dill.

**\* Kefir**

Mmm. The original probiotic, if you like. It evolved as the famous horsemen of the region galloped the steppes: (mare's) milk, which they carried in saddle bags, would slowly ferment, forming a not unpleasant but entirely different drink. To this day *kefir* is a popular drink in places such as Uzbekistan and Kazakhstan. In the West it is more often the bacteria itself for which we use the term. You can buy it as grains or already developed (when it looks like something that Fungus the Bogeyman might have dreamed up): it is self-propagating (my, how it grows), and enthusiasts are usually happy to share their cultures (how nice). It is phenomenally good for you.

# Yayla Çorbasi

# TURKISH HOT YOGURT SOUP
# WITH CILANTRO DUMPLINGS

This is Turkish comfort food. The creamy dairiness of it, with the naughtiness implied by the dumplings—it's all too easy to over-indulge.

*Yayla çorbasi* (literally "plateau" or "pasture" soup) is traditionally served without the dumplings, but I find the addition thereof makes for a fabulous Sunday supper dish. I found umpteen quaint versions of how the soup got its name; I was almost tempted to invent my own ... Suffice it to say that it was/is staple fare for mountain shepherds.

Hot yogurt is a tricky one, but by adding either egg or flour or both to it before heating, you can stop it from curdling.

SERVES 4

generous ¼ cup /2¼ oz/60g rice (long- or short-grain)

4 cups/32fl oz/1 liter really nice vegetable stock

generous ¾ cup/4½ oz/125g all-purpose flour*

1 egg

3–4 garlic cloves, minced (optional)

1lb 2 oz/500g whole-milk plain strained yogurt

scant ½ cup/1½ oz/40g vegetarian shortening

half bunch fresh cilantro, washed and chopped

salt and pepper to taste

1 tablespoon butter

1–2 tablespoons dried mint

Cook the rice in the stock—this should take about 20 minutes. In the meantime, whisk ⅓ cup/1¾oz/50g of the flour along with the egg and the garlic into the yogurt. Pour a ladle of the stock into the yogurt and beat well to mix before pouring the whole lot into the soup, stirring well all the time and in the same direction (the yogurt can otherwise "crack").

Next the dumplings. Gosh, I love dumplings. Sift the rest of the flour* into a bowl, mix in the shortening and the cilantro, together with a pinch of salt and enough water to bind the mixture (about 4 tablespoons). Form into dumpling shapes.

Season the soup to taste, and drop the dumplings in. Cover the pan and simmer for around half an hour more.

To serve, melt the butter in a frying pan, and when it is sizzling throw in the mint. After a couple of minutes, take it off the heat and drizzle across the soup.

\*

Two schools of thought about this. Neither of them very Middle Eastern. Convention says the dumplings should be made with self-rising flour so they rise and look pretty. But in fact they have a much better flavor with all-purpose—the way my mom taught me. Try it and see.

*Tarkhineh*

# GREEN SOUP WITH *TRAHANA*

Food ethnology is awfully exciting: tracking the course of an ingredient or the evolution of a recipe across the globe, looking at how important food customs are in cultural rituals, describing social phenomena and predicting social change through changes in eating patterns—well, this girl gets off on it anyway.

This ingredient, *trahana*, is a very good example of the food treasure trail. It crops up all over the place. The names and methods may be different, but it is fundamentally the same stuff—cracked wheat mixed with fermented milk or yogurt, which is then dried and used as a sour pasta to plop into soups and stews. In Egypt it is known as *kishk* (not to be confused with the Iranian *kashk*, or whey); in Iraq *kushuk*; in Turkey *tarhana*; and in Greek Cyprus, *trahanas*.

This is basically my mother-in-law's recipe. Actually, that's not entirely true, because she says that no one bothers making their own *trahana*—it is something you just buy along with your package of sugar and carton of milk (and it is widely available in Greek and Turkish stores). But she did "acquire" this recipe for me. *Trahana* (*tarkhineh* in Farsi) is not common in Iran, but my in-laws are from the far west of the country, where Kurdish and Turkish influences are felt. And she has been making soup with *trahana* in it ever since me and the man started courting. It is extremely wholesome, and also great invalid food.

The recipe below is enough for 3–4 batches of soup.

SERVES 8
FOR THE *TRAHANA*:
1¼ cups/10fl oz/300ml whole milk, warmed
1¼ cups/10fl oz/300ml plain yogurt
1 teaspoon lemon juice
1lb 2oz/500g bulgar (cracked wheat)

⅔ cup/3½oz/100g all-purpose flour
generous ½ cup/3½oz/100g semolina
10 eggs, slightly beaten
2 teaspoons salt and pepper, as desired
2 teaspoons dried mint

Mix the milk, yogurt, and lemon juice together in a bowl, cover it, and leave it somewhere "ambient" overnight to sour.

The next day, mix the bulgar, flour, and semolina together, and then beat in the soured dairy mixture and the eggs, together with the seasoning and the mint. Pour into a pan, bring to a boil, and then allow to simmer for 10 minutes, stirring regularly. Take it off the heat and set aside for 30 minutes.

Next heat your oven to 225°F/110°C, and then spread the mixture in flattish lumps on a baking sheet, pop it in the oven and leave to dry for about 4 hours.

(continues overleaf)

Once it is hard, you can wrap it in a dish towel and bash it with a meat tenderizer to break it up, or blast it briefly in the blender, before storing it somewhere cool and dry.

Congratulations! You have just reproduced one of the world's oldest forms of processed carbohydrate. You can use it in soups and stews—it reconstitutes very quickly. And it is pretty indestructible—it will keep for up to 2 years.

OK, that was the hard part. The soup is easy. You can use vegetable stock rather than water, but it's not essential.

FOR THE SOUP:
6¼ cups/50fl oz/1.5 liters water, or vegetable
    stock
12oz/350g *trahana*
1lb 5oz/600g spinach, washed and roughly
    chopped

2 garlic cloves, peeled and chopped
1 large onion, peeled and chopped
1 teaspoon ground turmeric
a little oil, for frying
salt and pepper

Bring the water to a boil in a pan, plop in the *trahana* (which will break up and soften as it hits the water), and then, after around 10 minutes, add the spinach. Fry the garlic, onion, and turmeric together in a little oil—cook until the onion becomes quite brown, and then add to the soup. Bubble away for 10 minutes more, season to taste, and then serve with warm bread and some crumbly white cheese on the side.

If you don't feel like making *trahana*, or cannot get it from your local Mediterranean deli, just use pearl barley in its place.

# Vospapur

## ARMENIAN GREEN LENTIL, GARLIC, AND SPINACH SOUP

Given that the Middle East is an entity formed of disparate cultures and obeying few collective rules, Armenia is an oddity in a class of its own. It was the first nation formally to embrace Christianity, and to this day remains an Orthodox enclave in a largely Islamic landscape. It is landlocked and thus largely dependent on its neighbors—but is at loggerheads with Turkey and Azerbaijan, which border it to the west, south, and east. Its most ancient claim to fame was that the Ark came to rest there—although Mount Ararat, where Noah eventually alighted, has now been, er, moved to Turkey.  In fact, the country's own name for itself is Hayk, or Hayastan, and Hayk was a great-great descendant of Noah and apparent founder of the Armenian nation. So now you know.

This recipe, I am told, was designed to help one withstand the harshest of mountain winters. Although it came to me by way of London. Mind you, winter in London can be pretty grim too.

You can use vegetable stock rather than water, but it's not essential. As for the tomatoes, you can use ones that are past their best, and which wouldn't pass for salad.

SERVES 4

generous 1½ cups/10½oz/300g green or
     brown lentils
knob of butter (3½ tablespoons/1¾oz/50g)
1 large onion, chopped
7–8 garlic cloves, peeled
1 teaspoon ground coriander
1 teaspoon ground cumin

1 teaspoon ground paprika
1 level tablespoon dill
4 cups/32fl oz/1 liter water (or stock)
salt and black pepper
10½oz/300g fresh (or equivalent frozen)
     spinach, washed and roughly chopped
4–5 medium squidgy tomatoes, chopped
1 cup/3½oz/100g walnuts, roughly crushed

Firstly pick through the lentils. Even supermarket-processed lentils contain small stones sometimes, and it is always worth checking through them before rinsing them.

Next melt some butter (adding a dash of oil will stop it from burning) in a suitable soup pan, and fry the onion until it just starts to color. Finely chop half of the garlic and add this, followed by the spices and herbs, followed by the lentils, stirring merrily all the while. Add the water (or stock), and stir well before setting to simmer for around 40 minutes, or until the lentils are softish. At this stage, season the soup to taste, add more water if required, together with the spinach, tomatoes, and most of the walnuts, and cook for another 5 minutes.

Finally slice the remaining garlic and fry it, with the remaining walnuts, in a little oil.

Ladle the soup into bowls and garnish with the browned garlicky nutty stuff. Serve with warm *barbari* bread. Preferably sitting around the fire.

# Domates Çorbasi ve Raki
## TOMATO, FENNEL, AND *ARAK* SOUP

Tomato soup. Guaranteed to put a smile on the face. And a stain on the tie. Well, this one isn't quite the "Cream of" variety upon which we in the West are partially raised. There's more than a hint of the exotic about it.

Instead of *arak*, you could use *raki* or *ouzo*, or even Pernod in a pinch.

SERVES 4

1 large onion, chopped

1 large bulb fennel, chopped

1 red pepper, chopped

olive oil, for cooking

2 garlic cloves, finely chopped

1 teaspoon fennel seeds

½ teaspoon thyme

1 tablespoon tomato paste

scant ½ cup/3½fl oz/100ml *arak*

1 can (14oz/400g) tomato *concasse* (chopped tomatoes)

1½ cups/12fl oz/350ml vegetable stock

4 medium tomatoes

TO SERVE:

sour cream or crème fraîche

chopped parsley

flatbread croûtons

OK, so you fry the onion, fennel, and pepper in a little olive oil; as they begin to soften, add the garlic, fennel seeds, and thyme, followed by the tomato paste. Add the *arak*—if you are confident so to do, you can flame it as you pour it in, but this is not essential—and chase it with the *concasse* and the stock. Bring the soup to a boil and simmer for about 15 minutes. Roughly chop the fresh tomatoes, lower these in to the soup—this gives the soup a more artisan, less homogenized feel—and cook for around 15 minutes more.

Serve the soup together with sour cream/crème fraîche for swirling, a scatter of chopped parsley, and flatbread croûtons.

# Ezo Gelin Çorbasi
## THE SOUP OF EZO THE BRIDE

Don't you just love red lentils? You need do little more than show them where your soup pan is and they all but cook themselves. This recipe is really simple and one that you can dress up for party occasions or slob around with on lazy days.

Quite a few sappy movies and soppy folk songs seem to have sprung up around the figure of Ezo Gelin. She was reputedly a beautiful young girl from Southern Turkey who wasn't too lucky on the marriage front: her first husband was a bum, and her second came with a monstrous mother-in-law as part of the deal. She had nine children, and died wretchedly and prematurely. This soup reflected the poor girl's efforts to appease said mother-in-law. Food with a story attached always has more flavor, no?

This soup seems really popular in Turkey, and, according to more than one of our customers, is to the Turkish hangover what eggs and bacon is to the West.

The recipe is similar to *Kolkeh*, a Syrian red lentil soup—which is hardly surprising, as Ezo's second husband was in fact Syrian.

SERVES 4

butter/oil, for frying

1 large onion, finely chopped

2–3 garlic cloves, finely chopped

2–3 tomatoes, diced

½ teaspoon ground cumin

3 tablespoons paprika

1 tablespoon tomato paste

1 tablespoon *biber salçasi* (pepper paste—buy ready made or see p.226)

1½ cups/10½oz/300g red lentils, cleaned and rinsed

¼ cup/1¾oz/50g long-grain rice

generous ½ cup/3½oz/100g medium bulgar (cracked wheat)

8 cups/64fl oz/2 liters water or vegetable stock

salt and pepper

2 tablespoons dried mint

Melt a little butter in a soup pot, add some oil to stop it from burning, and fry the onion. As it begins to soften, add the garlic, followed one minute later by the tomatoes, cumin, and half the paprika. Stir for a further 1 minute and then add the tomato and pepper paste, and then the lentils, rice, and bulgar. Stir in the water, bring to a boil, and then turn down to a simmer. The soup should be ready after about 40 minutes, at which stage you should season it to taste. You may also need to add more water so that it remains of a soup-like consistency.

In the meantime melt a little more butter in a small pan (no oil this time), and when it is sizzling throw in the mint and the rest of the paprika, stirring well to stop it sticking. Serve the soup garnished with the minty paprika. Other accessories include plenty of warm *pide* or flatbread, a bowl of yogurt, and some lemon wedges.

# Harira

## MOROCCAN TOMATO
## AND ONION SOUP

Actually this is another lentil soup. But I am wary of lentil overkill and so have chosen to stress the other two important ingredients. Mind you, one can't downplay the importance of lentils in the Middle East; there was the business of Esau selling his inheritance to Isaac for a bowl of the stuff.

*Harira* is Morocco's most famous soup. It is a big hit, especially during Ramadan, when it is often used, alongside dates and sweet tea, to break fast. I tend to think of it as a vegetarian chicken soup: it's got all the right stuff in it to blast those coldy, flu-ey blues. It is actually so well known that it is readily available in canned and packaged form in Middle Eastern stores.

SERVES 4

2 medium onions, chopped

2 sticks celery, chopped

splodge of oil, for frying

1 teaspoon ground cinnamon

½ teaspoon ground ginger

½ teaspoon ground cumin

½ teaspoon ground smoked paprika

1 teaspoon regular ground paprika

1 teaspoon turmeric

3–4 tomatoes, chopped

¾ cup/5½oz/150g green or brown lentils, sorted and washed

1¼ cups/10fl oz/about 300ml cold water

1 can (14oz/400g) cooked chickpeas (or about scant ¾ cup/2¾ oz/75g raw, soaked and cooked)

2 "nests" of vermicelli (about 2¼oz/60g)

1 tablespoon all-purpose flour

1 tablespoon lemon juice

½ tablespoon tomato paste

big handful each of chopped fresh cilantro and parsley

Fry the onion and celery in a little oil, and when they have softened add the spices, followed by the tomato, and then the lentils. Pour in the water, bring to a boil, and then add the chickpeas and pasta. Set the pan to a simmer for 30 minutes, or until the lentils are cooked.

Blend the flour, lemon juice, and tomato paste in a bowl, add a ladle of the bubbling soup, whisk well and pour the whole lot back into the pan to thicken it, stirring all the while. Season the *harira* to taste: we actually like it with some harissa dolloped in, but some don't like it hot. Serve liberally sprinkled with the fresh herbs and with extra lemon wedges.

*Trivia night bonus point:*
The mixture of flour, lemon juice, and tomato paste used to thicken the *harira* is known as *tadouira*.

# Shorbat Yaqteen

# PUMPKIN AND RICE SOUP WITH
## *ZA'ATAR* CROÛTONS

This is one of the (many) recipes in the book which I should not have endeavored to write while hungry. It is the comfort blanket of the Middle Eastern soup world.

Pumpkin, you know. Rice too, I'm guessing. *Za'atar* is the wacky one in this concoction. It literally means "thyme" in Arabic (although there is some debate as to whether this means thyme itself or the family of herbs to which thyme belongs), but the term also applies to one of the Middle East's greatest spice mixes, a blend of ground thyme with sumac, a little salt, and sesame. Of course, every household makes it differently. The mix is most commonly used with olive-oil-dunked-bread, and is now to be found throughout the Arab world. But it is also great as a seasoning for vegetables (or fish or meat) or whisked into salad dressing. You can make your own (aim for half thyme, half sumac, with salt and sesame according to taste), but it is readily available in Arabic stores.

### A note on seeds

Pumpkin seeds and sunflower seeds are famously good for you. In the Middle East they are consumed in vast quantities alongside zucchini, gourd, and melon seeds, roasted and salted in their shells, and quite often spiced too. Anyone who has been to Spain during fiesta will testify to the carpet of discarded "pipas" shells on the floor when the crowds have parted—well, the Spanish have got nothing on Iran and the Levant. Unless you are part-parrot or have been raised on the stuff, it is very hard to understand the appeal, or indeed to learn the art of cracking seeds. My beloved can get through hundreds per minute (I know, as I get to empty his pockets of an evening), whereas I end up with a nasty soggy mess. But you've got to admit, the general principle of enjoying all parts of a vegetable or fruit—waste not, want not and all that—is pretty cool.

### SERVES 4, GENEROUSLY, WITH LEFTOVERS

about 2lb 4oz / 1kg pumpkin

oil for frying (peanut is good here, but any will do)

2 medium onions, peeled and chopped

2–3 garlic cloves (optional)

½ teaspoon turmeric

1 teaspoon cinnamon

1 teaspoon curry powder

½ Scotch bonnet chili (or something less fiery if you're a chili wuss)

generous ⅔ cup/6oz/175g short-grain white rice

4 cups/32fl oz/1 liter good vegetable stock

1–2 slices of stale bread, cubed

2 teaspoons *za'atar*

salt and pepper

Peel and chunk your pumpkin, retaining the seeds. Heat some oil in your pet soup pan, and fry the onion until it softens. Add the garlic, spices, and chili, followed by the pumpkin, stirring well. Pour the stock on top, bring to a boil, and add half of the rice before setting the pan to simmer.

In the meantime, boil the rest of the rice in water for about 15 minutes or until it is soft, and then set it to drain.

After 30 minutes, the pumpkin mixture should be cooked. Take it off the heat and blend it, before returning it to the pan and adding the drained rice. Set it back to simmer gently while you make the croûtons. Heat a little oil in a frying pan and toss the bread cubes in. Once they start to color, add the pumpkin seeds, stirring constantly, and then the *za'atar*. Cook for 1 more minute, and then take off the heat.

Season the soup to taste, and serve garnished with the *za'atar* croutons.

# MIDDLE EASTERN PATENT SPICE MIXES

What's not to love about spice? Nothing in the culinary world has such power to transport the diner to another level, a different place, a time before. I get tremendously excited when traveling anywhere that has anything as exotic as a spice market, although it is an unfortunate fact that the pretty and photogenic piles of stuff for which gullible tourists like me go ga-ga usually prove to be tasteless and unexciting back home. My streetwise husband has taught me that in Middle Eastern countries the freshest ethnic ingredients are often to be found in the less attractive backstreet stores (i.e. where the locals shop).

Anyway, *za'atar* (see p.98) is only one of a range of famous and important Middle Eastern spice mixes. Each of them offers a key to the essential flavors of their country of origin. Yes, they're a bit of a hassle to make—but it is worth the effort, as you will see when you come in tired after a day's hard work and you realize that half the work for dinner is already done. There is, of course, scope for culinary license with any of these, as every household has its own recipe—so the following is but a guide.

ADVIEH: Iranian spice mix (and also the Farsi word for spice). Iranians use two basic mixtures: *advieh pulao*, or rice spice, and *advieh khoreshti*, casserole spice. The former usually contains ground

cardamom, ground rose petals, ground cinnamon and saffron, although on grounds of economy the saffron is often replaced with turmeric. The latter contains ground cumin, coriander, cinnamon, and turmeric. Both are very useful to have in your cupboard, especially the rice spice, as it is simply stirred through cooked rice—a very simple way to transform the stuff.

BAHARAT: This literally means "spice" in Arabic, and has become the generic name for a number of seven-spice mixes that are used in a wide range of dishes, particularly in Syria and Iraq. If you want to make your own, you can use whole spices and grind them yourself, or ready-ground if they are of good quality. I won't be very popular for saying this, but try not to rely on supermarket stuff—it is hideously expensive and usually stale. The most important ingredient is black pepper: use two tablespoons, together with the same of paprika, and then 1 tablespoon each of cumin, coriander seed, cloves, cinnamon (or cassia—practically the same thing), and cardamom. Use as a rub on grilled veggies (or fish or meat), or incorporate at the sealing/frying stage into soups and casseroles.

DUKKAH: Before peanut butter was invented, people were possibly more creative with their bread consumption: *dukkah* is another mix (this time from Egypt) used in conjunction with olive oil to spice up the daily loaf. It's fabulous in salads or used as a seasoning/crusty coating with cooked veggies. Toast equal quantities of raw hazelnuts (or almonds) and sesame seeds with half that amount of cumin and coriander seeds. Grind roughly with some salt and black pepper.

GARAM MASALA: Literally, this means "hot mix" in Hindi. Trouble is, there are almost certainly as many recipes for it as there are households in the Indian subcontinent. It has found its way into this tome by virtue of the fact that really hot variations of it are used widely in Afghanistan and Kashmir. This is what I use: 2 teaspoons ground black pepper, 1 teaspoon chili flakes, 1 teaspoon ground ginger, ¼ teaspoon ground nutmeg, ½ teaspoon ground cardamom, ½ teaspoon ground cumin, 1 teaspoon ground coriander, ¼ teaspoon ground fenugreek seeds, 1 teaspoon ground fennel seeds, 1 teaspoon ground caraway seeds, 2 teaspoons ground cinnamon, ½ teaspoon ground cloves, 3 crushed bay leaves. Yes, it does sound a bit like we've just emptied the cupboards, but it works. As with all the mixes above, it is better to use whole spices and grind them to order, but if you have sourced fresh ground spices from a reputable local store (ahem), then go for it.

HAWAYIJ: A mix from Yemen/Saudi. Yemeni Jews also took it with them when they migrated to Israel. It gets itself around, this blend, popping up in coffee and seasoning soups. And it is used with bread. It is used to great effect in *Zhug*, a famous fiery relish from the region (see p.218). To make it you will need 6 teaspoons black peppercorns, 3 teaspoons caraway seeds, 2 teaspoons turmeric, 1 teaspoon podded cardamom seeds, ½ teaspoon saffron strands (should be more, but not until the price of saffron comes down). Grind together and store in an airtight jar.

RAS EL HANOUT: This is what every tourist who goes to Morocco brings back from the souk. The words translate as the "head of the shop," and the blend is quite often something that stall holders/storekeepers use as their signature product. It is a combination of up to 50 spices, and recipes vary considerably. Our (restrained) recipe uses no more than a dozen ingredients—but you'll be glad to know that *Ras el Hanout* is fairly easy to source in the West. To make your own you will need 1 teaspoon of each of the following: allspice berries, cardamom seeds, cumin seeds, coriander seeds, black peppercorns, white peppercorns, mustard seeds, fennel seeds, rose petals, caraway seeds, and cloves, together with 2 cinnamon sticks. Grind and store in a dry, airtight jar.

# Eshkaneh

# PERSIAN EGG AND ONION SOUP

This is regarded as a dish for peasants in Iran—which is a shame, as it is really a dish fit for kings. Many Iranians, being inveterate snobs, will deny ever having sampled it, let alone prepared it. Their loss.

It's even simpler to make than its fancy French cousin.

### SERVES 6

6 medium onions

2–4 teaspoons vegetable ghee, or butter

1 teaspoon ground turmeric

4 teaspoons flour

4 cups/32fl oz/1 liter water

salt and pepper

1 egg per person

### OPTIONAL EXTRAS—BUT NOT ALL AT THE SAME TIME:

¾ cup/2¾oz/75g broken walnuts or

10½oz/300g fresh spinach, washed and
      roughly chopped or

1 cup/7oz/200g pitted sour cherries (or
      soaked prunes/apricots)

### FOR THE GARNISH:

1 onion, finely chopped

4 teaspoons dried mint

2–3 eggs

2–3 slices stale bread

Slice the 6 onions very finely and then fry them in hot melted ghee or butter. Once they are quite soft and starting to color, add the turmeric, and the walnuts (if using); cook for a few moments more, and then stir in the flour. Add the water, stirring constantly, and continue to heat so that the soup starts to thicken. Add the fruit and/or spinach if using, season to taste, and set to simmer for another 20 minutes.

Now prepare the garnish. Fry the onion in a little oil until it starts to brown. Add the mint, and cook until the mixture darkens; then set aside. Beat the eggs for the garnish with a sprinkle of salt and pepper. Cut each slice of the bread into six, dunk the resulting squares into the egg, and then fry in hot oil until browned. Keep them hot.

Just before you want to dish up, gently crack the eggs one by one into the *eshkaneh*, let it bubble for a few minutes until they start to set, and then carefully ladle the soup into warm bowls (obviously ensuring each person gets an egg). Float 2–3 eggy-bread croûtons in each bowl, and then top with a criss-cross of the minted onion mixture. Serve with fresh warm bread and raw onion.

# Ash-e-Sholeh-Ghalamkar

## KHALEH FIZZY'S

### *ASH-E-SHOLEH-GHALAMKAR*

Khaleh Fizzy is actually my husband Jamshid's Aunt Farzaneh. His family is originally from Kermanshah in the West of Iran, and he has three (diminutive, cuddly) aunts still living there. I am always astonished by their effortless thrift and tireless industry: they pick their own mountain herbs, preserve their own vegetables, make their own tomato paste, jams, pickles ... Any visitors leave with a suitcase full of beautifully prepared ingredients and copious instructions on how to use them.

The Persian word for chef is *ash-pas*, which basically means soup-maker. *Ash* is a particular range of nourishing herby soups—they constitute a cherished part of Iranian cuisine, and hence the ability to make them has become the mark of a good cook. Thus there is *ash reshteh*, which is with noodles; *ash anar*, which is with pomegranate paste; *ash-e-jo*, which is with barley; and this one, which literally means "scribe's soup," and is traditionally with wheat. Some of them originally comprised baby meatballs or shredded chicken, but quite unnecessarily in my opinion: all the flavor is in the herbs.

This particular *ash* is also one of a number of dishes that are made as a *nazri*, an offering, wherein friends and neighbors all contribute ingredients and help in making a huge pot of communal food in order to create good will. The idea is that each and every one of the participants pray for or think of someone who needs their help—usually a sick relative.

SERVES 4–6

1 cup/7oz/200g wheat berries, soaked overnight

scant ½ cup/2¾oz/75g kidney beans, soaked overnight, or 1 can (14oz/400g)

splash of sunflower oil

3 large onions, peeled and chopped

1 large leek, washed and chopped

1 teaspoon turmeric

½ teaspoon cumin

scant ½ cup/2¾oz/75g chickpeas, soaked overnight, or 1 can (14oz/400g)

scant ½ cup/2¾oz/75g cannellini beans, soaked overnight, or 1 can (14oz/400g)

scant ½ cup/2¾oz/75g mung beans

generous ⅓ cup/2¾oz/75g brown lentils

⅓ cup/2¾oz/75g short-grain rice

1 bunch cilantro, sorted, washed, and chopped

1 bunch parsley, sorted, washed and chopped

½ bunch dill, sorted, washed and chopped (or 1 heaped tablespoon dried dill)

handful of fresh basil, sorted, washed, and chopped

handful of fresh tarragon, sorted, washed and chopped (or 1 tablespoon dried)

2 teaspoons dried savory (if available)

salt and pepper

1 tablespoon dried mint

2 tablespoons *kashk* (see p.85) or yogurt (optional)

¼ teaspoon ground saffron, steeped in a tablespoon of hot water

This is far simpler than the long list of ingredients suggests: perhaps it is for this that the soup is known as "scribe's soup"—because it took such a long time to write out…

Rinse the soaked wheat, and then place it in a pan, cover it with cold water and bring it to a boil, skimming off any husks that rise to the surface. Allow to simmer for around 40 minutes, or until cooked, at which point you should drain it, reserving the stock.

If using dried kidney beans, bring them to a boil in cold water, and cook for 10 minutes before draining.

Heat a little sunflower oil in a big pan and add two of the onions together with the leek. When the vegetables begin to soften, add the spices followed a few minutes later by the kidney beans, chickpeas, and cannellini beans (although if you are using canned, you can add these with the other beans later on) and about 8 cups/64fl oz/2 liters water. Bring to a boil, and set to simmer.

After around 30 minutes, add the mung beans and the lentils. After a further 15 minutes, add the rice.

If you are using any dried herbs, fry them briefly in very little oil. Then add them to the soup together with the fresh herbs. Cook through for another 20 minutes or so, adding more water if necessary, before seasoning to taste.

Fry the remaining onion until it starts to catch, and add the mint, stirring for a minute or so more. This is a very common soup garnish in Iran and is known as *nana dagh*.

Swirl some *kashk* or yogurt over the *ash*, streak it with the *nana dagh*, and finally drizzle the liquid saffron over the top.

In Iran *ash* is usually served with sweet tea to counteract the effects of all those beans. This is because of the Iranian adherence to the millennia old system of eating a balanced diet using the principles of *sardi* and *garmi*—"hot" and "cold" foods eaten in proportion. This is not hot and cold as in temperature, but rather refers to the properties of the foods and the body's ability to digest them. Put as succinctly as I can manage in an appended paragraph, some foods are "cold," and take a while for your body to deal with, while others are "hot" and get processed very quickly. If you have too many of the former, you will end up feeling light-headed, bilious even: alcohol is cold (hence the hangover), so are coffee, fish, and many vegetables. Too many hot foods will leave you lacking energy and potentially febrile: these include cheese, salt, red meat, and sugar. The system is complex and far from obvious—but to my mind it works. So the sweet tea adds warmth to all the "cold" ingredients of *Ash-e-Sholeh Ghalamkar*. Er, and hopefully rids you of any flatulence…

# Shorbat Jazar wa Hail

## CARROT AND CARDAMOM SOUP

Tricky one, cardamom. It has a very distinctive flavor and aroma. In rice, with desserts, in sauces—well, thanks to the mother-in-law, I've come to value its subtlety, its lingering fragrance. Actually, I'm a bit obsessed with it. But please don't put it in my coffee. Ever. Arabs seem to love it in coffee, and it does kind of work, but some of us prefer our coffee uncontaminated.

This is a lovely recipe: carrots and cardamom are a match made in culinary heaven. And it's oh-so-good for you.

SERVES 4

a knob of butter (3½ tablespoons/1¾oz/50g)

1 medium onion, chopped

6 large carrots (about 1lb 2 oz/500g), peeled and chunked

2 garlic cloves, peeled and chopped

a knob of ginger (½in/1cm), peeled and chopped

1 rounded teaspoon ground cardamom (or the seeds of around 8 pods, crushed)

½ teaspoon ground turmeric

1 tablespoon all-purpose flour

3 cups/25fl oz/750ml vegetable stock

scant ½ cup/3½fl oz/100ml orange juice

juice of 1 lime

scant ½ cup/3½fl oz/100ml coconut milk (unauthentic optional extra)

sugar, salt, and pepper to taste

Melt the butter in a saucepan, add the onion, carrots, garlic, ginger, cardamom, and turmeric, and brown gently. After a few minutes, add the flour, and stir in the stock, orange juice, and lime juice. Bring to a boil and set to simmer on a low heat for 30 minutes, or until the carrots are soft. Add the coconut milk (if using) towards the end.

Take off the heat and blend, adding sugar, salt, and pepper to taste.

This is especially sumptuous served with rich brown or rye bread, but any chunky, dunky bread will do.

legumes

This was a difficult chapter: I couldn't possibly fit in all my favorite beany recipes. Hummus, falafel... there's a lot of ground to cover here.

The Middle Eastern diet is a pretty healthy one. Lentils, chickpeas, and fava (broad) beans have been cultivated in the area for at least 8,000 years, not least because they are *vetches*, beans and legumes that actively improve and bind the soil.

Nowhere is this love of legumes more obvious than the inclusion of beans in the daily regime. Simple and tasty dishes. As a result of which, children grow up squabbling over the last bowl of fava beans rather than seeing any green matter on their plates as a punishment.

# Loubia bi Harissa
## FIERY GREEN BEANS

To start: a confession. I find green beans awfully boring. There—I said it; years of pretense off my chest with just a few taps on the keyboard. Green beans are the worst—they are inevitably served either over-cooked or under-cooked and taste of, well, water. Runner beans at least have flavor of their own, but are still in need of a little tarting up, methinks.

*Al dente* is an unheard-of concept in the Middle East, where food trendiness is something that happens over millennia and not over the Sunday newspapers, and food is cooked just the way it is. And so these beans are properly cooked, and then left to sit around in the sauce while the flavors mingle.

This is a go-anywhere recipe, something you can throw together with nonchalance as an appetizer, or a side dish, or a salad.

### SERVES 4 AS A SIDE DISH

10½oz/300g green beans or runner beans (or be radical and use a mixture)

butter, for frying

1 red onion, finely sliced

8 cherry tomatoes

3 garlic cloves

juice and zest of 1 lime

1 teaspoon rose water

2 teaspoons harissa paste (see p.230)

5 tablespoons olive oil

Top and tail your beans, and string them if you're using runners. Green beans should be cut in half, runners cut on the diagonal into 2in (5cm) striplets. Now blanch them in boiling water for about 4 minutes and set to drain.

Heat a knob of butter in a pan and throw in the onion: once it has softened add the tomatoes and garlic, turn the heat down, and leave them to sweat a little. After about 5 minutes, add your green beans and sweat stuff a little more before taking it off the heat.

Whisk the rest of the ingredients together. Check the seasoning—you may need to add salt, although harissa paste is usually well seasoned. Stir the dressing gently through the beans and then leave the whole thing to cool. You can serve this hot or cold, but it is undoubtedly at its best at room temperature or above.

Green beans have never been so exciting.

# Salat Lubia wa Jarator

# FAVA BEAN SALAD WITH SESAME

The beginning of the fava (broad) bean season is an ugly time in our household. We buy them by the case, you see, and then fight over the last portion. Traditional Iranian *taruf*, or politeness, does not apply here. In Iran they are a very popular street snack, boiled simply in their pods and served with salt and *golpar* (ground Persian hogwort—see p.169).

This salad sees them teamed and steamed with their early-summer chum, asparagus, and then drizzled with a lemony sesame dressing. If you happen to be reading this in midwinter, all is not lost: canned or bottled asparagus and frozen fava beans work pretty well too.

To clarify butter, melt it and then strain.

### SERVES 4 AS AN APPETIZER

2 tablespoons sesame seeds

2½ cups/9oz/250g fresh fava (broad) beans (out-of-pod weight)

1 bunch asparagus (or 1 can, or 1 jar)

4 garlic cloves, smashed

2 tablespoons chopped fresh chervil, if available, or parsley

4 perfectly hard-boiled eggs (or use the eggs *hamine* on p.67)

2 teaspoons *tahina*

2 tablespoons water

scant ¼ cup/1¾oz/50g clarified butter

2 tablespoons olive oil

juice of 1 lemon

salt and coarse ground black pepper

Dry-fry the sesame seeds in a small pan and set them to one side.

Shuck the fava beans if they are anything other than early summer babies, and trim the woody end bits from the asparagus (usually up to where the white part starts to merge into the green). Put the vegetables and the garlic in a steamer (or a colander suspended over boiling water), and steam for about 6 minutes, or until both beans and tips are tender. If you are using canned asparagus, just drain it.

Allow the vegetables to cool a little; chop the garlic roughly and stir it back into the salad with the chervil. Quarter the eggs and arrange them prettily over the top.

Now for the dressing. Beat the *tahina* and water together, and then whisk in the butter and the olive oil, followed by the lemon juice.* Season to taste.

Pour the dressing over the salad, and sprinkle the sesame seeds on top.

*

If you are cooking ahead, or wish to chill the salad before use, add a little more water to the dressing, as it will set in the fridge.

# Fasulye Pilaki
## TURKISH EVERYDAY BEANS

This is one of the most widely enjoyed dishes in Turkey, and it is wonderfully simple to make. It traditionally underpins a good *mezze* spread but is also great fridge food: you can gobble it hot on a winter's day or savor it cold when the living is easy. It fits nicely into sandwiches and crêpes, works as a salad, and is a good base for other dishes (try topping it with spicy stir-fried tofu).

*Pilaki* just refers to the method of preparation: anything *pilaki* denotes it is served cold with olive oil. *Fasulye* are white beans: traditionally navy beans, but quite often cannellini beans are used instead. *Fasulye pilaki* has a sister dish, *barbunya pilaki*, which is the same except that it uses borlotti beans in place of white ones. So now you know.

SERVES 6

2 cups/12oz/350g cannellini beans (or navy beans), soaked overnight
olive oil, for cooking
2 medium onions, finely diced
3 sticks celery, finely diced
2 carrots, peeled and finely diced
3–4 green chilies (optional), chopped

1 large peeled potato, finely diced
4 garlic cloves, chopped
scant ½ cup/3½fl oz/100ml extra-virgin olive oil
juice and zest of 2 lemons
1 bunch parsley
salt and black pepper

Drain the beans, rinse them, and place them in a saucepan with some fresh water. Bring them to a boil and simmer for 35–40 minutes, or until they are cooked; then drain them again and set to one side. Dash some olive oil into the pan, heat it until sizzle-point and then add the onions, celery, carrots, and chilies. Cook for around 5 minutes, stirring occasionally, and then add the potatoes and garlic. After a minute or so more of stirring constantly, add about scant ½ cup/3½fl oz/100ml cold water and stir in the cooked beans. Turn the heat right down low and let the beans bubble softly to themselves for 20 minutes, or until they are really tender. Remove the pan from the heat.

Next whisk the olive oil with the lemon juice and zest, and stir it through the cooling beans. Add the parsley, and season to taste. Serve as you wish, but I think it's best at room temperature.

# Ful Medames

## ABU ZAAD'S *FUL MEDAMES*

*Ful Medames. Foul Medammas.* Strange name whichever way you spell it. For the uninitiated, it is a Middle Eastern staple, and consists of dried fava beans soft-simmered with garlic and served with lemon and chopped herbs.

First, to dispel any fava bean confusion. In the West, we often eat fresh fava beans (sometimes known as broad beans) when they are young, green, and quite often still in their pods. The brown ones that constitute *ful medames* are simply the grown-up and dried versions of the green ones. Further puzzlement ensues over size: Egyptian fava beans are small and brown, while the Lebanese and Syrian versions are plumper and bigger. They are all (kind of) the same thing.

There would seem to be a huge cross-border debate on how the things are best prepared. The Egyptians serve them slightly mushy and seasoned with cumin, quite often with *hamine* eggs (see p.67) and raw onion wedges. At the risk of causing an international incident, I must admit that I prefer the Levantine version, which sees them served with *tahini*, optionally garnished with chickpeas. You can buy cooked and regionally seasoned *ful* easily enough, but it is a lot more satisfying making your own.

Quite simply the best *ful medames* that I have sampled are to be found at Abu Zaad, a bustling Syrian restaurant in Shepherd's Bush, London. And so this is their recipe, which Chef Ismail Abou Basel enthusiastically shared even though he couldn't entirely believe that I was writing a vegetarian cookbook: "What, not even just a little bit of meat?"

### SERVES 8–10 AS PART OF A BUFFET

1 lb 2 oz/500g dried whole fava beans, soaked overnight
1 teaspoon baking soda
2 teaspoons salt
1 teaspoon ground black pepper
juice of 1 lemon

1 generous teaspoon ground cumin
scant ½ cup/3½fl oz/100ml *tahini* (see p.56)
3–4 garlic cloves, chopped
generous ⅓ cup/3½oz/100g cooked chickpeas
½ bunch chopped flat-leaf parsley
2 tablespoons good olive oil

Drain the fava beans and then bring them to a boil in a covered saucepan. Add the baking soda, turn the heat way down low, and leave to simmer for around 2 hours, or until the beans are tender.

When they are cooked, drain them, season with the salt and pepper, and then stir in the lemon juice, cumin, tahini, and garlic.

Serve warm, strewn with the chickpeas, parsley, and olive oil. Onion wedges on the side are a traditional accompaniment, and can be used as scoops.

## Baking Soda

I have come to the conclusion in recent years that baking soda is one of the most useful substances known to mankind. Not only is it a baker's best friend, it has remarkable properties, and no Iranian home, at least, is without it. In the above recipe it serves to tenderize the beans: it is also used to make things such as falafel and *kufteh* swell and become lighter and fluffier. My mother-in-law frequently adds it to water when she washes herbs, as it is lightly disinfecting. For the same reason it is often to be found in Middle Eastern medicine cabinets: you can dab it on stings and cuts, and it soothes burns. A teaspoon in a glass of not-too-cold water remains one of the world's best hangover cures; make it 2 teaspoons, and you've got a remedy for constipation. My mother swears by it to cleanse tea-browned flasks and mugs. The accumulation of all this information only serves to enhance my reputation locally as a quack. Hey ho. I'll let you know when I manage to turn it into sulphur, or mercury, or gold.

# Qorma-e-Maash
## MUNG BEAN CASSEROLE

The mung bean is a very neglected and misunderstood legume. At least in the West. Firstly, he's a pea and not a bean, and secondly, he's always playing second food fiddle to lentils and bigger beans. Which is a shame, as he is cheap and nutritious, a valuable source of protein for vegans and vegetarians, and doesn't need pre-soaking. Furthermore, he does not, um, induce flatulence in the same way as other beans—mung beans, like chickpeas, are regarded as "warm" (see p.106) and thus easier to digest.

Fortunately in Eastern Iran and Afghanistan (where he is known as *maash*) the mung bean is given center stage in a number of dishes, and this is probably my favorite. It is a good, hearty winter warmer.

SERVES 1

1 big tablespoon vegetarian ghee (or oil)

1 teaspoon fenugreek seeds

1 teaspoon cumin seeds

3 garlic cloves, minced

¾in (2cm) knob of fresh ginger, chopped

1 Scotch bonnet chili (or 4 green chilies)

1 large onion, chopped

2 bell peppers (any color), chopped

2 medium potatoes, peeled

1 teaspoon ground turmeric

2 cups/12oz/350g mung beans, washed and sorted

4 cups/32fl oz/1 liter water or low-salt vegetable stock

1lb 2 oz/500g fresh spinach, washed and roughly chopped

3 tomatoes, chunked

juice of 2 limes

salt to taste

TO SERVE:

raw onion and chopped fresh cilantro

Heat the ghee in a heavy-bottomed pan, and sprinkle in the fenugreek and cumin seeds, followed after a minute by the garlic, ginger, chili, onion, and peppers. Sauté the vegetables until the onion is translucent, stirring regularly.

Cut the potatoes into ¾–1¼in (2–3cm) cubes and add them to the pan together with the turmeric. After a minute or two more, stir in the mung beans, and add the water. Bring the pan's contents to a boil and then set to simmer for 45 minutes, or until the beans are cooked. Then add the spinach and tomatoes, and allow them to bubble merrily together for a further 10 minutes. Add the lime juice and season to taste.

Sprinkle with the cilantro and serve in deep bowls with onion wedges on the side. Bread and rice are optional extras—the dish is pretty filling without any help.

# Soya Kufteh Tabrizi
## NO-MEAT-BALLS

The town of Tabriz in Northern Iran is the butt of a lot of jokes. In the culinary sense, it is famous for the saltiness of its cheese and the size of its meatballs. No, really—they make them big enough to encase a whole chicken. Well, obviously we couldn't be doing that in the context of this book but some sort of *kufteh* is pretty much essential for any book on Middle Eastern food. The idea is to shape a tasty, spiced casing around a hidden jewel of a filling—something unexpectedly crisp, such as nuts, or creamy, such as cheese, or sharp, such as this barberry filling.

SERVES 4

FOR THE *KUFTEH*:

1lb 5oz/600g TVP (textured vegetable protein)

½ bunch fresh parsley, finely chopped

2 medium onions, peeled and grated

1 egg

½ teaspoon chili powder

1 teaspoon dried savory or thyme

1 teaspoon ground cinnamon

1 level teaspoon salt

FOR THE FILLING:

generous ¾ cup/2¾ oz/75g barberries, soaked (or unsweetened cranberries)

scant ⅓ cup/1¾oz/50g dried apricots, chopped and soaked

knob of butter (3½ tablespoons/1¾ oz/50g)

⅓ cup/1¾oz/50g dried sour cherries, pitted

⅓ cup/1¾oz/50g walnuts, chopped

scant ½ cup/1¾oz/50g chopped pistachios (or almonds)

scant ¼ cup/1¾oz/50g (raw weight) white, short-grain rice, cooked

1 teaspoon turmeric

½ teaspoon ground cardamom

2 teaspoons tomato paste

FOR THE SAUCE:

2 medium onions, chopped

oil, for frying

2–3 green chilies (or ½ a hot red one), chopped

3–4 chopped tomatoes

1 tablespoon tomato paste

⅔ cup/5fl oz/150ml sour grape juice (or dry white wine with a squeeze of lemon)

3 cups/24fl oz/850ml vegetable stock

First, make the casing: Just pound all the *kufteh* ingredients together. The moisture from the egg and the onion should be enough to reconstitute the TVP and allow it to swell. If you happen to make it too wet, just add some breadcrumbs or flour to bind it. Once you are happy that it is thoroughly mixed, cover it and pop it in the fridge to chill.

Next the stuffing. Drain the barberries, checking for barbs/stones, and the apricots. Melt the butter in a frying pan and spoon in the fruit and nuts, stirring well. After a couple of minutes add the cooked rice, spices, and the paste; cook through for a minute or so more, and take off the heat.

For the sauce, sizzle the onion in some hot oil in a large saucepan, and then add the chilies and the tomato. After a few minutes add the paste, sour grape juice, and stock, and bring to a boil.

To assemble the *kufteh*, use wet hands to shape the casing into 8 large (or 12 slightly smaller) balls. Using a finger, poke a hole into each one, and spoon a generous amount of the stuffing into each, molding the casing back around it so that the stuffing is completely enclosed. Very carefully lower the *kufteh* into the bubbling stock, and cook them for around 30 minutes, turning them over with a spoon from time to time.

At the end of the this time, retrieve the *kufteh* with a slotted spoon, and crank up the heat so that the sauce reduces a little. Serve the *kufteh* on rice or with warm bread, with the sauce in a bowl on the side. Yogurt and fresh herbs are suitable accompaniments.

# FAVA BEAN MASH

Another indulgent foodstuff. Where hummus abrades and challenges the tastebuds, *besara* soothes and comforts. Like mashed potato, only better, and in many cases interchangeable. In the Middle East it is usually eaten as a dip, but I often serve it as a "sauce" for other vegetables, or as a base for fried or casseroled foods. This version is mostly Moroccan.

SERVES 4, AS A SIDE DISH

scant 1¼ cups/7oz/200g dried split fava
    beans, soaked for 6 hours or overnight
splash of olive oil
1 large onion, peeled and chopped
1 teaspoon green cumin seeds (optional)
1 level teaspoon smoked paprika

juice of 1 lemon
salt and pepper

TO GARNISH:
olive oil, for frying
extra-virgin olive oil, for drizzling
pinch of paprika

Drain the fava beans. Next heat a little oil in a saucepan and fry the onions and cumin seeds together for a few minutes, followed by the smoked paprika and most of the drained beans (keep a handful back). Stir well before adding about generous 2 cups/17fl oz/500ml water. Bring to a boil and then simmer for about 1 hour, or until the beans are really mushy and most of the water has been absorbed. (Do check during the cooking process that the liquid has not actually dried out—if it looks dry, just add another glass of water.) Once the beans are cooked, blend or mash them together with the lemon juice and season to taste.

Finally heat a little oil in a pan and fry the remaining beans until they are browned and crispy. Spoon the *besara* into a bowl, scatter the fried beans on top, and then swirl the surface with olive oil and paprika.

This is a dish that is best enjoyed fresh and still warm: serve with crusty bread, extra lemon wedges, and perchance some crudités.

# CHICKPEAS WITH GREENS, GARLIC, AND MINT

The five-minute lunch or dinner. It is based on an Iraqi lamb stew: I have literally stripped it of the meat element. You can find mint sauce in European delis and some supermarkets.

SERVES 1

2 garlic cloves

splash of olive oil

about 3½oz/100g fresh leafy greens

2 tomatoes, chunked

1 can (14oz/400g) chickpeas, drained

1 teaspoon mint sauce

salt and coarse black pepper

Sauté the garlic in a little oil, and tip in the greens, stirring well. After a couple of minutes, add the tomatoes, chickpeas, and mint sauce, and allow to cook through for a few minutes more, then season to taste. Tip into a bowl, and enjoy with flatbread: creamy yogurt is an optional but desirable extra. And you've still got half an hour of your lunch break left...

# BLACK-EYED PEA AND LEMON HOTPOT

This hotpot is a blend of Greek *lemonato* sauce and Persian casserole wizardry. It is so delicious that you'll want to keep on eating it long after you are stuffed.

SERVES 4

5 sticks celery, washed

3 carrots, peeled

1½ sticks/6oz/75g butter, plus a splash of oil

2 onions, sliced

1 teaspoon ground turmeric

1½ teaspoons dried basil

1 tablespoon dried dill

zest and juice of 2 lemons

generous 1 cup/7oz/200g black-eyed peas

2½ cups/20fl oz/600ml good vegetable stock

2 medium potatoes, peeled and quartered

salt and ground black pepper

big handful of chopped fresh parsley

Firstly cut the celery and the carrots into slender batons around 2½in (6cm) long. Heat the butter and oil in a pan, add the carrots, celery, and onions and fry until they all begin to soften. Add the turmeric, herbs, and lemon zest followed by the black-eyed peas, lemon juice, and stock. Bring the pan to a boil and set to simmer for 10 minutes, then add the potatoes. Cook through for another 30 minutes, or until the potatoes are really soft and the beans cooked. Season to taste, and dollop out into a big tureen. Sprinkle liberally with parsley and serve with warm bread. Or *kritheraki* (rice-like pasta). Or rice.

# 1001 WINNING WAYS WITH HUMMUS

It is a well-known fact that hummus holds the fabric of the vegetarian space-time continuum together. Without it the vegetarian race would face a grim existence: what else could they possibly put in their sandwiches or stick their crudités in? Actually, the stuff has run the gamut of vegan jokes and culinary satire, and come out a winner. It is more popular than ever, with suburban 4-year-olds demanding it in their lunchboxes, and local diners churning it out with sandwiches.

*Humous* is the Arabic word for chickpeas, and the correct name for the dish under discussion is *humous bi tahina*. So calling anything else hummus is a bit of a misnomer. Chickpeas are one of the earliest foodstuffs known to mankind, and the origins of this dish are unsurprisingly lost in ancient urban legend and medieval embellishment.

It is not hard to make, but for what it's worth I proffer my standard recipe below, with a couple of variations.

## Houmous bi Jahina

# HUMMUS

The most important thing about hummus is that you eat it fresh. As someone who has worked her fair share of Mediterranean kitchens, anything that could be made ahead in big batches always got my vote. This recipe isn't one of them; after a night in the fridge, it can start to acquire a tang. I would also advise against cheating by using canned or jarred chickpeas—they never have the same flavor.

SERVES 4–6

1¾ cups/7oz/200g dried chickpeas, sorted through, washed, and soaked overnight

4 tablespoons *tahina*

2 tablespoons really good extra-virgin olive oil

juice of 2–3 lemons

about 4 garlic cloves

salt and pepper, to taste

TO SERVE:

olive oil, for frying

paprika

Reserve a handful of soaked chickpeas, put the rest in a pan, cover them with water and bring them to a boil. Turn down the heat, allow to bubble for around 10 minutes, and then skim off any foam or detritus that has risen to the top. Cook for a further 1 hour, or until they are soft and can easily be squidged between finger and thumb. Do not drain, but remove the pan lid and leave them somewhere for half an hour or so to cool a tad.

You can do the next bit by hand—but it is so very much easier with a blender. Ladle about half of the chickpeas into the blender, including quite a bit of the cooking liquid.

Add half of the *tahina*, olive oil, lemon juice, and garlic, and blend until smoothish, adding more liquid if the mixture is too solid. Repeat with the rest of the ingredients, and then mix the two batches together well and season to taste.

Heat a little olive oil in a pan and fry the remaining chickpeas, stirring constantly, until they are golden and crisp to bite. Drain them on a piece of paper towel and then roll them in a little salt.

Serve the hummus on a plate—if you bash the bottom of the plate against the palm of your hand, the dip will spread evenly across the surface. Sprinkle the fried chickpeas across the hummus, and follow it up with a pinch of paprika.

Serve as a dip or a sauce or a sandwich filling.

# GREEN PEA HUMMUS

Same thing—only green. And much easier to prepare at the last minute. I am, of course, working on the principle that everyone keeps frozen peas in their freezer. Again, this dish is best eaten fresh. Although, unlike real hummus, this actually freezes pretty well. It is, if anything, even more versatile—try this with crispy fried onions as a baked potato filling.

SERVES 6–8

1lb 2 oz/500g frozen peas
2 tablespoons *tahina*
juice of 1–2 lemons
2 tablespoons extra-virgin olive oil
2–3 garlic cloves, peeled
1 level teaspoon ground cumin

½ bunch fresh parsley, washed
salt and pepper, to taste

TO SERVE:
extra-virgin olive oil
pinch cayenne

Bring the peas to a boil in a pan of water and cook for around 5 minutes, then drain and refresh under cold running water.

Pop them in the blender along with the *tahina*, lemon, oil, garlic, cumin, and parsley. Give it all a quick whizz—it will probably be far too stiff, so add about 2 tablespoons cold water to loosen it up. Season it to taste, and serve in a bowl with the olive oil and cayenne drizzled/sprinkled on top. Yummy.

*A Poetic Aside*

The chickpea is so well ensconced in the Eastern kitchen that some of its more prolific writers took it quite to heart. There is speculation that because chickpeas contain tryptophan (which generates serotonin i.e. it makes you happy), they were recognized as feel-good food. Rumi even wrote about them:

*A chickpea leaps almost over the rim of the pot where it is being boiled.*
*"Why are you doing this to me?"*
*The cook knocks him down with a ladle.*
*"Don't you try to jump out.*
*You think I am torturing you:*
*I'm giving you flavor*
*So you can mix with spices and rice*
*And be the lovely vitality of a human being.*
*Remember when you drank rain in the garden?*
*That was for this."*
[Translated by Coleman Barks]

Cool, no? Though if the chickpeas are actually talking to you, it's possibly a good idea to get some help.

# SWEET HUMMUS

Hummus, sweetened with honey and infused with the gorgeous scent of cinnamon and cardamom. The best of the bunch in our trio of hummus-y things. If it wasn't so infernally rich, I could eat it with a spoon for breakfast every day. I have used this in tarts (spread it across a pastry base and then smother the top with flaked almonds), to sandwich cakes (make a fatless sponge cake with a mix of chickpea flour and regular flour, and use this as the filling), and with much jolliness to create a dessert *mezze* (see below).

*Oh yes — the dessert mezze.*

This is great fun. *Mezze* is far too good a concept to reserve for savory stuff. The idea is to serve your guests a range of fruit crudités and sweet dips, including this hummus recipe. Use your imagination: for crudités, try apple, pear, pineapple, celery, carrot, cucumber, melon. Cut up the fruit in advance, and dunk into acidulated water (water with lemon juice added) to stop discoloration.

And for the dips? Well why not try sweet *çaçik*? Mix yogurt and honey with freshly chopped mint. I also like to serve a chili fruit salsa as part of this: just finely dice a combination of fruits—kiwi, strawberry, mango, banana, pear, and nectarine all work well—with some very hot chili, and dress it with a little rose water, sugar, and lime. Shove it in the fridge to chill, and serve it piled with mascarpone and garnished with pita bread nachos.

SERVES 6–8

1¾ cups/7oz/200g dried chickpeas, sorted and washed, and soaked overnight

2 cinnamon sticks

4 tablespoons *tahina*

2 tablespoons sugar

2 tablespoons date syrup (or honey)

2 teaspoons ground cinnamon

1 teaspoon ground cardamom

TO SERVE:

splash of oil

sugar

ground cinnamon

runny honey

Put a handful of the chickpeas aside and boil the rest in water for 10 minutes, then skim off any foam/residue that has appeared. Add the cinnamon sticks and continue to cook for another 1 hour, or until the chickpeas are well cooked, then take them off the heat and set them aside to cool a little. Do not drain them.

Once the contents of the pan have cooked somewhat, ladle half of the contents into the goblet of your blender, including some of the cooking stock, together with half of the *tahina*, sugar, date syrup, and spices. Blend to a smooth, creamy paste, and then repeat with the other half.

Heat a little oil in a frying pan and fry the reserved chickpeas until they are golden in color; drain them on paper towel and roll them in sugar.

Serve the hummus (still warm or well chilled) in bowls, sprinkled with cinnamon and drizzled with honey.

# FALAFEL

If you are a vegetarian living in the US, chances are you dream in falafel. They are the ubiquitous veggie stand-in, sold in restaurants and (Greek- and Turkish-owned) snack bars up and down the land. It is an undeniable fact that the falafel pocket is probably to the merry veggie what the gyro is to the drunken carnivore.

You can buy felafel ready-made, or frozen, or in packaged mix. You can dress them up and call them dinner, or shove them in some bread and call them lunch. When they're good they're very, very good, but when they are bad they are horrid: dry, over-cooked, crumbling, or tasteless.

They really are easy to make at home—but only if you have a blender or a strong arm. Call me fussy, but I think falafel are probably best consumed fresh—even when tightly wrapped, they still dry out when you store them for more than a day. Good news is that the mixture freezes well, and the finished product can also be frozen if you handle them with care.

There are two schools of thought on how to make them: the Egyptians, who invented them, make them with fava beans and call them *tami'ya*, while the Lebanese and Syrian convention is for chickpeas. American falafel are usually based on the latter. The tastiest are produced by a hybrid of methods, as here.

MAKES PITA POCKETS FOR 5–6

scant 1½ cups/5½oz/150g dried chickpeas, soaked overnight

scant 1 cup/5½oz/150g dried split fava beans, soaked overnight

½ bunch fresh cilantro, washed

½ bunch fresh parsley, washed

½ teaspoon baking soda

1 teaspoon ground cumin

½ teaspoon ground chili (optional)

4–5 garlic cloves, peeled

1 large onion, peeled and chunked

salt, to taste

oil, for cooking

Empty out the soaking water and rinse the beans and chickepeas well, then leave to drain for about 10 minutes. Discard the stalks of the herbs, and then place all of the ingredients (except the cooking oil, naturally) into the goblet of your blender—you will probably need to do this in two batches. Blend for a couple of minutes: you should end up with a moist green paste. You can, of course, make this by hand—but you will need to make sure everything is pounded, chopped, and grated really finely.

Heat some oil in a saucepan or deep fryer. Using wet hands, roll the mixture into balls of around 1¼–1½in (3–4cm) in diameter and then flatten them slightly between your palms to make UFO-shaped discs. Slide these into the hot oil (again, you will need to do it in batches) and cook for around 2 minutes per side (i.e. 4 minutes in total), or until they are golden in color. Scoop them out with a slotted spoon and drain on paper towel.

Fill hot pita pockets with sliced tomato, cucumber, and the herb and onion salad on p.55 and then spoon a few falafel on top of each one. Serve with lemon wedges and tahini (p.56) or chili sauce, or hummus, or yogurt.

*Troubleshooting:*
If the mixture seems too wet, add a little flour to bind it. If it is crumbly and won't come together, just add a (very) little bit of water.

# Kushari

## EGYPTIAN STREET FOOD

The first time I sampled *kushari* it was prepared by a fellow sous-washer-upper at some restaurant in which I was working, and I looked on skeptically as he combined rice and pasta and lentils—it looked like a rather bad experiment. But it worked, and came to be a popular staff supper. (Trade secret: some of the best restaurant meals are born out of staff dinner experiments—but shh! You didn't hear it from me.) Took me a few years to work out that it is, in fact, the joint favorite Egyptian national dish (one of three), and probably Cairo's best-selling street fare.

It evolved as a nutritious and fast dinner for Coptic Christians, who spend 210 days of each year fasting and following a vegan diet. They hold that Man started in on carnal pleasures (yes, that includes meat eating) only after his fall from grace, and that good Christians should aspire to renounce such things as often as possible.

It is especially good Monday evening fare: after the over-indulgence of the weekend, this simple concoction of tomatoes and carbs hits the mark.

### Note

There are many recipes similar to this in the Middle East, although none are perhaps as extravagant with the ingredients. *Mojadarra* is popular in the Levant, and consists of lentils with rice or wheat, topped with fried onions. *Adass Pulao* is one of Iran's famous rice dishes, and again comprises lentils and rice: it is a common accompaniment to casseroles and stocks. *Kitree*, or *kecheri* (the ancestors of European kedgeree) is popular in Afghanistan and the Gulf, and once again is spiced lentils with rice.

SERVES 4

2½ cups/10½oz/300g basmati rice
1¼ cups/9oz/250g brown lentils
3 large onions, peeled
oil, for frying
3–4 green chilies, chopped
2–3 garlic cloves, minced

8 tomatoes
1 tablespoon tomato paste
2 tablespoons red wine vinegar
¼ cup/2fl oz/50ml water
salt
2½ cups/10½oz/300g whole-wheat macaroni
    (or other small cut pasta)

Wash and cook the rice: turn it off before it is quite cooked and leave to steam. Pick through the lentils and put them in a pan with some water: they will need about 30 minutes to cook.

Slice 2 of the onions and fry them in a little oil until they are crispy and golden brown: remove them with a slotted spoon and set them to one side. Chop the remaining onion and fry it in the same pan together with the chilies and garlic: once the onion has softened, chop the tomatoes into the pan, and after a couple of minutes add the tomato paste, vinegar, and water. Season to taste and set to simmer while you attend to the pasta, which just needs to be cooked for a few minutes (follow the package instructions).

Drain the pasta, rice, and lentils. In a large shallow bowl, layer first the rice, then the lentils, and finally the pasta. Spoon the spiced tomatoes over the pasta, and top the whole thing with the crispy onions. Serve with some extra hot sauce on the side for your more masochistic guests. I also serve it with a tomato and onion salad.

rice and grains

Perhaps the second most important foodstuff in Veggiestan, after bread, is rice. It might have different names across the region—from *plov* to *biriani*—but its intrinsic value to the culinary culture of each country is the same. Its use originally denoted a certain opulence, and it is fair to say even today that "bread eaters" are often regarded as peasants (political correctness is not a strong point in the area).

I have tried very hard to hide my Persian bias in this tome, but the Iranians have turned rice into an art form. Lord Curzon observed that the rice of Persia "was prepared in a manner that no Parisian artist could emulate." So I make no apologies for the extra Iranian-ness in this chapter.

That said, all the countries in the area know how to turn what is a fairly basic carbohydrate into a feast.

In the West, there is a growing awareness of whole grains, and foodie fashion has been demanding ever more exotic varieties of the stuff. (You say *keynwoi*, I say *kwinoah*—there's a song in there somewhere.) Anyway, my Arab suppliers snort with amusement when I try to tell them that I have to have *moghrabia* because it was in the *Guardian*. *Freekeh* (green wheat), buckwheat, bulgar (cracked wheat), semolina, couscous—these are all everyday foods out Mid-East.

I find it extraordinarily satisfying contriving a dinner involving a carbohydrate that isn't bread, potato, rice, or pasta. And smug: you know the sort of superiority that you feel when you go to the gym before breakfast—well, clever healthy cooking can give you the same kick, really it can.

Thing is, wheat, agriculture, and cooking were almost certainly invented in Veggiestan. Well, the second two at any rate: wheat, I guess, was created. The oldest forms of cultivated grain known to mankind are *emmer* and *einkorn*, and they both made their first appearance in the area we broadly refer to as Kurdistan—Northern Iran and Iraq. It was in this region that previously nomadic tribes and family groups first put down roots—both literal, as they planted the soil, and social, as towns evolved around their patches of cultivated land. Archaeologists excavating an ancient village called Jarmo have found evidence of agrarian activity dating back 7,000 years.

# RICE — *ROZ* — THE BASICS

Rice is not indigenous to the Middle East. It's likely that the first taste of it was brought by traders from the Far East (the oldest evidence of rice cultivation, from 15,000 years ago, has been found in Korea), but the rice that is now grown in the region is actually descended from African stock.

Most of the countries of the region grow some rice of their own, most notably Iraq (where it is called *timman*), but few of them produce enough even for home consumption, and it is fiendishly hard to find these specialty strains abroad. Do look out for smoked *sadri* rice from Northern Iran—you will find it in some Iranian stores. It will cost you a bit more, but it is really special. Mostly it is long-grain rice that is used, although sticky rice and short-grain are used for sweet dishes and for stuffing.

I give you below a fail-safe method for cooking long-grain rice *à la* general purpose Arabic. And then I will aim to impart my enthusiasm for doing it the Persian way. Several Persian ways, in fact.

## RICE—A FOUNDATION COURSE

In a hurry? Use this method to produce perfectly cooked long-grain or basmati. Rice varies, not just from region to region but from batch to batch, and so some will require less water, and some rather more: Middle Eastern housewives usually cook a tiny quantity of a new sack of rice just to see how it is.

The important thing here is proportion. But, for the record, most rice measuring cups have a volume of a generous ¾ cup/7fl oz/200ml and will hold 5½oz/150g of uncooked rice, enough to feed one Iranian, or one-and-half mere mortals.

1 measure of rice per person
1 measure water per person
1 generous tablespoon butter or ghee per person
salt to taste

Rinse the rice well. Some people use boiling water to get rid of the starch, but be warned that over-washing removes many of the nutrients. Not that white rice has a lot of those in the first place.

Put the water, butter, and salt in a pan and bring it to a boil. Add the rice, bubble away for a few minutes, and then turn down the heat really low; wrap the lid of the pan in a clean cloth and simmer for another 20 minutes.

The rice should be perfectly cooked and the grains separated. Let it sit, covered, for another 5–10 minutes, then fluff with a fork and serve.

## RICE—INTERMEDIATE LEVEL

On to Iranian rice. Iranians are truly oryzivorous: bread may still be consumed more in rural areas, but in the cities rice has taken a firm hold. Residents of the North of the country (where the humidity allows rice to be grown) are famed for eating rice three times a day. And they eat it in quantity as well. As a guide, a standard rice measure is ¾ cup/ 5½oz/150g.

This gives a good Persian portion, but will produce at least twice as much as a regular rice eater can manage.

Iranian rice (and brown basmati) should be soaked in cold salted water for at least 1 hour before use, but Indian or Pakistani basmati rice does not need this.

There are three basic ways of preparing Persian rice (*berenj*, in its raw state), although they all depend on the absorption principle.

The first and most basic is known as *chelow*—plain white rice—and I have given the method of preparation for this below. The second is known as *pulao*—it is prepared in the same way as *chelow*, but is made more of an event by the addition of spices, vegetables, or fruit (or meat or fish) layered through the rice. You will find a few *pulao* recipes in the following pages.

The last is known as *katteh*, and is prepared by absorption, but the rice isn't drained after its initial boiling, and so the rice remains waterlogged and cooks into a glutinous lump. Rice prepared this way is very popular in the north of Iran; it is certainly more nutritious and filling, as the nutrients and starch aren't drained away, but it is, shall we say, an acquired taste.

*Katteh* does have one very important thing going for it—it is one of the world's best remedies for an upset tummy. Last time I was feeling bleurrgh, my very sweet husband insisted on forcefeeding me *katteh* with yogurt, which was actually the last thing that I wanted and caused me to behave like a spoiled child at the time. But d'ya know, within half an hour I felt like a new storekeeper. Just trust me and try it.

All Iranians aim to get a good *tahdik* on the bottom of their rice, regardless of how they are cooking it. *Tahdik* (literally, "until the bottom of the pan") refers to the golden, sticky crust that is encouraged to form in the bottom of the pan. And which will, of course, be the top of the dish once it is inverted on to a plate. It can be achieved with practice in a normal saucepan, but for those with a penchant for eating instant rice, I strongly recommend the purchase of a Persian rice cooker, which does all the hard work for you. They are built to last: my mother-in-law has two that have been working for over 20 years (though the removable inner pan has been replaced). They are readily found in Persian grocery stores.

## "Chelow"—White Rice

If you are using a rice cooker, wash and soak 1 measure (¾ cup/5½oz/150g) of rice per person, drain it, and then tip it into the pan with ¾ cup/6fl oz/175ml water per person; add 1 teaspoon of butter/ghee and ½ teaspoon of salt per person. Cook according to the instructions for your cooker model. To serve, simply invert a plate over the pan, and turn upside down—the non-stick interiors turn out perfect rice cakes again and again.

Now, on to the slightly harder stuff—the saucepan method. This assumes you have read the preceding paragraph and that you have thus washed, soaked (if applicable), and drained your rice. Bring a pan of salted water to a rolling boil, tip the rice in, and cook for around 7 minutes; the rice should thereupon be soft outside, but still hard inside—pinching a grain between your thumb and forefinger should determine this. Drain the rice thoroughly in a sieve (as clearly it would pass through a colander). Heat a dollop of oil or ghee in the saucepan, and add 2 tablespoons water. As soon as it starts to sizzle, carefully spoon a layer of rice across the bottom, followed by another and another until all the rice is piled into the pan. Resist the temptation to pour the rice into the pan, as this will weight it down and it will not have the legendary Persian fluffiness. Poke the handle of a spoon or a skewer down through the rice to the bottom of the pan—do this 5–6 times to make steam fumaroles. As soon as the rice starts to steam visibly, wrap the lid of the saucepan in a clean dish towel, and turn the heat down very low. The rice will take about 35 minutes to cook, although it will keep quite happily on that setting for a further 30–40 minutes, or until you are ready to serve.

To evict the rice from the pan (and it usually proves a little reluctant to move), sit the bottom of the pan in a couple of inches of cold water in the sink—the sudden cold will cause the rice to contract from the sides, and you should then be able to turn it on to an inverted plate with ease.

RICE—ADVANCED COURSE
Once you have achieved the above, you will be ready for the *tahdik* masterclass—wherein you will learn how to use assorted secret ingredients at the bottom of the pan to create the perfect crust. The most common variant is to use saffron, sprinkling a little steeped, ground saffron into the sizzling ghee just before you start to layer up the rice. Or there's always:

• *Tahdik* with yogurt
Mix a spoon of the hot, drained rice with 2 tablespoons yogurt and a beaten egg, then spread it into the hot oil—this gives a really tasty, glossy crust.

• *Tahdik* with potato
Peel and thinly slice 2–3 medium, waxy potatoes and lay these in the hot oil, then gently spoon the rice on top.

• *Tahdik* with bread
This is my favorite. Simply lay slices of flatbread in the sizzling oil—halved pita will do, or *lavash* bread, or best of all, halved Arabic *khobez*, which is already round and will fit the saucepan. Then pile the rice in as above.

# Morasa Pulao

# JEWELED RICE

This has to be the most stunning of Iran's famous range of *pulaos*, or rice dishes. This is Iran showing off.

It is very similar to another dish known as *shirin pulao*, or sweet rice. It is the stuff of banquets and weddings—glorious, jeweled, shimmering stripes of fruit and nuts across steaming saffron rice. It would traditionally be served with a simple citrusy stock that has been thickened with potato or beans (see p.137). Pictured overleaf.

## SERVES 4 AS AN APPETIZER

⅓ cup/1¾oz/50g each chopped pistachios and almonds

1⅓ cups/3½oz/100g barberries (or cranberries if you really cannot find barberries), soaked and drained

splodge of butter, for frying

scant ⅔ cup/3½oz/100g raisins, soaked and drained

2 medium carrots, peeled and grated

1 large onion, peeled and chopped

2¾oz/75g sour orange peel (see note)

dash of oil

4 measures (4 cups/1lb 5oz/600g) basmati rice

butter or ghee

salt and pepper

½ teaspoonful ground saffron steeped in a saucer of boiling water

3 teaspoons "rice spice," *advieh pulao* (usually 2 parts cinnamon to 1 part each ground cardamom, rose petals, and nutmeg, although recipes vary)

1¾oz/50g *nabat* (crystallized sugar), crushed (optional)

Firstly, make ready the nutty fruity bits. The nuts should be blanched (separately) in boiling water; the barberries should be fried in a little butter; the raisins should be fried in butter until they start to puff up; the carrot, orange peel, and onion should be sautéed in a little oil.

Now cook the basmati according to your preferred method (see preceeding pages), and just before it is cooked, stir through the liquid saffron and the rice spice.

Turn the rice out onto a dish, and then literally stripe each of the "jewels" across the top in pretty little rows (trying to contrast the colors).  Right at the last minute, pour a little boiling water over the *nabat* so that it dissolves a tad, and then strew the whole lot over the rice dish—this makes the whole thing glisten like real gems (well, with a bit of imagination it does, anyway).

(Some Iranians serve the "jewels" mixed into the rice, which makes the whole thing easier to prepare… but not everyone likes all of the ingredients, so serving the dish like this is easier on you, the chef.  It also looks more sensational segmented in this way.)

## Sour oranges

In Iran, the peel and juice of sour oranges (akin to the Seville oranges so prized for marmalade making) are both used.  The juice, known as *ab-naranj*, is used in northern regions in place of *ablimoo* or lemon juice to add sharpness to casseroles; the fresh fruits are also excellent when squeezed over fish.  But the grated peel, or *halal-e-naranj*, is used all over the country to add an extra dimension to rice dishes. Iranian shops sell a ready-grated, dried version, which may just be rinsed and fried, or you can make your own.  Even if you can't find Seville oranges to use, just pare the skin of a regular orange in very thin striplets, blanch it briefly in boiling water (to remove any nasty chemicals), and then spread it out and leave it in a warm spot to dry for a day or two.

A special bonus tip from my mother-in-law: oranges are such uplifting fruits that it seems a shame so much of their fragrance is wasted; next time you peel one, leave the peel on the radiator for a while and, before long, the whole room should be infused with a waft of citrus.

*Reshteh Pulao*

# NOODLEY RICE WITH RAISINS

This is an Iranian classic, popular during festive times, most notably at *Nowrooz*, the Persian new year. It comprises fragrant rice steamed with roasted noodles and buttered raisins, and is enjoyed accompanied by a pot of flavorsome stock (see opposite). The noodles are meant to represent the different strands of one's life coming together: a good omen for important occasions.

*Reshteh* are readily available in Persian and Arabic supermarkets but if you cannot find them, use roasted rice (or *udon*) noodles (available in Asian stores) or even whole-wheat spaghetti.

You can replace the cinammon, cardamom, rose petals, and nutmeg with 2 teaspoons rice spice—*advieh pulao* (see p.133).

SERVES 4

4 measures of rice (see p.130)
4 measures of water
salt and butter, to taste
1 teaspoon ground cinnamon
½ teaspoon ground cardamom
½ teaspoon crushed dried rose petals
¼ teaspoon nutmeg

½ teaspoon ground turmeric
9oz/250g *reshteh pulao*, broken into 1¼–
    1½in (3–4cm) lengths
knob of butter (3½ tablespoons/1¾oz/50g)
scant 1 cup/5½oz/150g raisins, soaked in
    cold water
¼ teaspoon ground saffron steeped in a little
    boiling water

Cook the rice according to the intermediate method on p.130. Once you have boiled it, mix it with the spices and the raw noodles before leaving to steam.

If you are using a rice cooker, just cook the rice normally and then add the spices and the noodles about 10 minutes before you want to serve, stirring well.

Melt a little butter in a pan. Drain the raisins and toss them in the butter, sautéing them for a few minutes. Turn the rice out, crack the *tahdik*, and streak the steeped saffron over it, mixing it into the rice a little. Finally stripe the raisins over the top.

Accompany with pickles, herbs, and yogurt.

Ab Sabzi Jaht

# VEGETABLE STOCK TO GO WITH *PULAO*

The recipe opposite also works well with Black-Eyed Pea Hotpot (p.121) but this is much simpler.

SERVES 4

3 sticks celery, cleaned and chopped

1 large onion, chopped

2 carrots, chopped

4 dried limes, rinsed and pricked

1 teaspoon turmeric

1 tablespoon tomato paste

4 cups/32fl oz/1 liter water

4 small potatoes, peeled and cubed

1 can (14oz/400g) white kidney (or butter or cannellini) beans, drained

1 can (14oz/400g) chickpeas, drained

salt and pepper, to taste

splash of oil

1 tablespoon dried mint

Put the celery, onion, carrots, limes, turmeric, and tomato paste in a pan, cover them with the water, and bring it to a boil. Simmer for about 30 minutes and then add the potatoes, beans, and chickpeas. Again, bring the stock to a boil, turn the heat down, and allow to cook for another 30 minutes, or until the potato is falling apart.

Heat the oil in a skillet and sizzle the mint in it until it becomes quite dark: stir this into the bubbling stock and season the whole thing to taste.

Serve in a big bowl alongside any of the Iranian *pulaos* in this chapter.

# Sib Pulao

# RICE WITH POTATO AND DILL

This is an easy, everyday kind of rice using easy, everyday ingredients. Serve it alongside the citrusy stock *Ab Sabzi Jaht* (see p.137) for a filling and comforting weekday supper.

SERVES 4

4 medium potatoes, peeled and diced
   (½in/1cm cubes)
2 tablespoons chopped spring garlic (or
   2–3 cloves regular garlic, chopped)
butter or ghee

4 measures (4 cups/1lb 5oz/600g) basmati rice
2 level teaspoons salt
½ teaspoon ground turmeric
3 tablespoons dried dill
¼ teaspoon saffron, ground and steeped
   in water

First, fry the potatoes and garlic for a few minutes in some ghee—you are aiming merely to start off the cooking process, so do not let them overcook. Next, wash the rice and bring it to a boil in a pan of water together with the salt and the turmeric. Cook for around 7 minutes (see the master recipe, for *Chelow*, p.131), drain, and then melt a little more butter/ghee in the pan. Mix the rice with the dill and layer it back into the pan, alternating with the garlicky fried potato cubes. Poke a few fumaroles down through the mixture to the bottom using the handle of a wooden spoon, and then wrap the lid in a dish towel and set the *pulao* to cook on a low heat (about 35 minutes should do it). If you are using a rice cooker, just add the raw potato and garlic in with the rice at the beginning and then stir the dill through just before serving.

Turn off the rice and allow it to sit for a few moments (you can do the same if you wish), before turning it out on to a serving plate. Crack the *tahdik*, or crust, which will have formed, and trickle the steeped saffron over the rice, mixing it lightly with a spoon. Serve with raw onion, yogurt, and fresh herbs, and, most importantly, *torshi*—this dish really needs pickles as an accompaniment.

Alternative recipe:

Another popular dish in Iran is *bogoli pulao*—rice with fava beans. It is made in just the same way as *sib pulao*, but substitutes peeled, fresh baby fava beans for the potato—just blanch the fava beans instead of frying them.

# Jimman Kamah

## IRAQI RICE WITH TRUFFLES

Truffles are known as *kamah* in classical Arabic, *terfas* in North African parlance, and *fagga* in Saudi circles. They have been enjoyed in the region for millennia (not least because of their reputation as an aphrodisiac): they were easy to forage for early humans, and became popular with ancient civilizations from Babylon to Rome. They are at their best enjoyed simply, poached or sautéed: the traditional desert way to prepare them is poached in camel milk, but I'm prepared to bet you're all out of that. Whipping them into an omelet also works well, while in Iraq they are shaved into rice with lamb. This Iraqi recipe combines all of these ideas, minus the lamb.

Fresh white truffles are almost impossible to source, but the canned variety are easy to find: most Middle Eastern stores carry them. Even canned, you will still need to peel and wash them: six months under the desert means that they are usually full of sand. If you simply can't find them, substitute morels or Chanterelle mushrooms. Using truffle paste to cook the eggs will also help lend an authentic flavor.

TO SERVE 6 (OVERNIGHT
PREPARATION REQUIRED)
2lb 4 oz/1kg canned white desert truffles
2¼ cups/1lb/450g long-grain rice, washed
    and drained well
butter or ghee, for frying

1 large onion, chopped
1 tablespoon *baharat* (see p. 100)
salt and pepper, to taste
¼ cup/2fl oz/50ml truffle oil
6 eggs
handful of fresh chopped parsley

Rinse and drain the truffles and check for sand. Put the drained rice into a tub, and roll the truffles in it. Seal the tub and bury it in the fridge for the night. This is a bona fide way of storing fresh truffles, but all we are aiming to do here is to infuse the rice with truffle-ness.

Next day, take the truffles out, brushing off the rice. Peel them, dice them finely and set them to one side momentarily.

Heat a little ghee in a pan and cook the onion; once it has softened, add the *baharat* and the rice together with a pinch of salt and about 3¾ cups/29fl oz/850ml water. Bring it all to a boil and then turn down the heat, cover the lid of the pan, and set to simmer for about 20 minutes.

Whisk the eggs together with 1 tablespoon water, plenty of black pepper and a pinch of salt. Warm the truffle oil in a frying pan, and toss the cubed truffles in. Sauteé gently for a couple of minutes, and then turn up the heat and pour in the egg mixture. Cook for a couple of minutes before sliding the pan under a hot grill. Once it is firm and lightly browned, slide the omelet on to a chopping board and chop through roughly.

Check that the rice is cooked, fluff up with a fork, and then spoon it all on to a platter. Strew the truffley omelet over the top, and sprinkle parsley on top of that.

Think of truffles, and most of you will immediately think of pigs and French forests. But in this context we are talking desert truffles. Strange white lumps of fancy fungus that grow under the sands in areas ranging from the Sahara to Iraq. Just as elusive (and expensive) as their European cousins, but with twice the mystery attached. They are also known as thunder potatoes, and they are regarded as the spawn of the desert storm. This is, rather wonderfully, one legend that is more or less true. Autumn storms in the desert produce lightning, which cracks the earth and provides the opportunity for the truffle spore to sprout: they attach themselves to the roots of rockroses, and grow during the winter under the sand. They are hard to find: come spring, experienced truffle spotters look for ripples in the surface of the land, but to the untrained eye the quest is well nigh impossible. Which is why they are the holy grail for 'shroomers.

# Maghluba
## PALESTINIAN UPSIDE-DOWN RICE

Upside-down stuff appeals to my inner kid. There are two reasons you should add this to your supper repertoire: 1) it is a lot easier than it seems at first glance; and 2) it really is one-pot cooking, perfect for those that prefer their tummies full and their sinks relatively empty. I make the whole thing in a sturdy wok.

*Maghluba* literally means "upside down" in Arabic, and refers to a style of food that has become popular all over Veggiestan. The dish is traditionally prepared either with lamb and eggplant, or with chicken and cauliflower. Our version sees the lamb replaced with a range of vegetables.

SERVES 4

2 large eggplants, calyx removed

canola oil, for frying

8 garlic cloves, whole but smashed a bit

2 onions, chopped

1 large zucchini, cubed

2 red peppers, roughly-chopped

2 teaspoons *baharat* (see p. 100)

1 teaspoon turmeric

1 tablespoon tomato paste

8 tomatoes, 4 chopped, 4 sliced

salt, to taste

2 tablespoons veggie ghee

3 medium potatoes, peeled and cut into
    ¼in/5mm slices

2½ cups/1lb 2 oz/500g long-grain rice,
    washed

4 cups/34fl oz/1 liter good vegetable stock

1¾oz/50g flaked almonds, lightly toasted

handful of fresh chopped parsley

Cut the eggplants into ½in (1cm) slices, and sprinkle them with salt to bring out the bitterness/excess moisture. After 30 minutes, wipe them dry, heat a little oil in a wok, and fry them on both sides until they are golden brown. Drain them on paper towel.

Add the garlic to the same pan; add a dash more oil if required. Follow it immediately with the onion, zucchini, and peppers, and cook them for a couple of minutes, then add the spices, tomato paste, and the chopped tomatoes at 1-minute intervals. After a further 2 minutes, season the mixture to taste and scoop it out into a bowl.

Melt a knob of ghee in the wok, and fry the potato slices. When they are tender and golden, spread them around the base and sides of the wok and layer the eggplants on top. Next, gently spoon the zucchini/pepper mix in, and arrange the sliced tomatoes on top. Finally, gently sprinkle the rice over the tomatoes, tapping the wok so that the rice kind of settles and fills any cracks in the "structure." Pour the stock over the rice, topping it up with water if necessary—the liquid element should come to just above the surface of the rice.

Woks don't usually come with lids, so improvise one by covering a tray with foil. Turn the heat way down low, and let the *maghluba* bubble and steam for 50 minutes to 1 hour, or until the rice is cooked. At the end, swiftly invert the *maghluba* onto a serving platter, potatoes and eggplants uppermost. Scatter with the almonds and parsley, and serve with pickles and a bowl of plain, creamy yogurt.

# MR. HADDAD'S PUMPKIN *KIBBEH*

*Kibbeh* (or *koubbeh* in Iraq) are another of those seminal Middle Eastern dishes, and a strong contender for the position of the national dish of Lebanon. There are many different varieties, although the original was made with raw pounded lamb and wheat. They can be made simply, without filling, or stuffed as in the recipe below. And they can be boiled, fried, or baked—ours are fried, as I think they are best that way. They are a must for *mezze*, a great fridge standby for busy households, a freezable asset for unexpected guests, perfect for picnics and, well, actually quite fiddly to make. In certain parts of Lebanese society, the measure of a good housewife is said to be on the texture of her *kibbeh*. Eek. I thought I'd better ask the professionals for help...

Mr. Haddad is one of our bakers and the boss of Dina Foods. Well, we actually suspect Mrs. Haddad is the real boss, in true Middle Eastern tradition. (You will find her recipe for spinach *fatayer* on p.22.) Mr. Haddad's pumpkin *kibbeh* are exceptional—but he does of course make an awful lot of them, and so I have helpfully converted the recipe he gave me for 300 pieces to one for 30.

MAKES 30 PIECES
FOR THE CASING:
14oz/400g pumpkin, peeled and cubed
2½ cups/16fl oz/600ml water
3½ cups/1lb 9oz/700g fine bulgar (cracked) wheat
scant 1⅓ cups/7oz/200g whole-wheat flour
2 teaspoons salt
½ teaspoon white pepper
2 teaspoons dried basil

FOR THE FILLING:
4 teaspoons canola oil
2½ cups/14oz/400g diced onion
1 cup/5½oz/150g diced celery
½ cup/3½oz/100g diced red pepper
1 tablespoon sumac
2 teaspoons citric acid
2 teaspoons ground coriander
1 teaspoon ground white pepper
2 teaspoons ground cinnamon
salt, to taste
1lb 5oz/600g cooked chickpeas, coarse-ground
canola oil, for frying

First off, boil the pumpkin in the water: when it is soft, drain it, reserving the stock.

Rinse the wheat and then set it to soak in the pumpkin stock: leave it for at least 1 hour.

Now make the filling. Heat the oil in a frying pan and cook the onion, celery, and pepper until they are soft. Add the spices and seasoning, stirring well, followed finally by the coarse-ground chickpeas.

Now drain any surplus water from the soaked bulgar, and pound it together with the pumpkin, flour, seasoning, and basil. A mixer would help—you need it to be well blended.

*(continues overleaf)*

So far, so easy, no? Now comes the tricky part. A bowl of water at your side will considerably ease the next part of the operation—keep dipping your best *kibbeh* hand in it to stop everything from sticking. Take a tablespoon of the casing mixture, and roll it into a fat sausage shape. Using your forefinger, poke a hole into one end of the sausage. Take a teaspoon of the filling and prod it into the cavity you have just created, and then pinch the casing with your fingers so that it encloses the filling. The resultant shape should, traditionally, resemble a football, fat in the middle, tapering to the ends (although you can, of course, make them any shape you like). Keep going until you have used all of the mixture.

Deep-fry the *kibbeh* in batches until they are golden and rise to the surface, and then scoop them out and drain them on paper towels.

Serve with lemon wedges, warm bread, and salad.

*Mansaf*

# JORDANIAN PILAF

This is Jordan's national dish. Well, it would be if it was prepared with lamb. But of course we won't be doing that. Instead we shall make a rich, spiced vegetable stock to go with it. The secret of *mansaf*, you see, is not in the meat, but rather the inclusion of *laban moutboukh* (which the Jordanians call *jameed* and usually make from dried *labneh*—strained yogurt), to make a sharp creamy sauce. In Jordan, *mansaf* is eaten at every conceivable important occasion, and so it would be remiss of me not to give it a mention herein. One proviso with this dish: you've got to eat it with your hands.

Jordan? Hmm—what can I say about it? If you want a gentle introduction to Middle Eastern culture, there are plenty of Arab-American neighborhoods in the US that you can visit: Atlantic Avenue in Brooklyn, New York; Patterson, New Jersey; or Dearborn, Michigan, to name a few. Feeling a bit more adventurous? Go to Jordan. At the time of writing, it is the region's jewel of friendly stability. They love tourists. It gained its independence from Palestine in 1946 and was guided through many years of peace by the late King Hussein; he was succeeded by his son King Abdullah II, who continues to provide competent rule. Quite apart from the fact that it is home to one of the world's most famous movie sets (the ruins of the city of Petra, which was built by the Nabateans in the first century BCE), there is more to see and do there than you can shake a cinnamon stick at. And no, I am not being paid by their tourist board.

SERVES 6
FOR THE RICE:
2¼ cups/1lb/450g long-grain rice
¾ stick/2½ oz/75g butter or veggie ghee
1 teaspoon ground turmeric
1 teaspoon ground cinnamon
3¾ cups/30fl oz/850ml water
salt, to taste

FOR THE VEGETABLES:
olive oil, for frying
1 large onion, peeled and chopped
3 garlic cloves, chopped
2 red peppers, chunked
7oz/200g button mushrooms

2 large eggplants, washed, cubed,
    and salted
1 teaspoon ground cumin
1 teaspoon ground allspice
6 large tomatoes, cut into large chunks
salt and pepper
*laban moutboukh* made with 14oz/400g
    yogurt (see p.74)

TO FINISH:
7oz /200g assorted seeds: sesame, sunflower,
    and pumpkin are all good
1–2 sheets *khobez* (see p.15) or other
    flatbread

OK, firstly rinse the rice and leave it to drain well.

Next get the veggies under way: heat some oil in a deepish frying pan, and add the onion, garlic, peppers, and mushrooms. Pat the eggplants dry, tip these in too, and fry, stirring regularly, until the onion is soft and the eggplants are at least halfway cooked. Next add the spices, tomatoes, and a sprinkle of salt and pepper. Cook on high for 3–4 minutes, and then pour in just enough water to cover the vegetables. Turn the heat down and cover the pan.

Back to the rice. Melt the butter in a saucepan and tip in the rice, stirring well so it doesn't stick. After a couple of minutes add the spices, then the water and a measure of salt to taste. Cover the lid of the pan with a clean cloth, reduce the heat, and leave it alone for 20 minutes. After this time is up, take the pan off the heat. Now you can peek; give it a quick fluff with a fork, then re-cover the pan and let it rest for 10 minutes.

Time to get the garnish ready: spread the seeds out on an oven tray, and either broil for milliseconds, or pop them in the oven for milliminutes.

Meanwhile, back in the vegetable pan … Spoon a little of the vegetable stock into the *laban moutboukh*, mix gently and then pour the whole lot into the pan, being careful to stir either clockwise or anti-clockwise but always in the same direction. Bring to a barely perceptible boil, check the seasoning and take off the heat.

Warm the bread and stretch it across your chosen serving platter. Pour a little of the warm veggie sauce over it, and then pile the rice on top. Spoon the vegetables into the middle of the rice, and cover with sauce—you may wish to serve any surplus sauce in a bowl on the side. Sprinkle with the toasted nuts, and serve with fresh herbs or a green salad.

The idea is that you break off pieces of bread with your hands, wrap them around some rice and sauce, and cram it all in. I won't tell anyone if you choose to use silverware, but I can guarantee it won't be as much fun.

# SPINACH, APRICOT, AND BULGAR SALAD

Diamonds were never a girl's best friend—that's a load of old baloney. Mind you, I'd be hard-pushed to say what is. Especially with the cat on my lap and the husband reading over my shoulder as I type. A cook's best friend? Well, ingredient-wise, bulgar (cracked wheat) has got to be up there as a prime candidate. It can get tossed into croquettes, mixed with fruit as stuffing, used hot as a rice type thing, or used to great effect in salads. The only time it has let me down was as a porridge substitute. So don't try it with milk.

The secret with this salad, or with any bulgar salad, is to make sure that there are plenty of the other ingredients: thus this is not bulgar salad with spinach, but spinach salad with bulgar.

It is a great summer lunch; it's got crunch, squidge, and oomph. Great picnic fare perhaps, as it travels well, and looks pretty too (picnics should always be pretty, don't you think?).

SERVES 4

generous ½ cup/3½oz/100g dried apricots, roughly chopped

generous 1⅓ cups/10½oz/300g bulgar (cracked wheat)

1¾ cups/14fl oz/400ml vegetable stock or water

1¼ cups/10fl oz/300ml apricot juice, or apple juice

5½oz/150g fresh, thoroughly washed spinach

1 well-scrubbed carrot

1 smallish red onion

4 tablespoons nice olive oil

2 tablespoons lime juice, and the zest of 1 lime

1 teaspoon crushed chilies

1 teaspoon ground cumin

salt and pepper

⅔ cup/3½oz/100g raw (unsalted) pistachio kernels (or almonds)

1 small bunch fresh cilantro, stalked, washed, and chopped

handful of fresh mint, washed and chopped

OK; firstly set the apricots to soak in tepid water (cold is fine, but tepid is quicker). Set your oven to 275°F/140°C. Spread the bulgar over the bottom of an oven tray (not forgetting that it should swell to about twice its bulk), and pour the stock and juice over it, mixing well. Put the tray into the oven for about 20 minutes, fluffing the bulgar with a fork halfway through.

In the meantime, rough-shred the spinach, coarse-grate the carrot, and fine-slice the onion. Whisk the oil, lime juice, zest, chilies, and cumin together with some salt and pepper. Drain the apricots. Once the bulgar is cooked through, let it cool a little and then scoop it into a bowl and mix with all the other ingredients, adjusting the seasoning to taste.

Great with flatbread and plain yogurt or *çaçik*.

# PANTRY TABOULEH

Cracked wheat is a grain of international mystery. It variously gets called *bulgar*, *bulghur*, *burghul*, and *pourgourri*, and this particular dish also has several aliases: *kissir* in Turkey, and again *pourgourri* in Greece. But most of us know it as tabouleh. Any which way, it is a salad made from wheat and varying degrees of herbs and vegetables. I have written out my recipe down below, but there is nothing stopping you from making it differently. Experiment.

In truth, if you have bulgar in your cupboard you can pretty much unroll a whole meal around it: serve it hot as the carbohydrate du jour, slip it into burgers and *kibbeh*, or turn it into an instant salad. OK, so I have already waxed lyrical about it above. Just one thing—don't be tempted to buy the tabouleh instant ready-mix packs unless you are really very lazy, as bulgar is by definition instant-cook and it takes nanoseconds to chop a few things to throw into it.

SERVES 4

1⅓ cups/7oz/200g medium bulgar
1 large onion, chopped
1 large handful fresh herbs of your choice, chopped
salt and pepper
a few handfuls, finely chopped, of the following:
 tomatoes, peppers, mild chilies, cucumber, zucchini, mushrooms, raw cabbage, shelled fava (broad) beans, podded peas, pitted olives, sugar snap peas, snow peas, corn kernels, broccoli florets, spinach, carrot, celery

OTHER OPTIONAL EXTRAS:

cooked chickpeas, beans, or lentils; cooked rice; sunflower seed kernels; pumpkin seed kernels; pine nuts; raisins; chopped apple or pear

FOR THE DRESSING:

¼–scant ½ cup/2–3½fl oz/50–100ml extra-virgin olive oil
and a splash of one of the following:
 lemon juice, tamarind paste, *pekmez*, pomegranate molasses, steak sauce, mint sauce plus vinegar, sour grape juice

I think you've kind of got the idea by now. Just douse the bulgar with boiling water, spread it out in a tray and pop in a warm oven (275°F/140°C) for about 20 minutes. Remove it from the heat after this time, tip it into a bowl and fluff it with a fork. Allow it to cool a little, then add your choice of the ingredients above. There you have it.

# ANISSA HELOU'S *TABBÛLEH*

What can I say about the lovely Anissa Helou? She is an authority on Levantine cuisine, and a veritable mine of historical and culinary knowledge. And she's a fellow fan of really big hair, so that's got to be good.

As I deem her *tabbûleh* recipe to be definitive, there seemed little point in offering you anything else—so here it is, authentic and unabridged. She goes to great lengths to point out that the real deal is a parsley salad, with wheat as an added extra.

SERVES 4–6

¼ cup/1oz/30g fine bulgar (cracked wheat)

1lb 5oz/600g very best tomatoes

1¾oz/50g scallions, washed and trimmed

14oz/400g washed flat-leaf parsley
  (that's one very big bunch, or two
  regular bunches)

2½oz/70g fresh mint leaves, washed

¼ teaspoon ground cinnamon

½ teaspoon *baharat* (see p.100) or
  ground allspice

¼ teaspoon ground black pepper

sea salt, to taste

juice of 1 lemon

⅔ cup/5fl oz/150ml extra-virgin olive oil

Wash the bulgar several times, drain it well, and then spoon it into a large-ish bowl. Continue to fluff it occasionally with a fork as you get the rest of the dish ready.

Next finely dice the tomatoes and scallions, setting the former in a colander to drain. Discard the woodier parts of the parsley and chop the rest finely with a knife (Anissa suggests that you avoid the temptation of using a mezzaluna, as it tends to make the herbs clump and become unworkable); do the same with the mint. Add the tomato, scallions, and herbs to the bulgar together with the spice and black pepper and mix well before sprinkling in salt to taste. Pour the lemon juice and olive oil over the *tabbûleh* and stir one more time before serving. It is traditionally piled into the middle of an array of lettuce leaves, which are in turn used as scoops.

# COUSCOUS

Gotta love couscous. It is an edible blank canvas, ready for you to fill out any way you like. And it is easy to cook once you grasp the basic principles of steaming and forking and fluffing. The "big secret" behind couscous is to keep all the grains separate at every stage of preparation. Here's my fail-safe 5-point plan:

1) sprinkle some water over the couscous in a colander or sieve, massaging the grains between your fingers;

2) bring some water or stock to a boil in either a couscousier or saucepan;

3) spoon the couscous into the top of the couscousier, or fit the colander in which your have just moistened the grains securely over the boiling stock;

4) after 20–30 minutes, tip the couscous into a bowl, add 2–3 tablespoons water and some oil or butter, toss it well, and sprinkle it with salt;

5) set it back over the bubbling stock for a final 20–30 minutes, then serve with more butter dotted through it.

You can, of course, ignore all of this and just chuck a jug of boiling water over your couscous, leave it for 10 minutes and then fluff it with a fork—but in my opinion it is never quite the same as the properly steamed stuff.

SERVES 4

1 large onion, washed

2 cinnamon sticks

2⅓ cups/12oz/350g whole-wheat (or white) couscous

1 stick plus 1 tablespoon/4½oz/125g butter

olive oil, for cooking

2–3 garlic cloves, peeled and chopped

½in/1cm fresh ginger, peeled and chopped

1 yellow pepper, chopped

3 medium sweet potatoes, peeled and cubed

1 generous teaspoon curry powder

¼ teaspoon ground nutmeg

4 chopped tomatoes

scant ½ cup/3½fl oz/100ml water or veggie stock

1 can (14oz/400g) chickpeas

½ cup/1¾oz/50g flaked almonds

scant ⅓ cup/1¾oz/50g raisins (optional)

1¾oz/50g fresh coconut, roughly chopped

Peel the onion and drop the skin, together with the cinnamon sticks, into the base of your couscousier/saucepan. Cover with about 3in (7cm) water and bring it to a boil, preparing the couscous as outlined above, using about half of your butter allocation.

Chop the reserved onion and fry it in a little oil, adding the garlic and ginger and pepper. After a couple of minutes, add the sweet potato to the frying pan with the spices. Stir constantly so the potato doesn't stick (add more oil if necessary) for 2–3 minutes, then add the tomatoes, vegetable stock, and chickpeas. Simmer for about 20 minutes, or until the sweet potato is cooked through and then season to taste.

Heat the remaining butter in a little pan and toss in the almonds, raisins, and coconut: sauté for a couple of minutes.

To serve, mix the nutty raisins through the couscous, arrange the latter in a pile on a serving tray, and spoon the curried potatoes on top. Harissa (p.230) is an optional side dish.

*Firik Pilau*

# TURKISH GREEN WHEAT *PILAU*

*Freekeh* is quite simply one of the tastiest carbs that I've come across. It has been used in the kitchen for centuries and gets a mention in medieval Baghdad texts. Young green wheat is sundried, scooped into a stack, and then torched. Because there is so much sap inside the wheat, only the chaff burns off, leaving the inner kernel roasted but intact. The wheat is then rubbed and thrashed, and left in the sun a little more: it is either packed whole or cracked so that it resembles coarse bulgar.

It is a versatile and nutritious grain: like most of its agricultural peers, it can be used in soups, salads, cakes and bread, as a cereal, and, as here, as an accompaniment, taking the place of rice. In fact, this recipe has got enough going on to be the main event—just serve it with a little yogurt on the side.

It is broadly available—but you can substitute roasted buckwheat.

SERVES 4

1¾ cups/12oz/350g whole *freekeh*

a good glug of olive oil, for cooking

4 garlic cloves, peeled and minced

2 sticks celery, washed and chopped

2 carrots, peeled and diced

2 bunches scallions, washed and chopped

1 teaspoon ground allspice

½ teaspoon ground cardamom

3¼ cups/27fl oz/800ml vegetable stock

knob of butter (3½ tablespoons/1¾oz/50g)

⅔ cup/3½oz/100g pine nuts or sunflower seed kernels

⅔ cup/3½oz/100g chopped pistachios

⅔ cup/3½oz/100g chopped almonds

⅔ cup/3½oz/100g currants, soaked in water

salt and pepper (Aleppo pepper would be nice, but cracked black will do)

generous quantity of fresh chopped dill and parsley

First off you need to rinse the *freekeh*, checking for stones or any other unwanted bits of countryside. While it is draining, heat some oil in a heavy saucepan and fry the garlic, celery, carrots, and scallions. Once the celery has started to soften, measure in the spices followed by the *freekeh*, and after a few minutes of vigorous stirring, pour in the stock. Bring to a boil, turn the heat down real low, and wrap the lid of the pan with a clean dish towel, fitting it so that the pan closes well. The wheat will take about 35 minutes to cook: it should be pleasantly chewy. (Actually, *freekeh* is pretty hard to overcook, and retains its bite whatever you do to it—this is part of its charm.)

Melt the butter in a skillet and toss in the nuts. Drain the currants and add these in too, and cook until the currants puff up and the pine nuts turn golden brown.

Season the *freekeh* to taste, gently stir the nuts and the fresh herbs through it, and then pile the whole thing on to a platter. Serve on its own with yogurt, or top it with naughty buttery fried eggplants, zucchini, and onions, or use it as an accompaniment for Saffron Vegetables, p.53.

# Burger Nabati
# BURGHLERS

These are the original veggie burgers, and something like this recipe has been prepared for centuries. Bulgar patties are often served cold as part of a *mezze*— but this version sees them sizzled and served in buns. They are a squillion times nicer than the average meat infested burger: your carnivorous friends will be so jealous.

SERVES 4

¾ cup/4½oz/125g fine bulgar (cracked wheat)

½ cup/3½oz/100g red lentils

1 tablespoon whole-wheat flour

1 large onion, peeled and chunked

2 tomatoes, chunked

1 carrot, peeled and chunked

½ bunch of cilantro, washed

2 tablespoons *tahina*

¼ teaspoon ground cumin

½ teaspoon ground coriander

¼ teaspoon smoked paprika

½ teaspoon chili powder

salt and pepper

peanut oil, for frying*

TO SERVE:

shredded lettuce, sliced tomatoes, sliced
    pickles, fried onions

Onion and Herb Salad (see p.55)

*Çaçik* (p.61)

4 large whole-wheat buns

*

These don't respond very well to the barbecue treatment—they are too soft to start. But few real vegetarians would actually want their food cooked on a grill that is in all likelihood covered in meat drippings.

Put the bulgar in a bowl, and cover it with about generous ¾ cup/7fl oz/200ml boiling water. Mix it with a fork, cover it, and leave it to do its thing for a while.

Wash and pick through the lentils, tip them into a saucepan, cover them with around 1¼ cups/10fl oz/300ml of water, and bring it all to a boil. Cook for around 20 minutes, or until they are soft, and then drain them. Put them in a blender if you have one, together with the remaining ingredients, and mix well. If you don't have a blender, then grate the onion and carrot, dice the tomatoes, finely chop the cilantro, and pound it all with a potato masher. Tip the contents of the blender goblet on to the soaked bulgar and mix well with your hands.

Using wet hands mold the mixture into 4 large burger shapes. Heat a slosh of oil in a frying pan and lower the patties in: cook for 3–4 minutes either side.

Serve the burgers as you would any other burgers, with a plethora of add-ons, and a shedful of fries.

# Kasha

## TOASTED BUCKWHEAT SALAD

*Kasha* is toasted, roasted buckwheat. It is yet another foodstuff that traveled to Veggiestan from Russia "with love." It found particular fans in Armenia, Georgia, and Israel.

Buckwheat is a great pantry standby, and cooks up just like risotto or barley. Weirdly it is not actually wheat at all, but rather the seeds of a distant cousin of rhubarb. Not a lot of people know that.

This recipe works best hot, but you can enjoy it as a salad too—just add some olive oil and vinegar.

Toasted buckwheat is a rich, reddy brown; untoasted is pale in color.

### A SIDE DISH FOR 4–6

1 bunch scallions, washed and trimmed

canola or sunflower oil for frying

1 small head of fennel, finely sliced

1⅓ cups/7oz/200g toasted buckwheat

1¾ cups/14fl oz/400ml vegetable stock

1 bunch radishes, trimmed, and roughly sliced

1½ cups/5½oz/150g sugar snap peas, rinsed and sliced

1 bunch of fresh dill (or 1 good tablespoon dried dill)

generous ½ cup/3oz/85g raw peanuts, roughly chopped

salt and black pepper

Chop half the scallions, and cut the rest into striplets. Heat a little hot oil in a frying pan and toss in the chopped scallions and half of the fennel. Add the buckwheat, followed straight away by the stock. Bring the stock to a boil and then turn it way down low: it will need about 40 minutes to cook through, but you should fluff it with a fork after about 20 minutes.

Once the *kasha* is cooked, heat a little more oil in another pan and throw in the other half of the fennel and scallions. To this add the radishes, sugar snap peas, and dill, and cook on a high heat for around 2 minutes, so the vegetables are hot but still very crispy. Sprinkle in the peanuts and cook for 1 minute more, then take off the heat.

Season the *kasha* well, and then stir the crispy vegetables through it. Serve with a big dollop of sour cream or yogurt.

# Plov, Osh, Pilavi
## CARROT AND CHICKPEA *PILAF*

This is a terrific barbecue rice: fragrant, but not too fussy. It supports the main event admirably, but is tasty enough to be the main event for vegetarians. With the best will in the world, the barbecue was not designed with veggies in mind, and the burned vegetable offerings that pass as vegetable kebabs can be woefully inadequate. Serve this with a pot of yogurt, and you've got the best part of supper sorted, al fresco, al living room, or anywhere else.

The dish (or variations thereof) is popular across Turkistan, and has been since the emergence from Ergenekon.* When cooked with lamb, it is more or less the national dish of Uzbekistan. It is quite an oily affair—yet another that was originally made with lamb tail fat—and is lent character by the dark color of the fried onion.

*

Turkistan is one of those gloriously vague terms that can have all sorts of geographical and historical associations. But it is broadly understood to refer to all of the Turkic speaking nations and their lands, from Central Asia westwards to Turkey itself. The story goes that the ancient, pre-Turkic inhabitants of the land fled from goodness knows what terror: the lone survivor, a boy, ended up in the mythical valley of Ergenekon in the Altay Mountains and was raised by a wolf. The years passed, some better-not-to-think-about-it breeding took place, and a new tribe evolved. It soon grew in numbers to the extent that they decided they needed more room to do whatever it was that proto-Turks did. Trouble was—no one knew the way out. The valley was deep and its walls impenetrable. Their leader, Bumin Khan, summoned the village blacksmith, and he made a huge pair of bellows and proceeded to huff and to puff and to knock a great hole in the mountains. As you do. The people were then led out to a shiny new Turkic existence by another wolf, Asena. The Turks have a thing about wolves to this day.

SERVES 4

scant 1½ cups/5½oz/150g uncooked dried chickpeas, soaked for at least 6 hours, or 1 can (14oz/400g) cooked
1½ cups/10½oz/300g long-grain rice
quite a lot of ghee or canola oil, for frying
2 large onions, peeled and chopped
½in/1cm piece fresh ginger, peeled and chopped
4–5 carrots, peeled and cut into thin batons
2 teaspoons *baharat* (see p. 100)

2 teaspoons sugar
2¾ cups/22fl oz/650ml veggie stock
1 (small–medium) whole bulb garlic, rinsed
salt and pepper, to taste

TO SERVE:
1 big knob of butter (4 tablespoons/2oz/55g)
1 onion, sliced
1 grated carrot
1½ teaspoons brown sugar
about 1 cup/9fl oz/250ml thick yogurt

Cook the chickpeas in boiling water (or open the can). Rinse the rice and leave it to drain.

Heat the ghee/oil and toss in the onion, ginger, and carrots. Fry until the onion is well browned and the carrots softened, and then add the *baharat*, stirring constantly. Follow it up with the rice, the sugar, the chickpeas, and finally the stock, together with a little seasoning. Flake off any loose outside skin from the garlic, and drop the whole bulb into the saucepan. Wrap the lid of the pan in a dish towel and fit it snugly in place, turn the heat right down and leave the rice (without interfering) to cook for about 20 minutes. At the end of this period, the rice should be soft and fluffy. Check the seasoning, re-cover the pan and let it rest for 10 minutes.

Melt a little butter or ghee in a frying pan, add the onion and carrot, and fry until crispy. Add the sugar and sizzle some more.

Pile the rice on to a platter, make a well in the middle, fill it with the yogurt, and then pour the buttery caramelized oniony stuff over the top. Strew the steamed garlic cloves around the edge.

# Dolmeh-ye-Kadu

# BARLEY-FILLED ZUCCHINI

Barley. It was one of the first grains to be harvested, and enjoyed great popularity in ancient times. It has now, to a large extent, been replaced by wheat, which is altogether easier to process into bread.

Barley is also one of our most seriously neglected cooking ingredients. There was a time when every granny's cupboard would have some pearl barley in it for dropping into soups. Where's it all gone? Out the window with all our other cooking lore. Anyway, this recipe uses pot barley (sometimes called Scotch barley), which you can't beat for nuttiness and chewiness and general goodness. I have twinned this stuffing mixture with zucchini, as they both have a slightly off-center flavor and complement each other—although you can, of course, use this barley mix to stuff anything you like, or even use it in place of rice or pasta in a meal.

## SERVES 8 AS AN APPETIZER. OR 4 AS A MAIN COURSE

8 fat zucchini, washed

1 medium onion, diced

3 green chilies, chopped

½in/1cm knob of ginger, finely chopped

1 green pepper, chopped

4 garlic cloves, finely chopped

½ teaspoon green cumin seeds

1 teaspoon cracked coriander seeds

olive oil, for cooking

⅔ cup/5½oz/150g pot barley, rinsed

4 tomatoes, chunked

2½ cups/20fl oz/600ml water or veggie stock

salt and pepper, to taste

big handful of chopped mixed fresh herbs
    (3–4 tablespoons)—choose from
    parsley, mint, cilantro, savory,
    or watercress

generous 2 cups/17fl oz/500ml tomato passata
    or juice

OK. So. There's two ways to stuff a zucchini, you see. You can cut it lengthwise, but then it's not really stuffed—more kind of filled. Or you can cut it across its diameter and hollow out the middle. Which is the method I prefer.

Halve the zucchini across their width, and use a combination of small pointy knife and teaspoon to hollow out the middle of each section. Retain the bits that you extract.

Next plunge the halves into boiling water and blanch them for 3–4 minutes—you are not aiming to cook them, merely to soften them. Turn the heat off, put the pan in the sink and run some cold water into it—this serves the twin purpose of arresting the cooking process and making sure that the veggies are cool enough to handle.

Time to start the stuffing. Fry the onions, chilies, ginger, pepper, garlic, and spices in a little oil. Once the pepper and onion have softened, add the barley; stir well to mix before adding the tomatoes and then start adding the water/stock, a little at a time. To all intents and purposes you can treat it like risotto rice. *(continued overleaf)*

Barley takes about 40 minutes to cook—if it looks a little dry, add some more water. The end product should be cooked but retain a little crunchiness around the edges. Take it off the heat, season to taste, and then stir the herbs through it.

Preheat the oven to 350°F/180°C.

Using a long spoon, poke some of the barley stuffing into each of the zucchini halves. Lay them in an ovenproof dish and pour the passata over and around them before covering the dish with foil. At this stage, if you like, you can involve some cheese: a sprinkling of halloumi or mozzarella is rather nice but blows the dish's vegan credentials. Bake in a medium oven for around 30 minutes.

Serve with warm bread and plain yogurt.

# WHEAT GRASS "MOUSSE"

If wheat has a history stretching back eight millennia, this recipe is in all likelihood nearly as old. I offer it as a curiosity—it is not, perhaps, something that you will all want to rush off and make. It is both strange and time-consuming. But it is possibly one of the first ever recipes. It is well nigh impossible to find this in books, but is rather passed on orally from mother to daughter. To get to the bottom of it I resorted to the best of methods, chatting to Persian and Afghan housewives.

It is usually made at the time of *Nowrooz* (Persian New Year)—it is one of the seven items beginning with the letter "S," which every house has to have to ensure a prosperous year. Its symbolism is clear: the wheat sprouts represent fertility and new life, the rebirth of the year, success for the months ahead. And as wheat grass is naturally sweet, the consumption of *samenu* is said to bring sweetness to the occasion. It is traditionally made overnight by the women of the household. Music and dancing accompany the creation thereof: who needs chick flicks and Chardonnay when you can sing and dance around a bubbling cauldron, huh? In Iran it is also made as a *nazr*, one of a range of foodstuffs prepared to share on certain anniversaries as a way of remembering the dead.

SERVES 4
(THIS TAKES ABOUT 6 DAYS)
1¼ cups/9oz/250g wheat berries

2lb 4oz/1kg whole-wheat flour, sieved
2 tablespoons chopped nuts (optional garnish)
Er, and that's it

Firstly you need to sprout the wheat berries. Pop them in a plastic tub, cover them with water and forget about them for 3 days. At the end of this time, drain them, wrap them in a wet cloth, and place the whole thing back in the tub. You need to leave it somewhere warm and dark for another day or two, wetting the cloth a couple of times a day, until the wheat has germinated. On the fourth or fifth day, spread the wheat out on a tray and cover the surface with paper towels: you will need to spray these with water 2–3 times a day for a day or two. Watch the wheat like a greedy crow: as soon as it starts to show silvery green shoots, pounce and harvest it. That is to say, crumble it all in your hands and wash it thoroughly twice. Then put about half of it in the goblet of a blender, add a couple of glasses of water (about 1 cup/9fl oz/250ml), and blend. Settle a cloth (muslin is ideal, a clean dish towel will do) into a sieve over a jug and empty the contents of the blender into it, pressing with a spoon to force the liquid through (it is the liquid extract that you are after). Twist the ends of the cloth together and squeeze some more, and then put the wheat grinds in a tub to one side while you repeat the exercise with the other half of the wheat. Repeat the whole thing twice over again with the two batches of ground wheat, adding more water, and liquidizing it all some more, and then squeezing the juice out into the jug: as long as the liquid is milky in appearance, you are still extracting good stuff.

Next put the wheat juice and flour in a non-stick pan and blend it to a smooth paste using a wooden spoon. Put the pan on the stovetop and cook the mixture gently until the liquid all evaporates and it becomes quite crumbly—you will need to stir it constantly (or delegate sensibly) at this stage. (Now you know why they throw parties to make this stuff!) After a few minutes, add some more water—about two glasses (1 cup/9fl oz/250ml)—and beat the mixture so it is once again homogenized. And now you leave alone for a bit: turn the heat down as low as it will go, pop the lid on and let it do its thing for about 30 minutes (a cursory stir after 15 minutes would be a good idea).

It should now be much thicker and darker. If you taste it, you will see how curiously sweet it is: this comes naturally from the wheat. To complete the thickening process, spoon the paste into an oven tray and put it into the oven on a very low heat (175°F/80°C; if you don't have an electric oven, 225°F will do, though slightly warmer) for about 30 minutes. Then turn the heat off and leave the *samenu* in the oven for at least another hour (or overnight). Scoop into a large bowl (or several smaller ones), garnish with the nuts if using, and chill until required.

I do suggest that you eat it very, very slowly, thus to appreciate all the work that went into it.

vegetables

It kind of seems daft having a chapter called "Vegetables" in the middle of what is patently a vegetarian cookbook. But that is exactly what this chapter is all about: roots and shoots, salad veggies, green veggies, winter veggies, summer veggies, squishy veggies, and scrunchy veggies. They are not naturally bedfellows, but they fall together by virtue of the fact that they didn't quite fit in anywhere else in the book. That is not to say that these are unwanted and friendless recipes: I actually wrote this chapter last, because it contains some of my favorite food.

Who needs meat when you've got eggplants and squash? They obligingly fill out the bulk of many a dish, while happily absorbing any flavors and seasoning you throw at them.

The eggplant is one of the chief protagonists in the Middle Eastern kitchen: he is eaten fried, mashed into dips, boiled in stews, stuffed, pickled, even as a jam.

Tomatoes and peppers—the stuff of a good salad. In the Middle East, salad is quite often just these vegetables chopped up small. Maybe with some onion, white cheese, and olives. But, of course, there's a lot more that you can do with them. Tomatoes are almost revered in certain countries—in Iran whole towns in the tomato-growing regions turn red for weeks after the harvest as the crop is spread over roofs and yards to dry and make into purée.

Our neighbors in the Near East look upon our vegetable consumption with amusement. The fact that the vegetable is something that traditionally comes in pairs with a lump of meat is actually fairly comical, if not sad. Vegetables in the Arabic and Indo-Iranian countries are a part of the cuisine, not an accompaniment to it. And nowhere is this more obvious than with green vegetables: none of this green, overcooked stuff on the side.

There are so many lovely Veggiestan recipes for beets, turnips, carrots, and radish. Oh, and spuds. It would have been easy to give them a chapter on their own.

One thing I have learned from my Iranian connections is that vegetables don't always need to be smothered with butter. Turnips, I had been led to believe, were something to be mashed and disguised: in Iran and Syria and Lebanon, they are often boiled and served au naturel (with a lone salt pot sentinel). In some of the following dishes I think that the real flavor of the star ingredients comes through: cherish it.

## *DOLMEH*—THE GENTLE ART OF STUFFING THINGS

It is a hotly debated matter as to who first stuffed what in Veggiestan. The Arabs call stuffed vegetables *mahshi khodar*: Persians, Turks, Cypriots, and Greeks call them *dolmeh, dolma, yemista,* or *dolmades* respectively. What is certain is that the Ottomans perfected the art, and that some of the best examples of stuffing come from the Turkish kitchen.

The important thing with stuffed vegetable dishes is to remain flexible—the stuffings are largely interchangeable. Some Middle Eastern home cooks make a range of vegetables all with the same filling; some just use different fillings for the same vegetable; some make different sauces (i.e. half sweet, half sour).

## CABBAGE AND VINE LEAVES

There are several *dolmeh* recipes dotted through this book, but the most famous one remains the vine leaf and its cousin, the cabbage leaf. I always use vacuum-packed vine leaves—I find the ones in jars too fragile. If you have access to fresh, blanch them for 10 minutes first. Likewise with cabbage leaves—they need to be blanched to make them malleable enough to roll. This is a fairly classic recipe.

MAKES ABOUT 30

1¼ cups/9oz/250g long-grain rice (short-grain or basmati would be acceptable)

1 large onion, very finely chopped

4 tomatoes, finely chopped

2 tablespoons dried mint

1 tablespoon dried oregano

1 teaspoon ground cinnamon

big handful fresh parsley, finely chopped

1 teaspoon ground black pepper

1 level teaspoon salt

3 tablespoons olive oil

9oz/250g vine leaves (1 vacuum pack), rinsed

juice of 1 lemon

3 tablespoons grape syrup (optional, but recommended)

Mix the uncooked rice with the onion, tomatoes, herbs, spices, seasoning, and 1 tablespoon of the olive oil. Spread a few of the vine leaves out on a flat surface—if any of them have holes, "patch" them with smaller leaves. The dull side with the veins showing should be face up, and the stalks should be pointing towards your tummy. Place 1 heaped teaspoon of the rice mixture in the middle of each leaf, near where the stalk and the leaf connect. Roll the two nearest points of each leaf once (away from you) around the mixture, and then "tuck in" the side bits of the leaf, before continuing to roll away from you. Each parcel thus made should be compact, but not too tight because the rice will expand during cooking. Repeat the exercise until all the whole leaves have been used. Invert a plate in the bottom of a large saucepan, and line it with any defective or part leaves. Arrange the stuffed vine leaves close together over the inverted plate, and layer up until they are all snuggled in. Put another inverted plate on top of the *dolmeh* to weight them down, and then pour in about 3 cups/1¼ pints/750ml of cold water, together with the rest of the olive oil, the lemon juice and the grape syrup. Bring to a boil and then set to simmer—you need to cook these for around 1 hour, 20 minutes—but remember to check that there is enough cooking stock in the pan at all times, and top up with water as required. If there is any left over rice mixture, you can just cook it as normal rice, or use it in other *dolmeh*.

Serve hot or cold with yogurt or lemon wedges.

# TOMATOES STUFFED WITH OLIVES

This isn't a classic *dolmeh* recipe, but as stuffing is involved and it is a gloriously simple affair, it had to be included. This one is high on the "ooh" factor.

MAKES 30

30 cherry tomatoes (but not too small)

1 small onion, very finely chopped

2 tablespoons chopped mixed fresh herbs—
    choose from chervil, basil, tarragon,
    parsley, and cilantro

drizzle of extra-virgin olive oil

pinch of sea salt and freshly milled
    black pepper

35 stuffed olives—pimento, garlic, or almond
    fillings are all good

Using a small vegetable knife, cut out and discard the core of each tomato so that you end up with a small cone-shaped pocket in each tomato. Take a teaspoon and scoop out a little more of the tomato's innards—but this time retain the excavated bits, and tip them into a bowl with the chopped onion. Mix in the herbs, a wee drop of olive oil, and some seasoning, and drop a little of this mixture into the cavity of each tomato. Finally, push a stuffed olive into each. The five extras are for you to thieve, as I know that you will find it impossible to resist.

And there, you've got it: a complete tomato and onion salad in one bite. You can serve these on cocktail sticks, or array them prettily on a bed of something green, or just drop them, incognito, into a bowl of dressed salad leaves and enjoy the surprise on the faces of those who bite into them. I like to serve them with *kufteh esfanaji* (see p.185), like a red and green checkerboard.

# PEPPERS FILLED WITH *MOGHRABIEH*

Peppers are one of the easiest things to stuff—they retain their integrity when cooked, and are obligingly hollow to start. They also have a bitter sweetness about them, which contrasts perfectly with the salty softness of most fillings.

*Moghrabieh* is actually a rather overrated ingredient and is often mistaken for Israeli couscous, which is the same, only smaller. They are both essentially spherical pastas, and bear little resemblance to the granular couscous of Northern Africa. And yet they are very much related: the word *moghrabieh* means "of the Maghreb," clearly denoting the stuff's origins. It has one redeeming feature: it is very absorbent, and so can be cooked like Arborio rice, sucking up flavorsome stock until it is plump and soft. You can substitute Israeli couscous, barley, or risotto rice if you cannot find any *moghrabieh*.

MAKES 8

8 large, pretty green bell peppers
generous 1 cup/7oz/200g *moghrabieh*
olive oil, for frying
1 red bell pepper, chopped
1 large onion, chopped
2 sticks celery, chopped
3 garlic cloves, minced
2 teaspoons paprika
½ teaspoon cayenne

1 teaspoon cinnamon
¼ teaspoon ground saffron, steeped in
    boiling water
generous 2 cups/17fl oz/500ml vegetable
    stock
large handful fresh cilantro, chopped
large handful fresh parsley, chopped
1 tablespoon fresh dill, chopped
salt and pepper
⅔ cup/5fl oz/150ml tomato juice or passata

Trim the base of the green peppers very slightly so that they sit up rather than all fall down. Then cut off the tops: retain them but discard the seeds. Blanch the peppers plus their "lids" for a couple of minutes, and then drain and arrange them snugly in an oven dish.

Blanch the *moghrabieh* for about 5 minutes in boiling water, and then drain—this will stop it from becoming gloopy.

Heat some oil in a frying pan, and when it is hot, slide in the chopped red pepper, onion, celery, and garlic. When they have softened, add the spices followed by the *moghrabieh*, stirring well so that all the globules get coated. Add the saffron to the vegetable stock, and then add this, bit by bit, to the *moghrabieh* until it is all absorbed. You will, in all likelihood, need to add a little water as well: the *moghrabieh* should be soft but not mushy, and the process should take about 25 minutes. Once it is cooked, take it off the heat, stir in the herbs and season to taste.

Spoon some of the mixture into the cavities of each of the peppers, topping them off with one of the blanched lids. Pour the tomato juice around the base of the vegetables, cover the dish with foil, and bake at 375°F/190°C for around 30 minutes.

If you wish, you can sprinkle some Parmesan over the hot *dolmeh*. Serve with warm bread and yogurt or *çaçik*. Like most *dolmeh*, they are also great cold for picnics.

# Imam Biyaldi

# THE SWOONING IMAM

The origins of this recipe are apocryphal. Some say the Imam swooned from delight when Missus Imam served it to him. Others recount how he had married an olive oil heiress and thus had a liquid dowry: when he realized how much of the commodity went into her cooking, he fainted in horror. You may surmise that he passed out on opening his cholesterol test results. Although we all know how good olive oil is for you ... To be honest, the dish, which comprises eggplants split lengthwise and crammed with tomato, garlic, and onion, does look like a cartoon imam lying on his back—black cape and hat and all.

Vegetables are often prepared in this way in Turkey, slow simmered with an indecent quantity of olive oil, and they are collectively known as *zeytinagli*— "olive oil foods." They are usually eaten cold or at room temperature, and are served as part of a summer *mezze*. If you want to make a less oily version you can just bake everything, but it won't have the same flavor.

SERVES 2

2 large, pert, glossy eggplants, rinsed

few tablespoons pure olive oil

4–6 garlic cloves, finely sliced

2 red onions, finely sliced

3–4 tomatoes, finely sliced

1 teaspoon paprika

1 teaspoon brown sugar

1 tablespoon *pekmez* (p.213) or lemon juice

salt and black pepper

about 5 tablespoons extra-virgin olive oil

shredded fresh mint, for garnish

Leaving the hat on the eggplants, score through the skin and peel it away in stripes. Then cut an incision along the length of each one and draw out the seedy bits. Chop these and set to one side. Sprinkle the cavities you have created with salt, and turn upside down on paper towels to drain for 30 minutes. At the end of this time, wipe the inside of the vegetables.

Now heat a slosh of pure olive oil in a broad frying pan. Pop the eggplants into the hot oil and fry for about 7 minutes, turning them occasionally, until they are lightly browned and somewhat softer. Remove them and again set them to drain. Add a bit more oil to the pan and fry the garlic and the onions together with the reserved middles of the eggplants; after 5 minutes, add the tomatoes, paprika, sugar, and *pekmez*; stir well and season.

Snuggle the eggplants into a frying pan, and prize open the cavities. Divide the onion mixture between them, compacting it well, and then drizzle the rest of the sauce from the pan across the top. Add the pure olive oil and a small glass (scant ½ cup/3½fl oz/100ml) of cold water, and put the pan on to the heat. Once it is bubbling, turn the heat way down low and cover it: the *imams* will need about 45 minutes to cook. At the end of this time they should be perfectly tender, swooning even. Just turn off the heat and let them cool.

Serve sprinkled with the mint, and accompany with plenty of mopping-up-bread. They will keep in the fridge for 2–3 days. The flavor does improve after 24 hours, so you can cook ahead.

# Basal Mahshi
## STUFFED ONIONS

There are more ways than one to stuff an onion. The redoubtable Claudia Roden suggests that you wrap your filling in layers of boiled onion, in much the same way as you would with cabbage leaves or vine leaves. You can also cut onions in two and fill the scooped out halves with your stuffing of choice. But we're not going to take either of those two options: we shall, rather, stuff the onions whole. Onions go with just about anything—it is pretty rare to find a recipe that doesn't list them among the ingredients—but here we'll go with a cheesy theme.

As with the other *dolmeh* mentioned in the book, you can serve them as an appetizer or main course, and you can mix and match them to make a *mezze* platter.

MAKES 6

6 large onions (Spanish are good)

scant ⅓ cup/2¾oz/75g short-grain rice

½ teaspoon ground turmeric

salt

olive oil, for cooking

2 sticks celery, chopped

scant ⅓ cup/1¾oz/50g raisins, soaked in water and then drained

½ cup/2¾oz/75g pine nuts (or chopped almonds)

3½oz/100g halloumi, diced

¼ teaspoon ground nutmeg

½ teaspoon allspice

handful of parsley, finely chopped

ground black pepper

Firstly cook the onions, whole, in a pan of boiling water for about 10 minutes. Then drain them and put them aside to cool a little.

Then cook the rice in boiling water along with the turmeric and some salt.

Once the onions are cool enough to handle, peel them and cut a little off one end of each to make them stable enough to sit without rolling. Cut about ½in (1.5cm) off the other end of each onion, reserving these "lids," then use a sharpish spoon to scoop out enough of the inner layers to make a stuffable cavity.

Preheat the oven to 350°F/180°C.

Roughly chop the onion you have excavated. Heat a little oil in a frying pan and tip in the celery. After 6–7 minutes, add the onion, followed a wee while later by the raisins, nuts, halloumi, and spices. Stir well until the halloumi and the nuts are browned and the raisins puffed up. Next mix in the drained rice and the parsley, and season the mixture to taste.

Snuggle the onions into an oven tray. Using the aforementioned pointy spoon, stuff the onions with the ricey cheesy mix, and then perch the lids back on top. Pour a glass of water into the bottom of the dish. Cook in the oven for about 30 minutes.

Serve on a bed of pretty green leaves.

# BARBECUED LEEKS AND SPRING GARLIC

This is more or less my father-in-law's recipe. He likes playing with matches, you see. Give him anything that looks like a fireplace, and he'll soon have it ablaze. It's not just him, of course: Iranians generally love fire, especially cooking over it. A bit of fine weather across London and the parks fill with Iranians (and Kurds, and Afghans) brandishing portable barbecues and generally upsetting the park rangers. In fact, come the Iranian New Year, a couple of the more po-faced London councils lock their parks to keep the party-loving Persians out.

Anyway, father-in-law likes nothing more than to cook dinner. Many Iranian houses actually have a "chimney room," where the family gathers around the fireplace to talk, eat, chat, and (in the winter) to keep warm. And over the years I have learned from him that some foods are simply better when simply cooked. These grilled veggies make for a cracking accompaniment to other barbecued foods, and if there are any left over, try them cold in sandwiches the next day. If you can't get baby leeks or spring garlic, use the regular varieties and chop them. You will not then be able to cook them over an open grill (use a frying pan or griddle instead), but the flavor will be almost as good.

A FUNKY SIDE DISH FOR 4

6–7 baby leeks
6–7 scallions
7–8 shoots of spring garlic
4 tablespoons olive oil
1 teaspoon salt
1 teaspoon black pepper
1 teaspoon chopped tarragon (fresh or dried)
1 teaspoon savory or thyme
½ teaspoon powdered *golpar*\* (Persian hogwort), if available (optional)

Trim the vegetables, chopping off the rooty bits and getting rid of any tired looking shoots. Wash them thoroughly.

Mix the olive oil with the seasoning and the herbs and bathe the vegetables in it, ensuring that each is thoroughly coated. Then tip the whole lot into a plastic bag and put it to one side: the roots and shoots need a couple of hours to marinate, and marinating stuff at room temperature in plastic gets the best results.

When you are ready to cook, heat your barbecue or griddle, shake the excess oil from each of the veggies, and sizzle them for a few minutes, turning regularly, until they are pleasingly charred without actually being burned. Serve hot. Or drizzle with a little olive oil, lemon, and freshly milled sea salt and serve at room temperature as a *mezze* dish.

\* *On golpar:*
Funny stuff, this. It is one of those foods that smells really rather bad (in this case, old socks) until you know what it is. It is Persian hogwort, and it is used as a spice in Iran. The whole stamens are used in pickle making, and it is also ground to sprinkle over a range of dishes from baked potatoes to boiled fava beans. It is incredibly tasty, and mysteriously, brings out the flavor of most vegetables. Iranians rate it as it is a "warm" food (see p.106), which works to reduce the, um, "flatulence inducing" effects of many veggies.

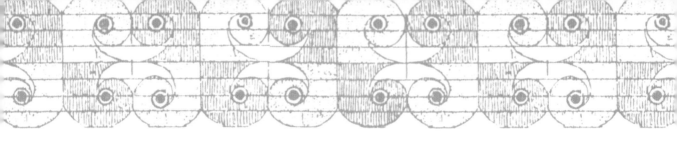

# ON HOW THE EGGPLANT GOT ITS HAT

There are few vegetables as anthropomorphic as the eggplant. It is just asking for cartoon eyes and cocktail stick arms and a carrot baton nose. It's the pixie hat that does it, you see. I've often wondered how come it was designed thus. I mean, vegetables do need a stalk, but the calyx is a cute add-on and quite unnecessary. And then I found this beguiling tale from old Arabia …

Once upon a time in old, old Babylon, there was a venerable market trader by the name of Hakim. He was a fruit and vegetable vendor, popular throughout the bazaar for his kindness and fairness, famed for the quality of his produce.

Each day he would rise before dawn to visit neighboring farms, where he would seek out the best and the juiciest goods. Every morning he would set out his stall, a riot of nature's finest in reds and greens and yellows. The most fragrant rose apples; the shiniest pomegranates; the pertest cucumbers; the plumpest tomatoes; flat, blushing peaches from Persia; syrup-oozing dates from the south; myriad green herbs fresh-plucked from the mountains, still wet with dew. By lunchtime his stall was nearly empty: housewives flocked to him from far and wide. His prices were the lowest, and he would always slip in a bit extra for those who had fallen on hard times. The other market traders could only look on with envy, although they knew that if they worked just a little harder and were a little less greedy, they too could succeed.

In the afternoons he would tend his own small holding, where he raised many of the vegetables

that he sold: strange, bulbous gourds, crispy white and pink radishes, tiny zucchini, chilies of every hue, *molokhia*, tiny diamond grapes, full hearted artichokes. He worked the earth tirelessly, bedding the plants with his own hands, watering the roots and caressing the leaves.

In the evening he would go home to his wife, herself a renowned herbalist, and together they would prepare plants and work on potions and remedies to heal the sick. Truly they were paragons of Ancient Babylonian virtue, living simple, blameless lives. There was but one sadness in their lives, a dark and heavy burden that left them so aggrieved that they rarely spoke of it: for some reason, the fickle Innana, whom some called Ishtar, had not seen fit to bless the pair with children. Heads were shaken and tuts were tutted: no-one understood how two people so productive in every other way could fail to be granted the ultimate produce—sons and daughters of their own.

One day Hakim noticed some chunky purple eggplants growing just beyond his own patch of land. Now in those days the eggplant was a sorry fellow, bare-headed, constantly water-logged owing to his spongy texture. It was as if the gods had created him and then changed their minds halfway through. He wasn't full of nutritious stuff like some of the other vegetables, and his soggy countenance and slightly bitter flavor meant that he was usually given to cattle.

It so happened that it was the time of rain in the Valley of the Euphrates, and Hakim could see that

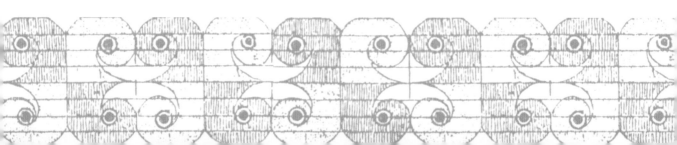

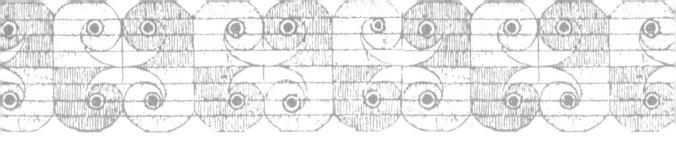

the vegetables were getting heavier and heavier as they absorbed more and more water. Which seemed a shame. And so he whittled a funky star-shaped hat for those of them that he could reach out of grasses and twigs. Unbeknownst to him, Ninhursaga, the mother of all things, was watching, and smiling: such care and attention for things of the earth was rare to find. She liked this Hakim.

That night in his dreams Hakim saw Ninhursaga, for this is a folk tale and that is how things are done. She told him to make sure that he took another look at the eggplant patch the next day: she probably told him lots of other stuff as well, but it is in the nature of dreams that they slip away no sooner have they arrived, and thus it was for our hero. The goddess also paid a discreet visit to Innana, the conceited.

The following day Hakim once again pottered over to the market gardens outside the city walls, and, as per his dream, went to study the rogue vegetables. Imagine his surprise when he saw that all of the eggplants now sported star-shaped hats. No longer were they sagging and soggy, but shiny and inviting. Ninhursaga had rewritten the vegetable constitution overnight, and it had been decreed that henceforth the eggplant should be a crowned prince among veggies. Astonished, he gathered a basketful and rushed home to his wife to see what could be done with them.

Together they peeled and chopped and sliced and diced and fried and boiled and grilled and baked and mashed and tossed and layered and dressed until they had a table full of appetizing eggplant dishes. So spongy and amenable was the vegetable that, whatever they did, it tasted wonderful. Just as before it had absorbed rainwater and silt, now it took in all the flavors of the dishes in which it featured.

Well, the next day at the market Hakim spread out all these new dishes for his customers to try. At first, no-one could believe that it was the lowly eggplant that they were eating. Word soon spread among the other traders that Hakim was trying to pass off cattle fodder as a swanky new product—but all those who sampled it had to agree that it was utterly scrumptious.

Day after day thereafter he toiled to keep up with demand, and before long he had taken on a couple of barrow boys to help him. His wife too had to take on help, as she was stuck from morning 'til evening in the kitchen, and it was not good for a pregnant lady to spend so long on her feet. Yes, Hakim was to be a father. For you see Ninhursaga the wise had persuaded Innana that the mark born by the eggplant, the star, was in fact a tribute to her, and that in return for this gesture of respect the least the younger goddess could do was to grant the hard-working couple the boon of fertility.

From that day on Innana adopted the eight-pointed star as her symbol.

Hakim and his wife had a plump baby boy. And another. And another. And it was for them he created the best-loved eggplant dish of all: *Baba Ghanoush*, which very literally means "spoiled by baba."

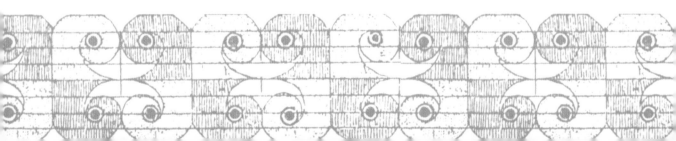

# Baba Ghanoush

## SMOKY EGGPLANT DIP

It would be hard to choose Veggiestan's best loved eggplant dish—but this has to be a strong contender. Smooth and creamy, it caresses the taste buds in a manner that even those who aver their dislike of eggplants seem to find irresistible. It does have several pseudonyms: it is also known as *moutabal*; in Greece they call it *melitzanosalata*, although it is made with baked eggplants and the skin is left on; and in Turkey *patlican ezmesi*, although yogurt is used rather than *tahina*.

The dish is a firm fixture on Arabic *mezze* platters, and works well as an appetizer.

TO MAKE A DECENT
BOWLFUL, FOR 4

2 large eggplants, washed and beheaded

3–4 garlic cloves still in their skin

3 tablespoons *tahina*

1 tablespoon extra-virgin olive oil, plus a swirl for garnish

juice of 1 lemon

salt and ground white pepper

½ teaspoon smoked paprika

In an ideal world … prick the skins of the eggplants in several places and pop them on to the rack of a hot barbecue: cook until tender, turning regularly. In practice … prick them and cook them under your broiler. Just before they are ready, thread the garlic on to a skewer and give this a little grilling too.

When the eggplants are soft, allow them to cool a little before flaking the skin off. Chop the flesh roughly and put it in a colander to allow any surplus water to drain away. In the meantime peel and chop the garlic. After about 15 minutes, tip the eggplant into a bowl, add the *tahina*, olive oil, and garlic and pound it with a potato masher or meat tenderizer. Once you have got a relatively smooth paste (it shouldn't be too homogenized), beat in the lemon juice and season to taste.

Spoon into a shallow bowl, and then use a fork to create an indented eddy pattern across the surface. Drizzle the extra-virgin olive oil over the top, and then sprinkle with the smoked paprika.

Serve with hot pita bread and crudités. Some warm sunshine, a light breeze rustling through the cedars, and the distant jingle of sheep bells would help too. Nothing wrong with whimsy.

# MUSHROOM *STIFATHO*

*Stifatho* is basically a Greek stew, infused with half a ton of cinnamon, made piquant by the addition of vinegar, and awash with wine. Heady stuff. It is most traditionally made with beef or hare, but this version sees it prepared with button mushrooms—much nicer.

SERVES 4

4½ tablespoons/2¼ oz/60g butter (or sunflower oil—but butter is better here)

1lb 2oz/500g baby onions/shallots (the smaller the better), peeled

1 red bell pepper, finely diced

1lb 2 oz/500g button mushrooms, wiped

4–5 cinnamon sticks

½ teaspoon coarse black pepper

1 tablespoon tomato paste

1 teaspoon sugar

2 bay leaves

5 tablespoons red wine vinegar

⅔ cup/5fl oz/150ml red wine

salt, to taste

Melt the butter in the bottom of saucepan, and toss in the peeled onions. Cook on high for about 5 minutes, or until they are starting to brown a little. Add the peppers and mushrooms, and continue to fry for another 5 minutes, then add the cinnamon, pepper, tomato paste, sugar, and bay leaves. Stir in the vinegar and the wine, bring to a boil, and then cover the pan and set it to simmer. The cooking liquid should be about level with the top of the veggies—if it looks a little low, top up with water.

Cook for about 1 hour, stirring occasionally, then season to taste.

Serve with rice. Although I actually eat it on its own, or with a little dunky bread if I am feeling really hungry.

# Sila bi Lubia
## SWISS CHARD AND BLACK-EYED PEAS

Funny stuff, Swiss chard. Firstly, it's not from Switzerland (according to Alan Davidson, it acquired the tag to distinguish it from French chard, which is different). It's like a hybrid between spinach and celery, except it has nothing to do with either. It is, rather, a cousin of the mangel-wurzel, and a distant relative of the cardoon. It first cropped up in Ancient Babylon, and is popular throughout the Middle East. There are several colors to collect: it comes in red, yellow, white, or pale green, so I suppose you could buy the one that goes best with your kitchen tiles. It is readily available and fairly easy to grow. You can use the leaves and the stalks, and these take slightly different times to cook.

This is based on a Palestinian recipe.

SERVES 2

generous ½ cup/3½oz/100g black-eyed peas

10½oz/300g Swiss chard, washed

1 fat leek, washed, trimmed and chopped

olive oil, for cooking

2 garlic cloves, sliced

¼ teaspoon ground nutmeg

½ teaspoon chili powder

big handful fresh cilantro, chopped

generous ¾ cup/7fl oz/200ml vegetable stock

2 tablespoons *tahina*

salt and black pepper, to taste

Cook the beans in water for around 40 minutes, or until tender, and then drain them.

While the beans are cooking, prepare the chard: separate the leaves and the stalks, chopping the former roughly and the latter more finely.

Toss the leek into some hot olive oil in a frying pan, followed by the garlic. Stir for a minute or so before, then add the chard stalks. Cook for another 2 minutes, and then add the chard leaves, spices, and cilantro. Stir well for a few moments and then stir in the black-eyed peas.

Pour a little hot stock on to the *tahina* in a bowl, whisk thoroughly and then tip it back into the rest of the stock, and whisk again. Next pour the stock on to the greens, season to taste, and bubble gently for about 5 minutes.

Serve with lemon wedges and bread—Iranian *nan-e-sangak* (see p.13) is great with this, but any warm flatbread will do.

# Broccoli bi Tarator

# BROCCOLI AND *TAHINA* BAKE

Broccoli and *tahina* go together like bread and butter. Or Samson and Delilah. Or Rostam and Rakhsh. Or—you get the picture. But it is so tasty that it is quite a good way to get even the most reluctant small person to indulge.

Broccoli is not indigenous to the Middle East—but that's not to say that it is not used and enjoyed in the region. I first tried something like this recipe at a Lebanese restaurant on the Edgware Road in London—this is my recreation of it.

You can make it into more substantial fare by making it a bit more "saucy" and serving it over spaghetti or tagliatelli.

SERVES 4

2 average stalks broccoli, washed
splash of peanut oil
1 onion, chopped
2–3 garlic cloves, minced
1 teaspoon dried thyme
1¼ cups/10fl oz/300ml boiling water
6–7 generous tablespoons *tahina*

2 tablespoons soy sauce
juice and zest of 2 limes
1 teaspoon Aleppo pepper (or
    paprika/cayenne mixed)
salt, to taste
3 tablespoons mixed pumpkin and sunflower
    seed kernels

Separate the florets of broccoli from the stalks, and cut through any that are over-sized. Cut away the outer skin from the stalk: the inner parts are great to eat as they are with a little salt, or you can add it to the dish.

Heat the oven to 350°F/180°C. Pour a little peanut oil in the base of an oven dish, and roll the broccoli in it so that it is coated, before sliding the dish into the oven to cook for about 10 minutes.

In the meantime, make the sauce. Heat some more oil in a frying pan and fry the onion and the garlic; after a few minutes, add the thyme. Trickle boiling water over the *tahina* in a jug and beat until you have a smooth, pourable paste. Add the soy sauce, the lime juice and zest, Aleppo pepper, and salt if required. Remove the broccoli from the oven and pour about three-quarters of the *tahina* sauce all over it, stirring to coat, before popping it back in the oven for another 10 minutes.

Scatter the seed kernels on to an oven tray and place them in the oven or under a hot broiler for a few minutes to toast.

Remove the broccoli from the oven, scatter with the toasted seeds, and serve with the reserved sauce in a jug on the side.

*Domatokeftethes*

# BABY TOMATO *KUFTEH*

This is kind of based on a Lenten Cypriot recipe. But it's got a splosh of Armenia and a sprinkle of Turkey in there too. You can make them to serve hot or cold as part of a *mezze* spread, accompanied by some lemon wedges—but I think they rock served over pasta with a smoky tomato sauce. It makes for a very red dinner, but red is good, no?

SUPPER FOR 3–4
FOR THE *KUFTEH*:
1lb 5oz/600g tomatoes
7–8 sun dried tomatoes, minced
3–4 garlic cloves, minced (optional)
2 bunches scallions, trimmed and very finely
　　chopped
big handful of fresh basil, finely chopped
½ bunch fresh parsley, finely chopped
1 cup/5½oz/150g flour
½ teaspoon baking soda
1 teaspoon salt and plenty of cracked
　　black pepper
pure olive oil

FOR THE SAUCE:
1 onion, chopped
2–3 garlic cloves
pure olive oil
1 teaspoon smoked paprika
1 teaspoon chili flakes
1 teaspoon sugar
generous 2 cups/17fl oz/500ml tomato passata
salt to taste

TO SERVE:
10½oz/300g of pasta of your choice

Chop the tomatoes, and then pound them together with all the other ingredients (except the oil, of course). Actually, do add a little oil to the mixture—it will make it easier to handle. You should end up with a thick paste—if it seems too dry, add some water. If it is hopelessly wet, add more flour. Cover it and pop it in the fridge to firm up while you make the sauce.

　　It's a simple sauce: fry the onion and garlic in some oil, add the spices and sugar, stir, stir, pour in the passata, season, bubble for 10 minutes, job done.

　　To cook the *kufteh*, use wet hands or a pair of teaspoons to fashion more or less spherical blobs of the mixture and shallow-fry them in hot oil until they are browned all over (4–5 minutes should do it).

　　Cook and drain your chosen pasta and pile it in to a serving bowl. Spoon the *kufteh* on top, and drizzle with sauce. Serve with plenty of green salad by way of color relief.

# Sarasura / Türlü / Güveç / Briami
## MIDDLE EASTERN RATATOUILLE

What a joy this dish is. A bit of chopping, shove it in the oven, and an hour or so later it is ready: a tender and aromatic composition of the season's and region's finest vegetables. With some garlic bread on the side it makes for a filling main course, although you can also serve it with bulgar or rice.

Yes, it does resemble ratatouille, and yes, if you are a vegetarian too much of it can wear thin. But do you know, I think it's due for a comeback. If shrimp cocktail, steak, and Black Forest cake are enjoying a renaissance, then ratatouille and vegetarian lasagne/moussaka are sure to follow.

In Turkey this dish is usually known as *türlü*, but there are huge regional variations. *Briami* is the name it goes under in Cyprus.

The recipe below should be pretty easy to follow all year round—but do add proportional amounts of seasonal stuff to it: summer peas and beans, okra, artichokes, or winter tubers. As a variation, throw some chunks of halloumi into the mix about halfway through the cooking time. Or make a few pot holes and drop a raw egg into each about 20 minutes before you want to serve.

This is Kim's recipe (I think) from Never on a Sunday, the name of a way-ahead-of-its-time taverna where I worked for a little while. (Also the name of a brilliant movie.)

## Bread Board

Of course, pizza and baguette-style garlic bread, dripping with butter or oil, are pretty much the universal accompaniment to tourist fare in Veggiestan just as everywhere else. The pizzeria continues its inexorable conquest of the world's food malls.

But the origins of the concept come, I suspect, from the Middle Eastern practice of dunking bread in oil followed by other flavorings and spices. If you ask for garlic bread in a regular Mustafa Bloggs café across the region, you will usually be presented with some warm bread, an olive oil pourer, a few garlic cloves and a pot of salt. The idea is to dip the bread in some oil, rub the garlic across it, and then season to taste. Hands-on food—much more fun.

If I am showing off, I like to use this approach with the *türlü* here. Serve two or three different types of bread and try mixing and matching with olive, chili, or herb oils, garlic, coarse sea salt or celery salt, *za'atar* or *dukka* (see pp.98–100), or freshly chopped mixed herbs.

SERVES 4

2 eggplants, cut into 1¼–1½in (3–4cm) chunks

2 zucchini, cut into 1¼–1½in (3–4cm) chunks

2 waxy potatoes, peeled and cut into 1¼–1½in (3–4cm) chunks

1 red pepper, cut into 1¼–1½in (3–4cm) chunks

1 green pepper, cut into 1¼–1½in (3–4cm) chunks

1 large onion, peeled and roughly chopped

8 garlic cloves, peeled and bashed

4 tomatoes, quartered

2 teaspoons dried oregano

3 bay leaves

salt and black pepper

1 large handful of chopped fresh parsley

Preheat the oven to 350°F/180°C.

Arrange all the ingredients bar the last two in a sturdy oven tray or casserole, turning gently to mix well. Add a splash of water: just enough to cover the bottom of the tray. Cover the dish and cook in the oven for 1½ hours, or until the potatoes are cooked and the other vegetables tender. Strew the parsley across the top just before you dish up.

Serve in earthy looking bowls with some interesting bread on the side.

# ARTICHOKE HEARTS WITH PISTACHIO SAUCE

This is a fancy treat—I mean, when did you last cook yourself an artichoke? It is not that artichokes are pricey, per se, but rather that they are fiddly. They are, after all, kind of inside out veggies, with the parts that look most appetizing mostly being discarded.

Actually my granny and I often used to buy them and scoff them when I had the privilege of living with her, and so I learned most of my artichoke lore from her. The most important thing she taught me was to keep a bowl of water handy with some lemon wedges floating in it: artichoke discolors really quickly once you start cutting and pulling at it.

The idea with this is to serve the vegetables warm with the pistachio as a dipping and dunking sauce. It's a great little appetizer or summer snack.

SERVES 6

2½ unwaxed lemons
6 smallish artichokes*
4 garlic cloves
⅔ cup/3½oz/100g unsalted shelled pistachios
small handful of fresh chopped tarragon
bigger handful of fresh chopped cilantro
2 teaspoons orange blossom water
6–7 tablespoons olive oil
salt and black pepper, to taste

Quarter one of the lemons, and then put half of it in a bowl of cold water. Prepare the artichokes: hack off the woodiest bits from the bottom, and the roughest looking tips from the leaves. If any of the outer leaves look spoiled, then they can go too. Once each vegetable has been trimmed, lob it in the lemon water until you are ready to cook.

Fill the bottom of a big pan with water to the depth of 1¼in (3cm), then add half a lemon, and bring it to a boil. Lower the artichokes in so they are sitting perfectly upright, cover the pan, and bring back to a boil. Turn right down and set to simmer for around 35 minutes. If you are using frozen chokes, just defrost and steam or boil for around 15 minutes.

In the meantime, make the sauce. Put the garlic in the goblet of your blender together with the pistachios, and give it a quick whizz. Juice and zest the second lemon, and add that to the pistachio mixture, together with the herbs and orange blossom water. Add a little cold water to make the mixture more malleable, and then trickle in the olive oil. The mixture should end up like a slightly runny looking pesto. Season to taste.

The best way to check if the artichoke is ready is to break off a leaf and nibble the base (which is, of course, the only bit of the leaf you eat): if it is soft and comes away as you scrape your teeth along it, it is ready to go.

Put the artichokes on a pretty platter (I usually use lettuce leaves to hold them upright), drizzle a little sauce into the middle of each, and then serve the rest of it in a bowl on the side.

\*
Artichokes are popular across the Middle East (they were in all likelihood first cultivated in North Africa), especially as part of *mezze*, poached and drizzled with olive oil and garlic. If you can't get whole ones, frozen artichoke hearts are a topping alternative. Canned come in third place.

## ABOUT PISTACHIOS

Well, Iran is streaks ahead of the rest of the world in volume and quality of pistachio production. Of course, I have had years of the husband telling me that Iran is superior in every way—in the pistachio department, this is certainly true. They are, sadly, hellishly difficult to import: there are very tight regulations governing nut health. This, combined with a less than enlightened perspective of all things Iranian at the port of entry, means that the pistachio trade is not for the faint-hearted.

In Iran the best pistachios come from Rafsanjan, which is "strongly affiliated" with Rafsanjani, the former president. In the nut world size matters, and pistachios are graded according to how many you get in one ounce—the fewer, the better since it means bigger nuts.

While in the West our encounters with pistachios usually involve "upmarket" bars and broken finger nails, or bright green ice cream, in Iran they get everywhere. Particularly in demand are *khalal-e-pesteh*, or chopped pistachios—they are sprinkled on everything from rice to cakes. They're never cheap, but they are such a pretty shade of green …

# Ardishawki bi Zeyt

## ARTICHOKES BAKED WITH OLIVE OIL

*You have your Lebanon and its dilemma. I have my Lebanon and its beauty. Your Lebanon is an arena for men from the West and men from the East.*

*My Lebanon is a flock of birds fluttering in the early morning as shepherds lead their sheep into the meadow and rising in the evening as farmers return from their fields and vineyards.* —Khalil Gibran, writing in the 1920s.

I've never been to Lebanon—but boy would I love to go. I've never thought of it as anything other than a land of bucolic bliss and ancient treasure, although I know that it has been riven by conflict. How can a land that is anything other than practically perfect produce such wonderful food?

This dish is one of my favorites, a top supper for summer—light, simple, and yet oozing with the flavors of (what I imagine to be) a warm Lebanese evening.

SERVES 4–5

1lb 5oz/600g artichoke hearts (fresh or frozen)

7oz /200g olives (any you like; I use pimento-stuffed ones)

scant 2 tablespoons/1¾oz/50g sun-dried tomatoes, chopped

2 bell peppers, roughly chunked

14oz/400g button mushrooms, wiped

1 large red onion, finely sliced

5–6 garlic cloves, peeled and sliced roughly

about 5 tablespoons extra-virgin olive oil

salt and black pepper

2 level teaspoons rosemary

2 level teaspoons thyme

1 teaspoon smoked paprika (inauthentic, but rather wonderful)

3 bay leaves

Preheat the oven to 350°F/180°C. Toss the artichokes, olives, tomatoes, peppers, mushrooms, onion, and garlic onto a large oven tray, mixing well. Drizzle with a goodly amount of olive oil, stirring so that everything gets coated. Season and then sprinkle with the rosemary, thyme, paprika, and bay leaves. Cover the dish with foil, and bake for 45 minutes, or until the pepper is cooked.

This dish works equally well hot or cold, although I reckon the hot option is slightly preferable. Serve with plenty of warm *khobez* or crusty bread.

# Bamia bi Tamaten

## OKRA WITH TOMATOES

You've got to feel sorry for the okra. He's like the bogeyman of the vegetable world, sending those he threatens reeling and squealing in horror. Well, at the very least turning their noses up and reaching for the takeout menu. Which is very unfortunate, as okra (ladies fingers) are full of healthy stuff: fiber, vitamins, folic acid, and amino acids. Not tempted? I see—it's the slime that does it. Okra are mucilaginous, you see: but it doesn't need to be that way …

Okra basics, then. If you buy big okra, you will need to remove the top of the stalk. Baby ones can be used as they are. Wash them—and then pat them dry with some paper towel; this is good anti-slime practice. And do not cut into the pod before cooking, which will result in the dreaded gloop being released. Then you can do one of two things: either seal them whole in hot oil—in fact, they are quite nice just like that, browned, and then sprinkled with salt and pepper and a squeeze of lemon. Or you can then add stock and other ingredients and simmer them. The other thing used to neutralize the slime is acid—that's acid as in lemon, or tomato—in which case, you can use them whole or sliced. You can either dunk the vegetables in acidulated water (water with a squeeze of lemon), or cook with tart ingredients—both ploys will work. If you can't get fresh okra, use frozen.

The first of these recipes is a dish common to practically all the countries of Veggiestan, combining tomatoes and light spices to make a lovely little supper dish—have it cold in the summer or hot in the winter.

SERVES 4

1 large onion, chopped

olive oil, for frying

4 garlic cloves, sliced

1lb 9oz/700g baby okra, washed and dried

12oz/350g cherry tomatoes, halved

2 teaspoons tomato paste

1 teaspoon ground allspice

salt and pepper

TO SERVE:

1 large *khobez* (or 2–3 slices pita bread)

Fry the onion in the oil, and then add the garlic. Once the onion has turned translucent, turn the heat right up and tip in the okra, stirring constantly. After a few minutes add the tomato, followed by the tomato paste and the allspice. Add a glass or two (scant ½–⅔ cup/ 3½–5fl oz/100–150ml) of water, season, cover the pan, and turn the heat down to the gentle simmer mark. Give the okra 35–45 minutes to cook through—you want them to be really tender—and then serve them atop a slice of warm *khobez*. Yogurt and raw onion would make good accompaniments.

# Bamia bi Zeyt
## MARINATED OKRA

The second okra recipe uses them raw and sliced: this is a good one for *mezze* spreads, as you can make it ahead.

SERVES 4

2lb 4oz/1kg baby okra, washed

7–8 garlic cloves, chopped

3–4 green chilies, chopped (optional)

juice and zest of 1 lime

juice and zest of 1 lemon

scant ½ cup/3½fl oz/100ml extra-virgin olive oil

big handful of fresh cilantro, chopped

freshly milled rock salt

Five-minute job. Slice the okra finely, and put them in a tub with a lid. Mix the rest of the ingredients together and pour over the okra, mixing well. Cover and refrigerate overnight. Stir well in the morning, and leave for a good few more hours before serving. This will keep in the fridge for up to 1 week, and is actually at its best after 2–3 days. You can enjoy it as it is, or incorporate it into salad dressings and other dishes.

# Kufteh Esfanaji
## PERSIAN MAGAZINE SPINACH BALLS

I tore this recipe out of a Persian magazine years ago, established it was both tasty and super quick to make … but I can't remember what magazine it was now. Sorry.

MAKES 25–30

4 slices white bread, crusts off (stale bread will do)

½ cup/4fl oz/125ml milk

1lb 2oz/500g cooked spinach

2 eggs, lightly beaten

2½ tablespoons all-purpose flour

2 garlic cloves, minced

3½ tablespoons/1¾oz/50g softened butter

salt and freshly ground black pepper

Soak the bread in the milk for about 10 minutes. Beat the rest of the ingredients together, and then add the soggy bread.

Roll the mixture into little balls, and place them on a lightly greased baking tray. Cook them at 350°F/180°C for about 35 minutes.

Serve warm or hot—they go brilliantly with stuffed tomatoes (see p.163), and make a fancy garnish for all sorts of dishes.

# VEGGIESTAN BREAKFAST FRY-UP

Now the residents of Veggiestan don't eat anything like the spread below for breakfast: fruit, cheese, and bread, washed down with black tea, is more the order of the day. And there are plenty of other sumptuous breakfast ideas elsewhere in the book: check out *ataif* (pancakes, p.248), *menemen* (p.75), or *ful medames* (p.115). This is simply a contrived way of incorporating a number of ideas that go well together as a platter, none of which merit a recipe page to themselves.

### SPICED HASH BROWNS

3 medium floury potatoes

1 tablespoon flour

2 teaspoons *za'atar*

¼ teaspoon ground cumin

½ teaspoon chili powder

salt and pepper

butter, plus canola oil, for frying

Peel and coarsely grate the potatoes, and then put them in a colander with a heavy weight on top to squeeze as much of the water out as possible. Mix the flour and spices together and season lightly before stirring gently through the drained potato. Melt a knob of butter in a non-stick pan and add a dash of oil to stop it burning. Spoon the spiced potato in and spread it evenly across the pan. Fry for 5 minutes, or until the first side is brown, then turn and cook the other side. Once cooked, cut into wedges and serve.

### SPICED HASH GREENS

2 zucchini, washed, topped and tailed

olive oil, for cooking

2 small red chilies, chopped

2 garlic cloves, minced

1 teaspoon dill

salt, to taste

1 handful fresh, chopped parsley

Grate the zucchini and squeeze out as much water as possible. Heat a couple of tablespoons of oil in a frying pan and tip in the chilies and the garlic, stirring well. Add the zucchini and the dill, and cook on high, stirring constantly, until the vegetables are nicely browned (they will not form patties in quite the way that potatoes do as they do not contain the same starch). Season, mix the parsley through, and then take the pan off the heat and serve— preferably next to the hash browns, as they offer a nice contrast.

### TURKISH BREAKFAST TOMATOES

8 cherry tomatoes, washed

1½ tablespoons *muhammara* (see p.227)

8 sprigs curly parsley

Preheat the oven to 350°F/180°C. Use a pointy knife to gouge out the core of the tomato, so that each one has a cone-shaped cavity. Fill each one with a teaspoonful of *muhammara*, and arrange them on a small baking tray. Cook in the oven for around 20 minutes, and serve be-topped with a sprig of parsley.

### HERBED SCRAMBLED EGGS

4 eggs

1 teaspoon butter

1 tablespoon milk

½ teaspoon chili flakes

1 level teaspoon savory or oregano

½ teaspoon turmeric

salt, to taste

parsley, to garnish

This is scrambled egg. You know how to make it, right? Plop all the ingredients in a pan, turn on the heat, and stir with your favorite wooden spoon until it looks like it is of the desired consistency (in my case, very runny). Garnish. Yum.

But maybe you haven't made scrambled tofu before ... Even if you are not a vegan, you should—it is one of the nicest ways to eat tofu:

### SCRAMBLED TOFU

oil, for frying

½ teaspoon asafetida

1 teaspoon paprika

1 teaspoon turmeric

1 teaspoon mustard seeds

1 tablespoon soy sauce

1 carton (12oz/350g) tofu (softer is better in this case), drained and crumbled

2–3 finely chopped tomatoes

handful of fresh cilantro

salt (if required)

Heat the oil in a pan, and add the spices, stirring rapidly. Follow them with the soy sauce and then the tofu. Cook for about 10 minutes, turning it over regularly with a wooden spoon, and then add the tomatoes, and cilantro. Check the seasoning and serve.

### MUSHROOMS WITH FENUGREEK

4 Portobello mushrooms (but any will do), wiped

big knob of butter (½ stick/2oz/55g)

1 tablespoon dried fenugreek leaves

¼ teaspoon ground fenugreek seeds

salt, if required

1 tablespoon lemon juice

handful of fresh parsley

Chop the mushrooms roughly. Melt some butter in a frying pan and add both lots of fenugreek, followed 30 seconds later by the mushrooms. Cook for about 5 minutes, season to taste, add the lemon juice and the parsley, and presto—it's ready.

Plate your Veggiestan breakfasts on top of warmed *khobez* bread (p.15), which is usually conveniently plate-shaped. The addition of grilled halloumi would make the repast pretty much perfect.

# ON OLIVES

Well, we all know that the olive was invented by Athena as a gift for the people of Athens, right? At the risk of upsetting my favorite Greek deity, it seems more likely that the first olive trees were cultivated across the Levant, in a belt from Palestine to Syria and thence up towards the North of Iran. Any which way, the olive has been cultivated across the Eastern Mediterranean for millennia—in fact, an impressive number of trees still bearing fruit are over 2,000 years old.

It is no wonder that both the Bible and the Koran wax lyrical about this unprepossessing, gnarly tree: it must indeed have seemed like God's gift to ancient farmers, as it flourishes in the dry, salty regions of the Med, and seems to like growing in awkward spots halfway up mountains.

The biggest producer of olives in the world is now Spain, and they are cultivated as far away as the Americas.

Now, there was a little official in the olive groves around Marathon in Greece whose daily sadistic pleasure it was to offer fresh olives off the tree to gawping gullible tourists. This was where I tasted my first fresh olive—and the pungent horror of it is with me still. This was also where I was disabused of the common notion that green and black olives come from different trees: black olives are just ripe green ones. Olives are drupes (meaning they consist of flesh that grows around a stone) and need to go through a number of processes before they become palatable, owing to the presence of something called oleuropein, which is a harmless bitter substance (actually it's very good for you). Usually

this involves washing them and then soaking them in several changes of water (over several days), then packing them in brine for a week or so. Black olives are often packed in dry salt, which really brings out their flavor and gives them that funny wrinkly appearance.

Olives are now big business and you can buy them stuffed with just about anything you like, from the common-or-garden pimento to the somewhat rarer orange and juniper. Home-stuffing is fiddly (unless you are time-rich and handy with a bodkin), and I shy away from it. But home marinating for olives is highly rewarding, and in the Middle East it is common practice to buy fresh olives and flavor them yourself. Buy about 1lb 2oz (500g) whole green olives in brine (black olives do not respond quite as well to marinades). Drain them and then use a small sharp knife to make a small cross in the bottom of each one. Cover them with extra-virgin olive oil and add one of the following combinations:

• 2–3 scored hot green chilies and 2–3 sprigs fresh thyme
• 1 quartered, finely sliced lemon and 1–2 tablespoons of dill
• 1 quartered, finely sliced lemon, 4–5 cloves of minced garlic and either 2 teaspoons of oregano or 3–4 teaspoons of cracked coriander seeds (in Cyprus, these are called *tsakistes*)
• 1 quartered, finely sliced orange plus 1 level teaspoon each of cumin and caraway seeds

Cover them and leave them in the fridge for a day or so: forget Athena—now we're talking Hestia, the original Greek domestic goddess.

# VEGGIE *SHAWARMA*

I have always liked *shawarma* kebabs, which is odd for someone who isn't really into fast food. So I decided to analyze what it is about them that makes them so irresistible to me. It comes down to the garlic sauce, the spice, the contrast of flavors and textures, and the chin-runningly tactile messiness of the general operation. And the garlic sauce. Did I mention the garlic sauce? You can use *tahini*, but the sauce I have suggested below (known as *thoom*) is the most authentic.

Mushrooms are one of the few veggies that you can marinate with great success—they have a spongy meatiness that soaks up all the spices you can throw at them.

MAKES 2

4 Portobello mushrooms, wiped

2½ tablespoons soy sauce (tamari is best)

2 tablespoons sesame oil (or olive oil)

1 garlic clove, minced

½ teaspoon ground cumin

½ teaspoon crushed coriander seeds

½ teaspoon paprika

½ teaspoon chili powder (optional)

FOR THE GARLIC SAUCE:

1 whole bulb garlic, peeled

big handful chopped, fresh parsley

1 tablespoon lemon juice

pinch of salt

generous ¾–1 cup/7–9fl oz/200–250ml
   olive oil

TO ASSEMBLE:

1 large *khobez* (although any pliable fresh
   flatbread would do)

3 spicy pickled cucumbers, finely sliced

1 sliced tomato

few slices cucumber

salad of choice: Herb and Onion Salad (p.55);
   coleslaw, or just use some chopped
   white cabbage, shredded lettuce,
   onion, and carrot

Cut the mushrooms into chunky strips. Whisk all the other ingredients for the marinade together, and swirl the mushroom strips around in it. Cover and refrigerate for 2 hours.

Next for the *thoom*. This is much easier with a blender. Lob in the peeled garlic, parsley, lemon juice, and salt. Blend well, and then very slowly trickle in the olive oil: we are making an emulsion and if you rush it, it will crack/curdle. If you want the sauce thicker, add more olive oil: if it turns out too thick, whisk in some more lemon juice or water. Pour it into a bowl, cover and chill—this too benefits from a little time to amalgamate.

Time to cook the mushrooms. Heat a frying pan or griddle to sizzle point, and then spoon the mushrooms in (or on). Cook until soft—just a few minutes should do it.

Warm the *khobez* just a little, and then split it into two discs. Stripe some pickled cucumbers, tomato, cucumber, and salad across the width of each piece of bread, just short of the middle so that two thirds of the bread is visible above it and the other third is peeking out on the side nearest you. Distribute the mushrooms between each wrap, and then spoon some of the sauce over. Roll the bread up, starting at the shorter end. Once you have rolled as far as the filling, use your little fingers to tuck in the excess bread flaps so that the filling is completely encased in bread. Roll it right up and then wrap it in a twist of paper to enjoy.

# Qorma-e-Zardak

## AFGHAN CARROT HOTPOT

This is a lovely, sweet, gloopy stew that truly celebrates the erstwhile humble carrot. It's also a great winter warmer. Afghan food is generally much spicier than that of its neighbors to the west: I reckon it's all those mountains.

*Qorma* is one of the mainstays of the Afghan kitchen. A thick tomatoey oniony sauce, usually with *nakhod daul*, or yellow split peas, it features a whole range of vegetables. I find it great lunch food: a bowl of this and some dippy bread does me proud. But it is a fine and upstanding dish to serve as a main course.

SERVES 4

2 medium onions, chopped

oil, for frying

2–3 garlic cloves, peeled and chopped

1 Scotch bonnet chili (see note on p.192)

½in (1cm) knob of fresh ginger, peeled and chopped

1 teaspoon ground turmeric

½ teaspoon ground cumin

½ teaspoon ground coriander

pinch ground cloves

1lb 5oz/600g baby carrots, scrubbed or grown-up carrots, peeled and chunked

1½ cups/10½oz/300g *nakhod daul* (yellow split peas)

1 tablespoon tomato paste

3 large tomatoes, chopped

salt, to taste

2 tablespoons sour grape juice or 2 teaspoons vinegar

about generous 2 cups/17fl oz/500ml water or vegetable stock

Just fry the onions in a little oil in the bottom of a big saucepan, and add in the garlic, chili and ginger. When the onions have started to soften, add in the spices, carrots, and split peas, followed a couple of minutes later by the paste and fresh tomato chunks. Sprinkle in some salt, add either the vinegar or sour grape juice, and then enough water to cover all the ingredients. Bring to a boil and then set to simmer for 45 minutes to 1 hour, or until the carrots and peas are cooked through.

Serve over plain white *chalau* rice (see *Chelow*, p.131), with yogurt and bread. And maybe the rather nice *salaata* below. *Naan Tiaris*! As we say in Londonistan.

SALAATA

3 small English cucumbers (or half a regular)

3 tomatoes

3–4 scallions

half a bunch of fresh cilantro, trimmed

handful fresh mint, trimmed

1 small regular onion

2 small, hot green chilies (optional, of course)

salt

juice of 1–2 lemons

Just chop all the ingredients together: we're talking bigger than a salsa here but much smaller than a regular chunk. Sprinkle with salt and drizzle with lemon, and then cover and pop it in the fridge for about 30 minutes (to let the flavors mingle and get to know each other).

*Notes:*

I like this served all chunky and au naturel, but in some parts of Afghanistan the carrots and *daul* are set aside for a moment while the rest of the sauce is blended to make it really thick.

You can make the same recipe using pumpkin—it is just as delicious. But you will then have to address it as *Qorma-e-Kadu.*

*Nakhod dual* (or *chana dal*) are slightly different from the peas used for European pease pudding; they hold their shape when cooked. Something to bear in mind.

# A FOOTNOTE ABOUT CHILIES

Chilies have an astonishing number of fan websites. They are really rather addictive, definitely food groupie status.

Like many addictions, the chili thing is a slippery slope: it starts innocently enough with a pert little *jalapeño* or two on the side of your plate, and then before long you're looking for excuses to sneak those little bird's eye chilies into all sorts of funny recipes, in search of an ever greater hit. Before you know it you're a *habanero* user and you've hit the bottom burner. If you see what I mean.

The addictive stuff in chilies is the same compound that gives them their heat: capsaicin. The idea is that the body releases endorphins to help kill the pain, and this makes you very happy, so you're left with the impression that chilies can show you a good time.

I use Scotch bonnet chilies (up there with *habanero*), as they are widely available, and are the top on the Scoville scale of hotness (yup, chilies have their own scale of measurement). The hottest chili in the world is a matter of contest between the *naga jolokia* and the red *savina habanero*.

Anyway, the initial point of this note was to warn you to be very careful. Wash your hands every time you touch a chili, or you will be in trouble. The best way is to rinse your hands initially in cold water—hot water opens up the pores and drives contaminants under the skin. Once you have washed away the heat, wash your hands again with warm water and soap. By way of a cautionary tale …

A friend of ours came home from work one evening to find her husband sitting in a bath of cold water. He was fully clothed from the waist up. He had been chopping chilies for dinner, and had, er, popped to the bathroom…

# Khudruwat Mehruseh
## SPICED CELERIAC/BEET MASH

This makes for a pretty little side dish: pale spiced mash topped with a slightly sweet beet purée, which is in turn swirled with yogurt (you can, of course, prepare and serve the mashes separately). This works well as an accompaniment to casseroles on those occasions when you don't fancy rice. And it is great comfort food too.

The recipe is frankly a hodge-podge, based on a whole host of Middle Eastern ideas. Celeriac (sometimes called celery root) is enjoyed in the region, but mostly chunked and dressed as a *mezze* dish, or raw in salads.

SERVES 4 AS A SIDE DISH
FOR THE BEET MASH:

6 medium beets

1 teaspoon sugar

½ teaspoon cardamom

1 teaspoon ground ginger

1 teaspoon balsamic (or raspberry) vinegar

1 tablespoon butter

FOR THE CELERIAC MASH:

1 small-medium celeriac

1 teaspoon salt

1 teaspoon freshly ground black pepper

½ teaspoon freshly ground nutmeg

1 teaspoon ground coriander

½ teaspoon ground cumin

2–3 tablespoons butter

TO FINISH:

1 cup/7oz/200g plain yogurt (or vegan option)

1 level tablespoon dill

1 tablespoon olive oil

salt and pepper, to taste

sprig of parsley

Peel and chop the beets and cook them in unsalted water for 40 minutes, or until soft. Drain them and mash them really well with the other ingredients.

The celeriac takes a little less time to cook: peel and chop it, and then boil it for 30 minutes, or until it is tender enough to mash. Drain it and then crush it (rather than mash it) with the spices and butter—this works well if it is left fairly "textured."

Finally mix the yogurt with the dill, olive oil, and seasoning.

Spread the celeriac across a plate, spoon or pipe the beet purée in a swirl on top of the celeriac, and then spoon the yogurt on top. Just add a sprig of parsley.

Tip:

Another nice Veggiestan mash option is to use *tahina* as well as butter. This works particularly well with potatoes and celeriac, and should be garnished with crispy, brown fried onions.

## *KOLOKASSI*

These recipes represent the solution of a culinary jigsaw puzzle. When I worked in Greek kitchens, a popular dish was *hirino me kolokassi*—pork with a pleasant root-type vegetable called *kolokassi*. The mystery vegetable was only available frozen, and so I did not put much thought into its pedigree or general appearance. Roll forward a few years: a combination of a Caribbean honeymoon and running a store in London sees me introduced to taro (or *dasheen*) and its leaves (which are sometimes known as *callaloo*). Turns out they are one and the same thing. It seems that *kolokassi* pops up all over the world using over a dozen different aliases. It appears uniquely at the Eastern end of the Med: Cyprus, Turkey, Lebanon, and Egypt.

It is a small hairy tuber with a couple of less than desirable properties. Firstly, like many vegetables, it can cause skin irritation: if you are a sensitive flower, best wear gloves to prepare it initially. And secondly it is, um, poisonous. Well, it is slightly toxic if you cook it all wrong. Many of the corms (technical word for this type of vegetable, which comprises sunken plant stems rather than bulbs or roots) contain high concentrations of calcium oxalate crystals, which is really bad news for the kidneys. But this doesn't prevent it from being extraordinarily popular in the parts of the world where it grows. And it will not deter us from cooking it. If you cannot find fresh taro, look for frozen *kolokassi* in Greek or Turkish stores. If all else fails, you can substitute yam or potato. I have included two recipes because I had a fit of girly indecision as to which was more fun.

If you do acquire taro leaves, cook them thoroughly and use them like spinach.

# LEBANESE *KOLOKASSI* WITH LENTILS

SERVES 4–5

1lb 9oz/700g *kolokassi* (taro), fresh or frozen
knob of butter (3½ tablespoons/1¾oz/50g)
    with a splash of canola oil
4 sticks celery, chopped
1 large onion
4 garlic cloves

1 tablespoon tomato paste
½ cup/3½oz/100g brown lentils
4 large, softish, chopped tomatoes
salt and pepper, to taste
handful of fresh chopped parsley and cilantro

Peel and wipe the *kolokassi*—do not wash it after you have peeled it. Then score around them at regular intervals with a sharp knife, but do not cut right through them. You are aiming to break fairly evenly sized pieces off. Both of these steps will prevent the corms from seeping mucilaginous goo while they are cooking. Frozen *kolokassi* will be all ready to rock and roll, so disregard the above.

Heat the butter and oil in a pan, add the celery, onion, and garlic; after a few minutes toss in the broken taro pieces, stirring well. Next mix in the tomato paste, followed by enough water to cover the vegetables by about ½in (1cm). Bring the contents of the pan to a boil, and then turn down the heat and leave to simmer for about 30 minutes (15 minutes will suffice if you are using frozen veggies).

In the meantime, pick through the lentils, put them in a pan of unsalted water, and bring to a boil. Cook until just tender (about 20 minutes), then drain and add to the simmering taro along with the tomatoes. Bubble for about 30 minutes more and then season to taste.

Serve for supper, strewn with the fresh herbs and accompanied by some crusty warm bread—try Olive Bread on p.23.

# Kolokassi me Skordalia
## CYPRIOT FRIES WITH
## GARLIC NON-MAYO

This recipe sees the *kolokassi* fried and served with *skordalia*, which is kind of like aïoli, but made without the egg. Vegan mayo, if you like.

Prepare the *kolokassi* as above, but once you have broken it from the main corm, cut the pieces into rough "fries." Fry them in pure olive oil until they are golden on the outside and well cooked inside. Just how a good fry should be. Again, if you can't find *kolokassi*, use yam, or sweet potato, or parsnips, or potatoes.

SERVES 6

6 garlic cloves, minced
1½ tablespoons white wine vinegar
6 thick slices (stale) bread, crusts removed,
    soaked in water, or 4 medium potatoes

2 tablespoons finely ground almonds or
    walnuts (optional)
1½ tablespoon lemon juice
¾ cup/6fl oz/175ml extra-virgin olive oil
salt and ground white pepper

Firstly macerate the garlic in the vinegar—30 minutes should suffice. Then tip it into the goblet of your blender. Squeeze the water out of the bread, and add that to the garlic along with the nuts and the lemon juice. Blend for about 1 minute, then slowly trickle the olive oil in: as with all emulsions if you add it too quickly it will curdle. Carry on until you have a thick paste, and then season to taste. Dip in before it's gone.

# POTATO *AFELIA*

This is a Greek recipe, but just as Turkey is slipping into Europe, the Greeks are really honorary Middle Easterners. They are, of course, part of that invasive clique that also comprises Turkey and Persia: always charging on to the neighbors' property and upsetting each other. Anyway, this is a gorgeous recipe, one that will bring out the worst in your dinner guests as they bicker over the last spoonful.

SERVES 6

2lb 4oz/1kg waxy potatoes

some nice olive oil

about 2 tablespoons coriander seeds

2 teaspoons sugar

salt

2 tablespoons red wine

Seriously easy. Just peel and cube the potatoes (¾in/2cm cubes will be fine). Actually, if the potatoes are newish and very pristine, don't bother with the peeling—just give them a quick scrub. Drizzle a very thin coat of olive oil across a non-stick oven tray, heat it 'til it sizzles, and then toss the potatoes in.

Preheat the oven to 400°F/200°C.

Wrap the coriander seeds in a clean dish towel and bash them until they are all "cracked," and then add them to the potatoes along with the sugar and a little salt. Put into the oven for 30 minutes, turning the potatoes after 15 minutes. Bring the dish out, add the wine, stir again, and put back into the oven for a further 15–20 minutes, or until the potatoes are golden cooked and sticky and oh-so-easy to pick at.

In the extraordinarily unlikely event that there is any left over, this stuff is great reheated for breakfast with a fried egg on top.

# ON BITTER GOURDS

I am a failure. There, I've said it. I have tried repeatedly to develop a culinary relationship with the *karela*, otherwise known as the bitter gourd or bitter melon. And I have failed.

It is, admittedly, used only in a small far Eastern corner of Veggiestan, but nevertheless I saw it as a challenge, and the fact that it looks like it grew on the Klingon homeworld kind of appeals too. You must have seen it in stores: it is dark green in hue, about the length of a zucchini, and frilly all over.

And it lives up to its name: it is bitter. Oh, so very bitter. Bitterer than the heart of the most callously jilted lover. I like bitter things—espresso, Guinness, spinach—but this got the better of me. And my best beloved thought I had poisoned his food. It is incredibly good for you (it's meant to be good at combating diabetes)—but that offered us little consolation on the two occasions that I tried to render it palatable.

It was my full intention to include *karela* as a recipe in this book, but I cannot bring myself to include something that I do not like and have failed to cook myself. Just in case you are really determined: you are meant to cut it open and remove the seeds. Then either slice it or leave it whole (for stuffing, for example) and salt it—this is meant to help draw out the bitterness. After 10 minutes or so, wipe and dry the gourd, and then boil it for around 30 minutes—this is also meant to reduce the bitterness. After 30 minutes drain it, and then you can proceed to use it in your chosen recipe. Try it sautéed with garlic butter, or stuff it with spiced rice. Good luck.

cooking with fruit

In the lands comprising Veggiestan, there is a lot about balance—and this is most obvious in the kitchen. Relics of Avicenna's theories on the four humors, and the Iranian tenets of *sardi* and *garmi* (hot and cold food, see p.106), are clear in the way dishes are constructed. Ingredients are paired to ensure that the dish pleases the system as well as the taste buds.

The inclusion of fruit in a lot of savory dishes is one example of this: the cook will strive for a balance of sweet and sour and salty and bitter. And this has unexpectedly delicious results.

The first time I was served rice made with sour cherry jam, I thought it was some sort of elaborate Persian joke, or at least part of a family initiation ritual, but golly-was-it-good.

So suspend your disbelief, if you will, and give the following recipes a shot...

# Melon Baal Canaf

## MELONS WITH WINGS

Melons are big in Veggiestan. In every sense. Watermelons are famously big anyway, but even Iranian muskmelons draw admiring gazes (melon envy, even) when we import them. They are like footballs—only way fatter. It seems likely that many species originated in the region, as they are embedded in the culture. In Turkmenistan they even have a National Melon Day, and in Iran melons are eaten in unfeasible quantities at various times of the year to stave off fevers and cool the body. They were also reputedly one of the favorite fruits of the Prophet Mohammed, and are mentioned more than once in the Koran.

This recipe was stolen from one of my customers, Amira, and it's a Yemeni specialty. The odd name reflects the popularity of the dish—no sooner is it served than it "flies" off the table...

Soaking the adzuki beans in water with lemon juice stops the redness of the beans from leaching.

Cantaloupe melons are ideal.

### Other nice things to do with melons:

Melons are so very much more versatile than we give them credit for over here. Even sweet, regular, muskmelons. Try throwing a load in the blender with some rose water and strawberry ice cream for a great smoothie, or chopping it into a salsa. I make a lovely salad by combining cubed melon with the chili marmalade on p.232 and tossing it with some warm cubed halloumi.

Watermelons are even better value. Try blending them and mixing them with chili and tiny diced croûtons to make watermelon gazpacho. They contrast well with cheese in salads, and with salty ingredients in salsas. They are also good in smoothies: add rose water, raspberries, and fresh mint. You can even fry them in butter (oh, yes, you can)—if you drizzle them with *sekanjabin* (mint syrup) they make a highly unusual *mezze* dish.

SERVES 4

1½ cups/9oz/250g adzuki beans, soaked
    overnight in water with a squirt of lemon
4 small sweet melons
sesame oil, for cooking
2 onions, finely chopped
½in/1cm piece ginger, peeled and chopped
2 green chilies, chopped
1 red pepper

2 teaspoons garam masala
2 carrots, coarsely grated
1 can (14oz/400g) chopped tomatoes
1¼ cups/9oz/250g long-grain brown rice,
    soaked for at least 1 hour and drained
about 2 cups/17fl oz/500ml vegetable stock
salt and pepper
1 bunch parsley, finely chopped
1¼ cups/10fl oz/300ml tomato passata

Drain the beans and bring them to a boil in a pan of fresh water: simmer for about 45 minutes, then drain and set to one side.

In the meantime, halve the melons and gently scoop out/discard the seeds. Scoop out most, but not all of the flesh and set that aside as well.

Heat a little sesame oil in a pan and fry the onions, ginger, chilies, and pepper until they are soft. Add the spice and carrot, followed 1 minute later by the tomatoes. Add the rice and enough stock just to cover the contents. Cover and simmer for 25 minutes, or until the rice is cooked through. Check the seasoning, then add the beans and chopped parsley.

Preheat the oven to at 350°F/180°C.

Divide the mixture into eight portions and spoon it into the cavities of the melons. Arrange the melon halves on a baking tray, and spoon some of the passata over each one, topping off with some of the reserved melon flesh. Pop the tray into the oven for about 30 minutes. Serve hot with lemon wedges, raw onion wedges, fresh herbs, and warm bread.

# Jeen Mahshi bi Jibnat Creama
## FIGS FILLED WITH SOFT CHEESE

Now there are some proprietary brands which, while incongruous to us, are hugely popular in the Middle East. It's a thing that always tickles me in the store: the fact that I am itching to sell exotic ingredients and yet I am maneuvered into selling such strange, old-fashioned commodities. Nescafé. Carnation milk. Liptons teabags (in Arabic and Persian, the word Lipton has come to denote teabag). And Laughing Cow cheese (which is usually known by its French brand name, *La Vache Qui Rit*). Anyway, Arabs just love this cheese. As do children of all sizes—stuffing something familiar like a soft cheese triangle inside something alien like fresh fruit is a sneaky way to bribe them to eat the good stuff. Anyway, feel free to substitute another soft cheese.

SERVES 4 *AS AN APPETIZER*

12 fresh figs (3 each), washed
olive oil
1 teaspoon salt and ground black pepper
about 1¾oz/50g clear honey
1 box Laughing Cow (or similar) soft cheese
   wedges

2½ teaspoons *ras el hanout* (see p.101)
3½oz/100g walnut pieces

TO SERVE:
1 tablespoon pomegranate molasses (see p.213)
few sprigs mint
endive or frissée

Preheat the oven to 375°F/190°C. Cut the hats off the figs and make a fairly deep cross in the top of each one, then dab each one with olive oil and sprinkle with salt and pepper. Arrange them on a greased baking tray (I use a muffin pan, as it stops them rolling around), and bake in the oven for about 5 minutes. Then whip them out of the oven and spoon a soupçon of honey over each one, then shove them back in for another 3–4 minutes to caramelize. Bring the tray out of the oven and put it to one side for a couple of minutes (the figs need to cool slightly, otherwise you will scald your guests).

Meanwhile, assemble the filling: Peel the cheese and beat it mightily together with the spice and the walnuts. Once it is well mixed, insert a spoonful into the top of each fig. Drizzle the top with just a tiny splodge of pomegranate molasses—if you are using the Iranian version, you will need to dilute it with a splash of water (the Arabic kind tends to be much runnier)—and top with a sprig of mint.

Serve immediately on a pretty platter supported by endive or curly frissée leaves.

You can use this lovely stuffing for other fruit:

Nectarines work particularly well. Just halve the fruits, take out the pit, and bake them in the same way, but note that they will need about 20 minutes in the oven (covered with foil) before you drizzle them with honey.

# Dolmeh-ye-Beh
## BAKED STUFFED QUINCES

Quinces are special. In more ways than one. They might be the ugly duckling of the fruit world, but they most definitely make up for it with their drop-dead gorgeous scent and flavor. In the Middle East they are often purchased specifically for their fragrance: a couple of these in a well-placed fruit bowl makes even the most well-intentioned aromatherapy habit redundant.

They are yet another fine illustration of the fact that Nature knows what she's doing: they are a fruit of the winter, and conveniently one of the best remedies for a bad chest/infant cough. The seeds, when steeped in boiling water, yield a strange mucilaginous substance that is a great bronchial soother.

Anyway, we are eating these ones for pleasure rather than as a remedy. The soft, delicate sweetness of the quince contrasts brilliantly with the salty, multi-textured sourness of the filling.

MAKES 4

¼ cup/1¾oz/50g yellow split peas (*chana dal*)

scant ½ cup/3½oz/100g short-grain rice

1 large onion, chopped

a little oil, for cooking

½ teaspoon ground turmeric

1 teaspoon ground cinnamon

1 teaspoon dried savory or thyme

generous ½ cup/1¾oz/50g barberries, soaked then drained

1¾oz/50g shelled walnuts, crumbled

salt and ground black pepper

4 medium quinces or cooking apples

scant ½ cup/3½fl oz/100ml water

3 tablespoons grape *pekmez* (p.213) or vinegar

2 tablespoons sugar

Cook the split peas in boiling water until they are just cooked, and do the same with the rice. Drain both and set them to one side.

Next fry the onion in oil, and when it has softened, stir in the spices and savory. After a few moments more, add the barberries and walnuts together with the cooked peas and rice. Stir well and season to taste.

Preheat the oven to 350°F/180°C.

To the quinces. Firstly rub any fur from the skin of the quinces: if you have sensitive skin, wear rubber gloves because this fluff can cause irritation. Then core them to within about ½in (1cm) of the base. Spoon a quarter of the filling into each one, and set the fruits into a small baking tray (the quinces need to fit snugly so they don't fall over). Add a drizzle of water to the tray, and bake the fruits in the oven for around 30 minutes.

Pour the scant ½ cup/3½fl oz/100ml water, *pekmez*, and sugar into a saucepan and heat them gently, mixing well. Pour this syrup over the fruit, and then slide the tray back into the oven for a final 10 minutes.

Serve hot—unlike other *dolmeh*, these are not quite right cold. They make a substantial appetizer or a great supper dish. Best of all, serve them as part of a *mezze*.

*Other nice things to do with quinces:*

Actually, you don't need to do much with them. They aren't great raw, but if you just peel them and quarter them without discarding the seeds you can cook them with a splash of water together with a little cinnamon and honey: possibly the world's best stewed fruit. The seeds contain a magic potion that turns everything a gorgeous shade of pink when cooked.

And quinces are, of course, much beloved of jam and cordial makers. They also sit well as a casserole ingredient alongside rich ingredients (such as meat, if you don't mind me using the "M" word).

# Khoresht-e-Aloo Bokhara
## PLUM, SPINACH, AND SPLIT PEA HOTPOT

This recipe packs a punch: it's got sweet, it's got sour, it's got fire, and yet it's strangely comforting.

*Aloo Bokhara* are golden plums, which are to be found across Central Asia and down into India; they are usually dried and consumed as a snack, but they have an underlying sharpness that makes them terrific in casseroles. If you can't find them (they are available in Middle Eastern and Indian stores), just substitute prunes. Although Rumi famously said, *"Enough, be silent; words cannot take the place of opinions, Just as pomegranates and apples cannot take the place of plums,"* we will for once ignore him.

Use Iranian or Indian yellow split peas (*chana dal*) if you can; they hold their shape in casseroles, unlike the more common American variety, which gaily turn to mush if you cook them too much.

**\* Sour grapes and verjuice**

Sour grapes crop up a lot in Persian cuisine: when Islam put a stop to regular viticulture, much of the land was used to grow sour grapes instead. Though they're pretty unpalatable in their natural state, the juice (which we know as verjuice) soon came to replace wine in food. It is also handy in salad dressings: it is like wine vinegar, without the wine or the vinegar. Many Persians drink it as a remedy for high blood pressure and cholesterol.

We import fresh ones during the summer months, and you can also buy them pickled: the whole grapes can be dropped into casseroles to add little bursts of sharpness. The juice is widely available in Middle Eastern stores, and you can also buy a dried and powdered version for use as a spice.

Be warned that you will find continental versions of verjuice (*verjus*) significantly more expensive than the Middle Eastern ones. If you really can't find any, you may substitute a mix of lemon juice and dry white wine in recipes.

SERVES 4

14oz/400g *aloo bokhara* or prunes
oil or veggie ghee, for frying
2 onions, chopped
2 red peppers, roughly chopped
1 Scotch bonnet chili, finely chopped
2 carrots, scraped
2 medium potatoes, peeled
2 medium turnips, peeled
1 teaspoon turmeric

1 teaspoon ground cinnamon
1 heaped tablespoon tomato paste
½ bottle (scant 1 cup/8fl oz/about 225ml) verjuice\*
1 tablespoon sour grapes (fresh or pickled, optional)\*
generous ¾ cup/6oz/175g firm yellow split peas (*chana dal*, or *lapeh*)
1lb 2oz /500g fresh spinach, roughly chopped
salt and pepper

Firstly set the plums to soak in water—they need about 30 minutes to swell and soften.

Heat a little ghee or oil in a saucepan and fry the onions, pepper, and chili. Cut the carrot, potatoes, and turnips into 1¼in/3cm cubes, and add them to the softened onion. After about 2 minutes, add the turmeric, cinnamon, and tomato paste. Stir well so that everything is coated with oil and spice, and then pour in the verjuice together with enough water to cover the vegetables by about ¾in (2cm). Add the sour grapes (if available) and the split peas, bring the pan's contents to a boil, and then turn things down to a simmer. After about 15 minutes, drain the *aloo* and spoon them into the *khoresht*; take a moment to check the liquid levels in the pan—you are aiming for thick and gloopy, but there should still be plenty of sauce. Cook for about 30 minutes, and then season to taste—you may need to add sugar if you feel it is too sharp, or a little more verjuice if it is too sweet. Now add the spinach, and replace the lid of the pan before cooking for a final 15–20 minutes. The vegetables should be tender, while retaining their integrity.

This dish should be served with plain white basmati rice, yogurt, and a decent salad.

# A TOKEN TAGINE—PRUNE AND TURNIP

Tagine is, of course, of Berber origin, from the Maghreb, and is the name of both a vessel and the food cooked in it. The dish is cone-shaped, the idea being that steam from the cooking stock is trapped and funneled back into the food, resulting in a uniquely tender and very flavorsome combination.

Tagines could take up a whole chapter of this book, and I would have been happy to write one: what's not to like? A perfectly balanced mixture of sweet and savory vegetables, spices, and herbs, multi-textured and colored, soft-cooked in the world's most photogenic cookware. But I have restrained myself, as to do so would have been to sacrifice other exciting corners of Veggiestan. This is admittedly one of my favorite tagines, but it is, nevertheless, a token. The original recipe was on the back of a postcard someone sent me from Essaouira.

The making of a good tagine is a state of mind rather than a culinary art. Once you have grasped the basic principles of seasoning, balance, and contrast, the opportunity is there to have fun creating your own. Play around. If you don't have a tagine pot, you can use a casserole dish, or just make the whole thing in a saucepan.

SERVES 4

2 tablespoons olive oil mixed with
    1 tablespoon butter or ghee, for cooking
about 12 shallots, peeled but left whole
1 teaspoon ground ginger
2 teaspoons ground cinnamon
1 teaspoon ground cumin
1lb 9oz/700g baby turnips (about 7–8),
    peeled and cubed (1¼in/3cm chunks)
2 carrots, peeled and cut into small chunks
1¾ cups/14fl oz/400ml vegetable stock

¼ teaspoon ground saffron, steeped in a splash
    of boiling water
10½oz/10½oz/300g soft pitted prunes (or dry
    prunes, soaked for 30 minutes)
1½ tablespoons runny honey
salt and black pepper

TO GARNISH:

1 tablespoons sesame seeds, lightly toasted
1 tablespoon flaked almonds, toasted
big handful of fresh cilantro, chopped

Preheat the oven to 325°F/160°C.

Heat the oil and ghee in a frying pan (unless you have a fancy cast-iron tagine), and toss in the shallots, stirring them so that they cook evenly. After a few minutes, add the spices together with the turnip and carrot. Let it cook gently for a few minutes more and then add the saffron and vegetable stock: when this comes to a boil, lower in the prunes and add the honey. Stir well and season to taste.

At this stage transfer the whole thing to your tagine pot or a casserole, put the lid on and pop it in the oven to do its thing—it will need about 40 minutes.

Serve, sprinkled with the sesame, almonds, and cilantro. Serve with couscous if you wish, although contrary to general belief couscous is not the inevitable companion of tagine but is rather a dish in itself (see p.151). In Morocco, tagine is most often eaten solo, or with bread and a colorful salad.

# Bonjon wa Jamur-Hindi
## GINGER AND TAMARIND EGGPLANTS

Ginger, tamarind, and eggplant are often found together in chutneys and relishes, but this recipe from Uzbekistan sees the eggplants fried with a spiced tamarind sauce. It's really good and vanishes quickly, so make sure you keep yourself a little plateful back in the kitchen.

*
Tamarind: the lowdown.

Gotta love the natural "packaging" of this fruit—not only does it have a dinky pod-like shape, it comes with a hard casing and an inner mesh of string, which you have to peel away. It is not entirely of this earth.

They are, of course, famously good for one's "system," and in Afghanistan and Saudi Arabia are boiled up to make a cooling summer drink.

Tamarinds come in two varieties: sweet or sour. The sweet are best to eat just as they are: peel and enjoy.

The sour ones are used more in cooked food: their sharpness works well in marinades and sauces, and they are particularly suitable for fish. If you can't buy tamarind paste in your 'hood (Indian grocery stores will have it, and nearly all Middle Eastern ones too), make your own from the whole fruit, which is widely available now, or buy a block of tamarind, which is formed from whole, peeled fruits that have been compressed. Steep in boiling water for 5–10 minutes, and then press the whole lot through a sieve.

### SERVES 4, AS A SIDE DISH

3 large eggplants, cut into ½in (1.5cm) slices
peanut oil (or canola), for frying
2 medium onions, chopped
2–3 garlic cloves, finely chopped
1–2 chilies, finely chopped
1¼in (3cm) knob of ginger, peeled and chopped
1 teaspoon ground cinnamon
pinch of ground cloves
3 tablespoons tamarind paste
2 teaspoons brown sugar
scant ½ cup/3½fl oz/100ml water
the flesh of 1 medium mango

First, sprinkle your eggplant slices with salt and set them to one side to drain for 30 minutes or so.

Next heat a splash of oil in a frying pan and add the onions, garlic, chilies, and ginger. Fry for a few minutes until the onion starts to soften, and then add the spices. Cook for a little longer, then scrape the ingredients into a bowl. Wipe the eggplants dry and fry them in the same pan (adding more oil if necessary) until they are golden on both sides, and then pop them somewhere to keep hot.

Now tip the fried onion mix back into the pan, and add the tamarind, sugar, and water. Bring to a boil, stirring well, and simmer for 7–8 minutes, then tip the whole lot into a blender with the mango flesh. Buzz for about 30 seconds and then pour into a serving bowl. Arrange the warm eggplant slices on a platter, splay some of the sauce across them and serve the rest on the side.

The sauce will, of course, go with all sorts of other things…

# Salad-e-Albaloo va Pulao
## SOUR CHERRY AND RICE SALAD

This is a twist on a Persian classic, *albaloo pulao*, which is a hot dish of meat and sour cherries layered with rice. Rice salad is not actually something you find in Veggiestan: rice is something that is eaten hot, and there are rarely leftovers anyway. But I think it is great.

Fresh sour cherries are fruit gold dust; rare indeed. But this recipe uses the dried version twinned with sour cherry jam, both of which are much easier to source. If you really can't find dried sour cherries, substitute unsweetened dried cranberries.

Instead of olive oil, you could use a mixture (half and half) of hazelnut oil and olive oil.

SERVES 4 AS AN
ACCOMPANIMENT
¾ cup/5½oz/150g red (Camargue) rice, or
    basmati or long-grain
1¼ cups/3½oz/100g dried sour cherries,
    pitted
1 bunch scallions, cleaned and chopped
½ cup/1¾oz/50g flaked almonds, toasted
½ bunch fresh flat-leaf parsley, chopped

FOR THE DRESSING:
2 juniper berries, crushed
½ teaspoon thyme
1 teaspoon sour cherry jam
2 teaspoons vinegar
zest and 1 tablespoon of the juice of 1 orange
5 tablespoons extra-virgin olive oil
salt and coarse ground black pepper

Cook the red rice in boiling water for about 30 minutes (it does take longer than regular rice), then drain it well and tip it into a bowl. Mix in the cherries, scallions, and almonds and stir well.

Whisk the ingredients for the dressing together, season to taste, and pour over the salad. At the last minute, stir the parsley through it—this way its greenness is preserved. This is otherwise a really red salad, and the colors merrily all leach into each other.

# Khoresht-e-Gheimeh Khalal
## BARBERRY AND ALMOND CASSEROLE

This is a hugely popular dish in Iran, although it is usually made with diced lamb. But as with so many Iranian *khoreshts* (casseroles to you), the meat is really irrelevant to the flavor. This is gloriously rich and tart, infused with the pungent flavor of dried limes, zinging with barberry goodness, and gloopy with tomatoes. A great show dish, and full of anti-oxidant super-powers too.

SERVES 4

2 onions, peeled and chopped

oil for frying (sunflower, to be authentic)

1 teaspoon turmeric

6 medium waxy potatoes, peeled
  and quartered

1 tablespoon tomato paste

2–3 dried limes,* washed, and pricked

scant 1 ⅔ cups/4¼oz/120g barberries,**
  washed and sorted

⅔ cup/3½oz/100g chopped almonds

4 large tomatoes

salt and pepper, to taste

Fry the onions in a little oil in a saucepan, and as they start to soften, add the turmeric, stirring well. Add the potatoes, the tomato paste and the dried limes, and then enough water to cover all the ingredients with ½in (1cm) to spare. Bring to a boil, spoon in the barberries and the almonds, and set to simmer.

Once the potatoes are al-dente-cooked (about 10 minutes should do the trick), halve the tomatoes and lower those in, and season the casserole to taste. Top up the liquid levels if it looks a bit dry. Allow to bubble gently for a further 20–25 minutes, or until the potatoes are really tender and the tomatoes soft.

Serve with brown basmati rice, plain yogurt, and fresh herbs. *Bah-bah*! (Which is Persian for "Yum!")

**\* Dried Limes**

Dried limes are one of the chief souring agents of Persian cuisine, and add a pungent and deliciously sharp undertone to many soups and casseroles. They are known as *limoo amani* in Farsi, which means Omani limes; this is simply because the concept of drying limes to use in food originated in Arabia. They are readily available in Middle Eastern stores, although you can make your own simply by drying fresh limes—preferably in the sun and not because you neglected them in the produce drawer of your fridge. In stores you will often find both pale ones and black ones: the darker ones are much stronger in flavor and are used more in Iraqi cooking. The paler ones have a more delicate flavor, and are even used to make tea by hardier sorts. *Limoo amani* are also ground into a spice (which then becomes known as *gard-e-limoo*): this you should use like any other spice, adding it in at the sealing stages of a dish.

To use dried limes, just rinse them, prick them with a knife or a fork and plop them into your cooking stock/sauce/soup. There is no need to remove them from the dish before serving.

** Barberries

Barberries (*zereshk* in Persian) are used extensively in Iran: chiefly in a dish called *zereshk pulao*, stirred through rice, which is then streaked with saffron. They are great in stuffings, their natural sharpness contrasting with sweeter fruits and nuts. And then they are used in casseroles to add ooh and aah.

To use barberries, you will first need to soak them in water—this is because they live up to their name and are naturally full of barbs, not to mention grit, both of which will settle to the bottom. After about 15 minutes, squeeze them out and then proceed to use. Don't eat them raw unless you have a cast-iron constitution; they will give you tummy ache. But they are really good for you, packed with vitamin C and an aid to digestion.

In most (but not all) recipes you can substitute unsweetened cranberries.

# Khoresht-e-Holu

## CHILIED PEACH STEW

Another Persian offering. The original recipe boasts chicken in place of lentils, and the chilies are my addition—you can just leave them out, although chili and fruit are an amazing combination. This is a gorgeous summer supper recipe.

SERVES 4

scant 1 cup/2¾oz/75g dried barberries or
    redcurrants or unsweetened cranberries
1 large onion, chopped
1 red bell pepper, chopped
7 tablespoons /3½oz/100g butter for frying
1 Scotch bonnet chili, chopped
    (or 2–3 green chilies)
½in (1cm) knob of ginger, chopped
1 teaspoon ground turmeric
1 teaspoon ground cinnamon

¼ teaspoon nutmeg
2 teaspoons tomato paste
2¼ cups/9oz /250g Puy (French) lentils,
    washed and picked through
about 2 cups/17fl oz/500ml water
¼ cup/2fl oz/50ml white wine (optional—
    replace with water if you like)
juice of 1 lime
1 tablespoon brown sugar
salt and pepper
4–5 nice peaches (or nectarines, I guess)

Pick through the barberries and soak for 10 minutes.

Fry the onion and the pepper in about half of the butter (add a splash of oil to stop it from burning), and as they start to soften, add the chili, ginger, and spices. Fry for a couple of minutes, and then add the tomato paste and the lentils, stirring well so that the latter get thoroughly coated with spiced butter. Add the water and the wine, bring to a boil, and then set the pan to a good simmer. After around 35 minutes, give it a quick prod—you want the lentils cooked but not mushy—then add the lime juice and sugar and season to taste. Check the liquid levels too: the casserole should be quite saucy and not stiff with ingredients, so add a little more water if necessary.

Halve and pit the peaches and cut them into wedges; it's also time to drain the barberries. Heat the rest of the butter in a little frying pan and toss in the fruit, poking it occasionally so it doesn't stick. Fry for about 2 minutes, or until the peaches are golden and the barberries plump, before spooning it into the casserole.

Stir gently and then spoon into a serving bowl. Best accompanied by basmati rice, a lovely leafy salad, and some very cold rosé.

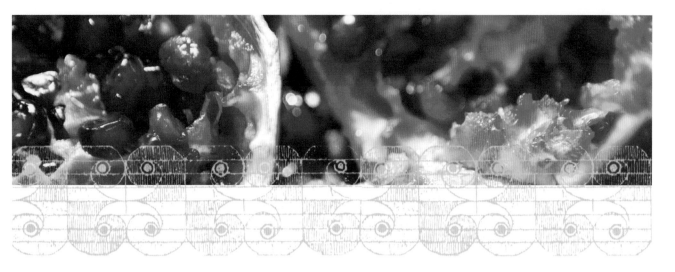

# WHY NO PANTRY SHOULD BE WITHOUT
# DATE SYRUP, POMEGRANATE MOLASSES, AND *PEKMEZ*

There are some ingredients that are pretty much indispensable, health police notwithstanding. Salt, for example. Cooking oil.

And then there are the ingredients that every cook makes their own: the wok king will perhaps throw a fit if he runs out of tamari, while the cake queen cannot live without her Madagascan vanilla, and the keen Thai weekend chef can't manage without *nam pla*.

I feel that way about many things, and am as faddy as the next chef, but my most recent props are all fruity: date syrup, pomegranate paste, and *pekmez*. I feel nervous if I run out and am constantly extending the range of things that I do with them. So here they are in turn, my current culinary playmates: if you happen to bump into them as you shop, stock up.

DATE SYRUP (*dibs* in Arabic, *shireh khormah* in Farsi): velvety and chocolatey, this is the sweetest of the three, and is similar to carob syrup. Like *pekmez*, it is often twinned with *tahina* as a breakfast favorite (especially in Iraq). You can use it in sweet dishes as you would molasses—it is great with steamed pudding, or in ice cream. In savory dishes it blends well with nuts, creamy stuff, and hot spices.

POMEGRANATE MOLASSES: makes a great marinade for just about anything (yes, including fish and meat). Great for sweet and sour dishes—mix with soy and honey and mustard. A drizzle in salad dressings and soups adds unexpected fruitiness. Try using it in place of ketchup (although it's not that great with fries).

*PEKMEZ*: this concentrated fruit syrup is made from boiled-up fruit bits, usually grape or mulberry. And it is really versatile. It is sharp enough to act as a counterpoint with strong salty flavors, but sweet enough to replace sugar in some recipes. It works in salads, and is often added to the cooking stock for things like *dolmeh*. It is a close bosom buddy of the maturing eggplant.

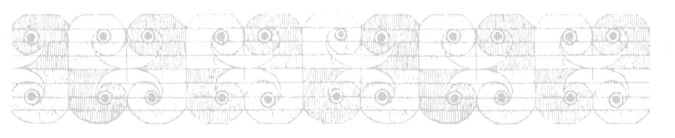

# Salata Tamr wa Jubnat Feta
## DATE AND FETA SALAD

Dates and cheese are common plate-fellows, found at breakfast tables all over Veggiestan, providing a simple lunch for desert nomads, or offering a nutritious repast for Ramadan sunsets.

This is quite a rich salad, but is a winsome accompaniment to sharp or tomatoey dishes. It is also a winner for *mezze*-style eating.

SERVES 4 A SIDE DISH
½ a stale *barberi* bread, or 1 stale *pide*,
    or 2 slices of stale white bread
pure olive oil, for frying
half a bunch of fresh cilantro, washed
1 bunch fresh arugula, also washed
12 fresh (or dried) dates
5½oz/150g real feta, cubed
about ½ cup/2¾oz/75g toasted hazelnut
    halves or walnuts

1 sweet white onion (use a red onion if you
    can't find a white one), finely sliced

FOR THE DRESSING:
4 tablespoons olive oil
2 teaspoons date syrup
3 teaspoons balsamic vinegar
handful of shredded fresh mint
salt and freshly milled black pepper

Cube your stale bread, and then fry it with a little oil in a pan, turning regularly, until it is a pleasingly golden color. Set the croûtons on a piece of paper towel to drain and cool.

Break the stalky bits off the cilantro, and separate the rest into pretty, curly fronds. Mix it with the arugula leaves, and pile them into your favorite salad bowl.

Next halve and pit the dates and mix them gently with the cheese, nuts, onion slices, and croûtons. Arrange the nutty cheese over the salad leaves, and then whisk the dressing together and drizzle it over the top.

saucing, pickling,
and preserving

The trouble with having everything in the stores all of the time is the fact that it has turned us all into spoiled brats. There was a time when seasons were seasons and we enjoyed what they had to offer. It's good to have something to which to look forward: the first fresh fava bean of the year does it for me. Oh, and the first quince of winter. And I am foolish enough to make a wish on all of these things: don't tell anyone.

Well, in the Middle East, expensive unseasonal items simply don't cut it. Fruits and vegetables are bought and consumed when they are at their optimum: the problem of a surplus (or a fetish for a particular item) is resolved by pickling or preserving said produce so that it's there for a rainy day.

I cannot overstate how pleasurable pickling and preserving can be. Not to mention satisfying. Expunge all thoughts of rivalry at country fairs (not that there is anything wrong with that concept, per se). Nothing (much) gets wasted and you end up with a pantry heaving with tasty and useful culinary solutions. I lob pickles into all sorts of places: sandwiches, salad dressings, sauces… And jam is always a good double as an ice cream sauce, or as an accompaniment to rich meats.

I have two special ladies to thank for my interest in this department: my grandmother, Jo-Jo, who taught me to have no fear in the kitchen (although she did have a remarkable ability to obfuscate recipes that were trade secrets) and my mother-in-law, who effortlessly captures the best of the year in a jar. An afternoon walk with the latter, even around the block, is an education: we invariably come back with pockets and handbags full of windfall fruit, which by the next day is preserved, labeled, and at the back of the pantry. Sour plums, crab apples, blackberries, mulberries, and barberries all grow nearby. Most things can be pickled within minutes: wash the fruit or veggies in question, pile them into a sterilized jar, and cover with vinegar and salt. Seal tightly, and label it with what it is and the date (you might think that you will remember, but in six months' time, trust me, you will scratch your head in puzzlement at the strange thing lurking at the back of the cupboard or the fridge, and then you'll throw it away).

The Iranians are probably the pickle kings of Veggiestan: they eat pickles (*torshi*) with most meals, as the sharpness offers a pleasant contrast with the richness of some dishes. (And as most pickles are cold, they provide balance within a meal that may contain a lot of hot ingredients; see p.106.) But, in truth, pickles (*mekhalel* or *achar*) are enjoyed all across the Middle East.

As are jams. The best jams in the region probably come from Turkey, but spiced fruits are enjoyed in many different formats, from thick thick preserves (*moraba* or *murabbiyat*), to whole-fruit conserves, to delicate syrups or *sharbat*.

So, aprons, pans, and wooden spoons at the ready?

# Zhug & Hilbeh
## YEMENI FIRE RELISH

If you thought harissa was hot... *Zhug* is a really fiery relish from Yemen. Why the Yemenis should need it when they live in such a hot country, I know not—it would make more sense if it was Eskimo food. All I can say is that they must have asbestos tastebuds: this is apparently standard breakfast fare over there. *Hilbeh* is *zhug* with extra stuff in it—and they are both really useful for dipping, marinating, and testing the mettle of your guests.

*Silly culinary tip of the day:*

Try mixing a couple of tablespoons of *hilbeh* with the same amount of olive oil, and toss a batch of freshly popped popcorn in it. Great with beer.

FOR 1 PINT JAR (1LB/450G)*ZHUG*:

6 dried chilies, soaked for at least 1 hour
3 cardamom pods
1 teaspoon caraway seeds
1 teaspoon black peppercorns
1 bunch cilantro, stalked and washed
1 bulb garlic, peeled
1 teaspoon salt

*HILBEH*—AS ABOVE, BUT WITH THE FOLLOWING EXTRAS:

1 tablespoon fenugreek seeds, soaked for at least 1 hour (until they go all gloopy)
1 tablespoon tomato paste

Blend the chilies with the spices, cilantro, garlic, and salt until you obtain a fine paste. Add the fenugreek and tomato paste, if using. That's it. Store in a small jar in the fridge, and use within 2 weeks. Great as a dip for bread, or to spice up soups and pasta.

# Torshi Liteh
## IRANIAN EGGPLANT PICKLE

In Iran, housewives are pretty much all minor domestic goddesses, and pride themselves on their range of house pickles. Few meals are complete without a tray of choice preserved vegetables being proffered, and these are sometimes brought out to be eaten with bread and herbs as an appetizer.

*Torshi* in Farsi just means sour stuff, and the word represents a huge range of vinegary pickles. It crossed the borders into Turkey, where it became *tursu*, and the word stem is in fact to be found all over the Middle East. This is in contrast with *shor*, which means salty, and is applied to pickles that have been preserved in brine rather than vinegar. One of Iran's most famous pickles is thus *khiar shor*, spiced, salted baby cucumbers.

Anyway, on to the pickle in hand. Strictly speaking, *liteh* is a blended mixed pickle, but as eggplant is the chief ingredient, this seems a fair translation. Eggplant is great in pickles (hence the inclusion of not one but two recipes in this chapter), as it naturally acts like blotting paper, absorbing every flavor you throw at it.

FOR ABOUT 2 QUART-SIZE JARS
(3LB 5OZ/1.5KG)

3lb 5oz/1.5kg eggplants

2 teaspoons nigella seeds

1 teaspoon golpar seeds (optional, as hard to find)

1 teaspoon coriander seeds

1 teaspoon black peppercorns

2 tablespoons salt

6¼ cups/50fl oz/1.5 liters vinegar (wine or grape vinegar works well)

1 bunch each fresh parsley and cilantro

handful each of fresh tarragon, mint, savory, and dill (or 1 tablespoon each dried)

Remove and discard the calices of the eggplants; wash the remainder and chop it into chunks. Put this into a pan together with the spices and the salt, cover with the vinegar, bring to a boil, and simmer for 5 minutes. Take off the heat and set aside to cool.

In the meantime, wash and roughly chop the fresh herbs. When the eggplant has cooled, mix the herbs in and either push it all through a strainer, or put it in the blender on pulse for a couple of seconds. You are aiming for a rough texture, not a purée: you should still be able to see lumps in the finished product. Just trust me—it really does taste better than it looks.

Pour the blended relish into sterilized jars,* label it, and tuck it away for at least 1 week: it will keep for up to 1 year.

*Liteh* is enjoyed in Iran with fish dishes and alongside kebabs, providing contrast to salty, smoky, or greasy food. In the context of Veggiestan, it is particularly good with barbecued vegetables and alongside *dolmeh*.

Useful pickle fact:
Pickles are pretty indestructible if you treat them right. In fact, some are better off with a Best After date than a Best Before date. But if you introduce foreign bodies or grease into the mix they will deteriorate very quickly. So always use a clean, dry spoon or fork to serve them. And make sure that all the pickle thieves in your household do the same …

I always thought there was some mystique to sterilizing jars for preserving stuff like this. There isn't. Just fill the jar with boiling water, sloosh it around and empty it again. Leave the jars upside down to drain and dry thoroughly. That's it.

# Batingas Makdous

## POSH MARINATED EGGPLANTS

This isn't exactly a pickle on account of it being preserved in oil. But it is one of our favorite Arabic treats, and it is both easy to make and stupid-money-expensive to buy ready-made. Like many of the numbers in this chapter, it makes a great foodie gift. In this new age of thrift, there is nothing like presenting friends with edible treats.

Buy good-quality walnuts; it's worth the investment.

TO FILL 1 QUART JAR
(2LB 4OZ/1KG)
8–9 dinky little eggplants, mauve or white
salt
7oz/200g shelled walnuts

1½ bulbs garlic, peeled and chopped
1 tablespoon chili flakes
about 1½ cups/12fl oz/350ml extra-virgin
olive oil

Take the hats off the eggplants, and prick them. Poach them in boiling salted water for about 15 minutes, then tip them into a colander to drain. When they have cooled enough to handle, make a small lengthwise incision in each one, squeezing gently to get rid of the water, then place them back in the colander with the incision facing downwards. Invert a heavy plate on top of them, and leave them to drain for at least another 1 hour (preferably overnight). This helps the vegetables to shed some of their innate bitterness.

Next chop the walnuts and pound them together with the garlic, chili flakes, a pinch of salt, and just a drop of olive oil—a pestle and mortar is good for this. Spoon a dollop of the mixture into each of the eggplant cavities, and then layer the stuffed veggies into a clean jar (see note on p.219).

Technically at this stage you should then invert the filled jars over a plate to let any remaining bitter dregs drain away. I saw some unfeasibly attractive Syrian goddess figure demonstrating this on one of the incessant cable channels to which my in-laws are permanently tuned. But I don't do this, and mine always turn out just fine. Just cover the eggplants with olive oil, wiggling a knife inside the jar carefully to ensure that there are no pockets of air left (air = potential mold = discouraged pickle maker). That's it. Seal the jar. And wait a week.

They do not need to be kept in the fridge. Enjoy them with bread and fresh herbs as a snack, or as a star *mezze* item.

*Exciting variation:*

Try cramming some *labneh* or feta into the walnut mixture. Scrumdiddlyumptious.

# BARTER AND HAGGLE:
## ON MIDDLE EASTERN STOREKEEPING

Funny job, storekeeping. While you would think that we are at the forefront of commercialism, in fact most small stores find themselves in the center of something far more primitive and fun. As few as 50% of the transactions that take place in my store actually involve people buying things for money. The other half are exchanges: ideas, recipes, services, favors, advice, orders, introductions, either verbal transactions of one kind or another, or actual goods swapped for other goods.

Each store inevitably creates its own community. There is an element of supply and demand about a good corner store that has nothing to do with the daily bread, and everything to do with matching people and things that need each other. Barter. It's human nature, and we've been at it for as long as we've been able to swap dinosaur bones and flints. Economies come and go, but the principal of matching like with like for trade has always been and will always be around. It was what made the silk route work, and enabled international trade to develop.

Haggling, on the other hand, does not come easily to everyone. This, I suspect, revolves around the basic notion that by haggling you are essentially calling into question the other party's integrity. Confrontational shopping. Always sends me scurrying for cover. But as the doyenne of a Middle Eastern emporium I am forced to deal with it every day, and with time have learned a degree of tolerance and even enjoyment of the sport. A properly haggled transaction is a game of strategy for the participants, and for the spectators it is a comedy of manners of sorts. Especially if the parties involved do not share a common language and at least one of them is a nervous tourist. Go on, admit it: you too have felt the peculiar sting of paying ten times the going rate for an item.

So why do Arabs haggle? And this is mostly an Arab issue we are talking about here: Iranian storekeepers are honor bound by *taruf*, a sort of Persian noblesse oblige, to offer goods for free, just as Iranian customers are obliged to insist on paying (even if they have just spent half an hour grumbling about your prices). It does ultimately come down to the fact that the Middle East saw the very beginnings of wide-scale trade: the Sumerians in Mesopotamia, the Egyptians along the Nile, and those nautical Phoenicians started it all off. All this rubbing up against other nations inevitably brought with it a degree of nervousness: after all, this was a time when your neighbor was as likely to invade you as ask for a cup of sugar. A buyer who didn't go through the motions of haggling was regarded as some sort of freak. The distrust and the expectation of being able to get a better price became embedded in the culture of the bazaar, and thus the ritual of negotiation.

And it is a tradition that some find it impossible to break. Omid Djalili may well joke about the shame of his mother haggling in McDonalds, but customers still try it on all the time in my store in Peckham.

Being both contrary and British I resent the persistent haggler, but delight in offering discount where none is solicited, and as we are importers as well as storekeepers, I am always well aware of the real bottom line. Of course, if I can see it coming, I simply put my prices up in anticipation of the fight to come…

Have we got any tips on the art? Only one. Never, ever let the vendor know how very much you want the item in question. Good luck.

# Mekhalel bil Tamaten
## TOMATO PICKLE WITH NIGELLA SEEDS

We're all the same, I'm convinced. We buy surplus fruit and veggies in a flurry of nutritional optimism (and also because they were cheap at the market), and then we get home and unpack them, thinking glowing domestic thoughts all the while. Then a few days later they start to taunt us from the bottom of the fridge, and we realize that rather than healthy ingredients in the making they have become a burden. The chief culprit here is tomatoes. Or it is in our house, at any rate. I buy them because they are good for my man, conveniently forgetting that he really doesn't like them in their regular guise. What to do, what to do?

Well, soup or sauce are the obvious solutions. But pickling them is much easier. And this recipe (which is a fusion of Greek and Arabic ideas) sees them stuffed with little bursts of spice and garlic, a distraction to such an extent that small people and fussy husbands will fight over the last ones.

FOR 1 QUART JAR (2LB 4OZ/1KG)
2lb 4oz/1kg small tomatoes, washed
salt
1 bulb garlic

3 teaspoons nigella seeds
2 teaspoons coarse ground coriander seeds
3 teaspoons chili flakes
about 2½ cups/20fl oz/600ml wine vinegar

First make an incision in the tomatoes: cut through from the stalk end to about halfway down the fruit. Next, prying each one open slightly, fill the gaps with salt, cover them, and set them to one side for 1–2 hours (this helps to draw out some of their water content). When this time has lapsed, or you can no longer bear the suspense, invert the tomatoes in a colander to drain.

In the meantime, peel and mince the garlic and mix it with the spices to form a paste. Smear a little of the mixture into the "cavity" of each tomato, and then layer them gently into a sterilized jar. Cover with vinegar, and seal with plastic wrap before putting the lid on the jar. This pickle will be ready in 4–5 days, and will keep for around 3 months.

A note about Nigella.
Nigella is an acquired taste, but a very important one. It is, you see, the source of black seed oil. The seeds (*Nigella sativa*) are part of the cumin family—it is often called black cumin, although that name strictly speaking belongs to *Bunium persicum*, which is a milder, sweeter, highly prized plant that grows in Iran and India.

Nigella is used in seed form in breads and salads and pickles, but the oil is used as a panacea. The Koran actually states that it is a remedy for all ills "except death." Studies do indicate that it is beneficial in the treatment of chest ailments, and also aids the memory, but in the Arab world it is used for everything from hair oil to an alternative treatment for cancer. It tastes utterly foul, and for that reason, should you wish to give it a shot, I do recommend that you disguise it heavily in orange juice or mix it with honey.

# Gashneetch

## AFGHAN CILANTRO CHUTNEY

I sampled this for the first time without realizing what it was (and for the record, it is not nice with coffee): one of my favorite Afghan customer ladies brought it in for me to try as a gift for filling out a form for her or some such. Ah, the joys of being a storekeeper ...

*Gashneetch* is super, somewhere between pickle and pesto—the sort of thing that is really handy to have skulking in your fridge. Afghans enjoy it with kebabs and bread, but it is versatile enough to tart up your sandwiches, toss into salad dressings, or use as a funky dip. It is one of those recipes that isn't too fussy about ingredients and weathers the worst storms of amateur improvisation.

I have to confess I have "toned down" this recipe; in its original Afghan glory it was, frankly, strong enough to make my eyes water. If you want to be authentic, and have a strong constitution, you should double the garlic and salt and use apple cider vinegar in place of the wine vinegar.

FOR 2 PINT JARS (2LB/900G)
2 bunches of cilantro
4–6 hot green chilies
6 garlic cloves, peeled
½ cup/1¾oz/50g shelled walnuts (or hazelnuts)
pinch sugar
3 teaspoons salt
scant ⅓ cup/1¾oz/50g raisins or chopped prunes (optional)
1 cup/9fl oz/250ml white wine vinegar

Simple, really. Remove the woodier bits of the cilantro stalks, wash the herbs thoroughly, and then chop them finely. Wash the chilies, and remove the stalk and most of the seeds, then dice them and add them to the cilantro. Grind the garlic together with the walnuts, sugar, and salt, and then add it to the herb mix together with the raisins and vinegar. Check the seasoning, and then spoon into clean jars, seal, and store in the fridge. This keeps for about 2 weeks.

# Biber Salçasi
## USEFUL TURKISH PEPPER PASTE

This is another of those things that any vegetable lover will enjoy having in their fridge. It is great with pizza, sandwiches, in salad dressings, as a dip, as a sauce with grilled vegetables ... Peppers are super good for the skin, and are full of vitamins A and C. Most importantly, there is no reason at all why tomatoes should get all the sauce action.

In Turkey there are two varieties of this *salçasi: aci*, which is hot, and *tatli*, which is sweet. The recipe below inclines towards the sweet, but obviously you can spice things up as much as you like.

It takes very little effort to make.

FOR 1 QUART JAR
(1LB 10OZ/750G)
1lb 2 oz/500g red bell peppers

1 teaspoon salt
2 hot-but-not-too-hot red chilies, stalks and
    seeds removed

Roast the red peppers in a hot oven for about 20 minutes, or until the skin blisters. Let them cool for a minute before popping them in a plastic bag or some plastic wrap—after 5–10 minutes, the skin should just flake off.

Remove the stalks and seeds and put the peppers in the blender with the chilies and the salt. Scoop the resulting purée into a shallow oven tray and put it back in the oven, this time on a very low heat so that any excess water can evaporate; say about 30 minutes ... This latter is, of course, in place of sun-drying: if you live in an area where you are able to sun-dry this paste for an hour or so—well, good for you.

Store the paste in a sterilized jar in the fridge: a thin layer of olive oil on top will prolong its life considerably.

# Muhammara & Çemen
## A PECK OF PURÉED PEPPERS

A pair of really handy little dishes from Anatolia, both using *biber salçasi* (see opposite). *Muhammara* is a popular dip, although I am not sure that I could eat it for breakfast the way that some Turks (reputedly) do. *Çemen* is used more as a rub or marinade (especially for *bastirma*, which is pressed fillet of beef), but it also makes a good sauce to have with bulgar or vegetable dishes.

## Muhammara—PEPPER AND WALNUT PURÉE

FOR 1 JAR (1LB 10OZ/750G)

1½ cups/1lb 2 oz/500g *biber salçasi* (see opposite)

2 tablespoons pomegranate molasses

1¼ cups/4½oz/125g shelled walnuts, crushed but not powdered

½ teaspoon ground cumin

1 teaspoon ground coriander

1 teaspoon chili flakes

2 tablespoons breadcrumbs

3 garlic cloves, peeled and minced

about ¼ cup/2fl oz/50ml extra-virgin olive oil

I usually mix this by hand, as it is better if it has got some chunk and texture to it. Mix all the ingredients, trickling the olive oil in last, until the paste is smooth and fairly stiff. Serve with hot bread or crudités, or use as a base for pizzas; it's pretty good with chips, too. Keeps for 1 week in the fridge.

## Çemen—FENUGREEK PEPPER SAUCE

*Çemen* is the Turkish word for fenugreek, and it is this that provides the overriding flavor for the paste of the same name.

FOR ABOUT 1 PINT JAR (1LB/450G)

¾ cup/9oz/250g *biber salçasi* (see opposite)

1 tablespoon tomato paste

1 teaspoon chili flakes

½ teaspoon ground cumin

1 teaspoon ground fenugreek seeds

½ teaspoon ground cinnamon

¼ teaspoon garlic powder

juice and zest of 1 lemon

2 tablespoons olive oil

Just mix all the ingredients together to a smooth paste. Use as a marinade or a sauce. Makes an excellent burger relish. *Çemen* will keep for at least 1 week in the fridge.

# Torshi Lefet
## PINK PICKLED TURNIPS

This pickle is worth making for the color alone (just don't call me shallow, now will you?). These are a Lebanese and Syrian staple, although I am sure that we sell as many in the store for their appearance as their potential flavor. I have already sung the virtues of turnips and beets to you: we really should all be eating more of them, and this is a fairly painless way to do it.

FOR ROUGHLY 2 QUART JARS
(3LB 5OZ/1.5KG)
generous 2 cups/17fl oz/500ml water
3 tablespoons salt
12 small turnips (approx. 3lb 5oz/1.5kg)

3 small beets
3–4 garlic cloves
big handful of celery tops
generous 2 cups/17fl oz/500ml white vinegar

First off, boil the water and salt together for about 5 minutes, then set it aside to cool. Next peel the turnips, cut each into 4–6 wedges, and then do the same for the beets. Finally peel and halve the garlic cloves.

Layer the turnips into sterilized jars, packing some beet, garlic, and celery between each layer. Combine the vinegar with the brine and pour the liquid over the vegetables, using a knife to wiggle everything into place and get rid of any air pockets. This sort of pickle doesn't like metal very much, and so if your jar has a metal lid, seal it first with some plastic wrap.

Your *torshi lefet* will be ready in about 2 weeks, and will keep for up to 6 months. It is great as a *mezze* dish, or as an accompaniment to pastry dishes such as *Piroshki* (see p.14).

*Harissa*

# HOMEMADE HARISSA

Harissa is probably the hottest hot chili sauce in the world. We're talking *seriously* hot. Middle Eastern cuisine is known for its subtlety as a general rule, but when it gets hot you know about it.

The beauty of making your own sauce is that you can control the heat. And the process is pretty good for clearing the sinuses while you are at it. Please read my guide to chili usage (p.192) before you get too carried away, though—and work in a well-ventilated room, or you could end up choking.

This works just as well if not better with dried chilies.

FOR 2 ½-PINT JARS (1LB/450G)

9oz/250g fresh hot chilies (or 7oz/200g dried whole chilies)

1 tablespoon caraway seeds

1 tablespoon cumin seeds

1 tablespoon coriander seeds

1 heaped teaspoon smoked paprika

4–5 garlic cloves, peeled

1 tablespoon tomato paste

1 teaspoon salt

juice of ½ lemon

glug of nice olive oil

If you are using dried chilies you will need to soak them in water for about 1 hour. Either way, you should remove the calices of the peppers, and some, if not all, of the seeds.

Dry-fry (i.e. toast) the spice seeds for a few minutes, being careful not to let them burn. And then put the chilies, spices, garlic, tomato paste, salt, and lemon juice in a blender. Whizz until smooth-ish, and then trickle in a little olive oil to make it even smoother. Check the seasoning (carefully—this is not the sort of compound that will have you licking the bowl); you will probably want to add a pinch more salt.

Store the paste in sterilized jars in the fridge: like a lot of sauces, a little olive oil poured across the surface will prevent mold from growing. Your homemade harissa should last for a couple of months.

Harissa is great as an accompaniment to couscous, although it is so hot I usually dilute it a little with some chopped tomatoes. It is also great with pizzas, paninis, as a marinade, or snuck into salad dressing.

# Limon Mekhalel

# PRESERVED LEMONS

Gosh, we sell a lot of these. Hardly surprising with the huge rise in the popularity of Morocco as a vacation and culinary destination: this is one of the most distinctive flavors of the Maghreb, and one of the main ingredients of tagine cookery.

They are readily available in stores, but they are also really easy to make at home. Here's how, if you want to give it shot.

FOR 1 QUART JAR (2LB 4OZ/1KG)
12 small unwaxed lemons (plus a few spare
   lemons of any variety)

4 tablespoons salt
1 bay leaf
about 6 peppercorns

Rinse the lemons, and then quarter them lengthwise to within ½in (1cm) of the base. Let me put that another way: do not cut all the way through. Pull the four segments of each one slightly apart and rub the exposed flesh generously with salt. Pack the salted fruits upside down into a big sterilized jar, pushing down so that a fair bit of the juice is squeezed out. Sprinkle in any remaining salt together with the bay leaf and the pepper. If there seems to be insufficient juice, push down harder: if that fails, then juice your reserve stock of lemons until the jar is topped up. Seal, not forgetting a layer of plastic wrap if your lid is metal. Your lemon preserve will be ready in about 1 month.

Apart from chopping them into tagines, try squidging them into salad dressings. And the not-entirely-vegetarians among you may find them delectable with fish.

## Variations:

You can spice these up a bit if you want—cloves, cinnamon, and coriander seeds are all optional extras. Commercially preserved lemons often have *safflower* added to make them an extra-pretty shade of yellow. But this is one culinary process that is, I think, best kept simple.

# Muraba-e-Murch-e-Surkh wa Piaz
## ONION, CHILI, AND MINT MARMALADE

This is a cracking relishy jammy type thing to have in your pantry. It is cool and spicy and sweet and sour all at the same time. We enjoy it with feta-style cheese and warm flatbread as a fancy cheese sandwich, but there are numerous uses for it. Try it with crispy fried vegetables, or spread on naan with melty goat cheese as a dinner party appetizer.

MAKES 2 PINT JARS (2LB/900G)

2½ cups/20fl oz/600ml water

1lb 2oz/500g superfine sugar

¾in/2cm knob fresh ginger, peeled and chopped

big handful fresh mint leaves, washed and roughly shredded

juice and zest of 2 (unwaxed) limes

2 large red onions, peeled

3 tablespoons brown sugar

7oz/200g assorted chilies of choice, washed, beheaded, and chopped

2 tablespoons balsamic vinegar

Put the water and sugar in a "non-reactive" (i.e. non-aluminum) pan, and bring it to a boil. Add the ginger and set to simmer. When the syrup starts to thicken, take it off the heat and add the mint, lime juice, and rind.

In the meantime, slice the onions finely and heat them in a frying pan together with the brown sugar and the chilies: stir regularly so that it doesn't burn or stick. When the vegetables start to caramelize (after about 20 minutes), add the balsamic vinegar; simmer for a few minutes more and take off the heat. Stir the red onions into the syrup, mix really really well, and then spoon into sterilized jars while still fairly warm, and seal. This is ready to rock and roll straight away but will keep for 3–4 months. Dare you to eat it for breakfast.

# Harosset

## GOOEY DATE PRESERVE

*He who ate the Sultan's raisins will pay them back as dates.* (Arabic proverb)

### On Dates

Hard to overstate the importance of dates in the Middle East. The first attempts at cultivation appear to have been in what we now know as Southern Iraq around 4000 BC, but the date palm is to be found all the way across Veggiestan.

Its popularity has as much to do with its very modest growing requirements and nutritional value as anything else. Dates are full of friendly carbohydrates and potassium, making them excellent food for traveling traders and wandering Bedouins, as well as the fast-breaking food of choice for Muslims during Ramadan. The fact that the tree has such deep roots and broad leaves makes it perfect for arid climes, as it indicates water, while providing both shade and food.

Marital demands compel me to assure you that the Iranian Bam date is in every way superior; it is gooey and chocolatey and really luxurious in flavor. But in truth there is a date to suit every taste out there (believe it), from the fulsome fruitiness of the Moroccan variety to the honied stickiness of Saudi dates to the gee-I'm-bigger-than-you swagger of their Californian cousins.

This recipe contains both. It is basically a Jewish recipe, enjoyed as part of the *Seder* at the beginning of the Passover. Like many of the foods consumed at this time, it is deeply symbolic: the word is derived from the Hebrew word for clay, and the dish is said to represent the clay of the Nile and the bricks that the enslaved Israelites were forced to make.

I haven't included many Jewish recipes in the book (there are many brilliant recipe books out there to take care of that), but *harosset* (or *charoset*) seems to me to contain the very essence of the Middle East, right down to its regional and seasonal variations. The date is one of the first of foods, and to many the best of foods, and this is a great way to enjoy it.

It is a really hearty preserve: more a spread than a jam. Enjoy with *matzos* or flatbread, or as a sweet relish with rich savory dishes.

### MAKES ABOUT 3 CUPS/750ML

generous 1¼ cups/9oz/250g soft pitted dates, chopped
1½ cups/9oz/250g raisins
2 apples, peeled, cored and sliced
1 teaspoon cinnamon
1 teaspoon allspice
scant ½ cup/3½fl oz/100ml Passover wine, or a sweet wine such as Madeira or Marsala
1 cup/3½oz/100g shelled walnuts, roughly chopped

Place the dates and raisins in a bowl and add enough warm water just to cover it. Leave to soak overnight.

On the following day, put the fruit together with the water in which it was soaked into a pan. Add the apple slices and the spice, and heat it gently. Cook for about 20 minutes, stirring constantly with a wooden spoon to squidge all the ingredients together. You should end up with a thick, fairly smooth paste. Take off the heat and allow to cool, then stir in the wine and walnuts.

# Gul Reçeli
## TURKISH ROSE PETAL JAM

This is gorgeous. So pretty, so fragrant. It is a close rival for the Number One slot on my Top Ten list of things to have on toast. But quite apart from its uses at breakfast and teatime, try using it in bread and butter pudding (make jam sandwiches and soak them in rose-water scented egg mix), or in cakes, or cookies, or with ice cream.

It is easy to buy ready-made but I do feel that we should be doing more than popping roses in vases and cooing over them. Ideally you should pick roses at dawn: they are at their freshest and most fragrant then. But this might give you the reputation of being a bit of a crank—depends on how twitchy your neighbors are. And you might need to harvest the neighbors' roses too, come to think of it.

FOR 2–3 PINT JARS
(ABOUT 2LB 4OZ–3LB/1–1.3KG)
1lb/450g unsprayed pink or red rose petals

1lb 5oz/600g sugar
2½ cups/20fl oz/600ml water
juice of 1 lemon

Trim the white base part of the petals and discard—this can result in unwanted bitterness (both in the jam and the chef). Wash the remaining petals gently, looking especially carefully for any multi-legged wildlife. Mix the damp petals with the sugar, cover, and leave overnight.

The next day, add the rose sugar to the water in a heavy-bottomed pan, bring to a boil, and set to simmer for about 20 minutes. Add the lemon juice, bring to a boil, and bubble for 5 minutes, or until the mixture is really quite thick. (If it does not seem to be rosy enough for your liking, now is the time to cheat and add a bit of rose water.) To test if it is of the right consistency, drop a little of the jam on to a cold saucer—if it sets and crackles, it is ready. Skim off any foam on the top of the jam (foam means air bubbles, and air bubbles mean potential mold), and pour it into sterilized jars. It should keep for 4–5 months.

## Talking Roses

*Of what use will be a dish of roses to thee?*
*Take a leaf from my rose-garden:*
*A flower endures but five or six days,*
*But this rose garden is always delightful.*

So wrote the Persian poet Sa'adi in the 13th century. He is right, of course, but don't let that put you off making the lovely jam above. I cite him by way of illustrating how very important the cult of the rose is in the Middle East. So important that Sa'adi wrote an enormous volume of poetry entitled *The Rose Garden* (*Gulistan*).

The rose was one of the most important metaphors for medieval writers—and with good reason. Not only are the flowers consumed as a medicinal tea, but they are of course the source of rose water. And rose water gets just about everywhere. Sweets, pastries, milkshakes, compôte, jams, creamed puddings—these are but the obvious uses for this fragrant distillate. In Sa'adi's day it was common for tired travelers to be offered rose-scented water to wash their hands or feet. But if that doesn't grab you, it is great for the skin: use it as a toner as it is mildly astringent. Or try a few drops in your iron, or in your ice tray. Just make sure you keep some in your pantry.

# Incir Reçeli
## FIG JAM WITH CHOPPED PISTACHIOS

Fig jam is pretty good stuff, whether you make it with fresh or dried figs. But, to be honest, fresh figs rarely sit around long enough in our house to make it to the jam pan, and so this recipe uses dried figs. Use squidgy Turkish-style dried figs rather than the baby Iranian ones.

Enjoy this with cheese, or in oatmeal, or why not be really radical and have it spread on bread and butter ...

SHOULD FILL AROUND 2
PINT JARS (2LB/900G)
2½ cups/1lb 2 oz/500g sugar
generous 2 cups/17fl oz/500ml water
1lb 2oz/500g dried figs

juice of 1 lemon
½ teaspoon ground aniseed
⅔ cup/3½oz/100g chopped pistachios (or almonds)
⅔ cup/3½oz/100g pine nuts

Put the sugar and the water in a pan and bring to a boil. Take any stalky bits off the figs, and chop them roughly, then add them to the pan with the lemon juice and the aniseed. Set to simmer, stirring regularly. Once the figs are soft (which should take about 30 minutes), add the nuts, cook for a few more minutes and then take off the heat. Cool a little, and then pour the jam into sterilized jars. Seal tightly. This should keep for up to 6 months.

# Moraba-ye-Kadu va Hail
## PUMPKIN JAM WITH GARAM MASALA

Pumpkin is a bit of a floozy, as vegetables go: it puts itself around and will go with practically anything. Hence its ability to go from soup to jam with ease.

This recipe reflects the Middle Eastern love of contrast, although its appearance in this tome perhaps has more to do with our own fascination with food used in unusual ways…

TO MAKE ABOUT 3 PINT JARS
1 fat pumpkin, about 3lb 5oz/1.5kg
2lb 4oz/1kg sugar
2 tablespoons garam masala

1¾oz/50g chopped fresh ginger
juice and zest of 2 lemons
about 1¼ cups/10fl oz/300ml water

First skin the pumpkin. (This always takes far longer than it should and involves a lot of huffing and puffing.) Remove the seeds and set them to one side, and then dice the flesh fairly finely. Mix the sugar with the garam masala, ginger, and the lemon zest and then layer it in a bowl together with the pumpkin. Drizzle the lemon juice over the top, cover the bowl, and leave somewhere cool overnight. This allows the flavors to mingle, and also draws some of the natural juice out of the pumpkin.

The next day, put the sugary pumpkin into a pan, add the water, and bring to a boil. Turn the heat down and bubble gently until the pumpkin has turned quite translucent, and the syrup is thick. Allow to cool slightly before pouring into sterilized jars. Toasting the reserve seeds with salt gives you a great snack—but I toast them without salt and drop a few into each jar of jam just before I seal them. Store in the fridge.

# desserts
## (because vegetarians need sweets too)

Like most ruthless and cynical retailers, we keep our best bits by the register and in full view: in our case, this is our range of tantalizing Lebanese pastries and Persian *shirinee*.

An old Persian story tells of a farmer traveling in to town to sell his wares. On passing a noted patisserie, he spies the storekeeper sitting in the doorway, sunning himself. In the window are cakes and cookies galore, moist, appetizing, beckoning. Approaching the man, he makes as if to jab his two fingers into the guy's eyes. The shopkeeper naturally recoils in shock and asks the farmer what on earth he thought he was doing, or words to that effect. The farmer apologizes, saying that he had wanted to check if the sweet seller was, in fact, blind: he could not see how the man could otherwise work in the shop without eating all the goodies on display.

Arabs and Indo-Iranians actually rarely consume dessert, as in something sweet after a meal. That is not at all the same as saying that they don't have a sweet tooth: they are guilty of some of the most heinous sugar crimes in the world, in fact. *Baklava*! Honey balls! *Halva*! And during the more opulent reigns of the more opulent leaders/despots/shahs/pharaohs (especially those decadent Ottomans), sorbets and syrups were a necessary part of the feasting.

Sweet things are more or less the constant companion of the teapot. They are also scoffed as anytime treats, or as something to fortify and energize an empty belly during Ramadan. And they are also a way of celebrating. If you are visiting someone's house, take a box of fresh pastries. If you have had good news—passed an exam, bought a new car, been given a new cookbook—it is customary to share the good fortune in the form of sweetmeats.

Anyway, there is nothing stopping you from enjoying the following as dessert. We do.

# NOAH'S PUDDING

This is simply glorious. And it's another recipe with a story attached. The tale goes that supplies on the Ark were just about finished when it went aground on Mount Ararat. Hoping to eke out a final repast while the flood waters were subsiding, Mrs. Noah literally emptied all of the ship's stores and cooked it into this—one magnificent, nutritious pudding.

Still to this day in Turkey it is seen as a meal to share, and is usually made by the vat-full. It is consumed during the holy time of *Muharram*, which is the first month of the Islamic calendar. The name *Aşure* refers to the tenth day of *Muharram*, which is a day of mourning and reflection, especially for Shi'ia Muslims because it is the day on which Imam Hussayn was martyred.

The pudding was originally made with bulgar, but barley is my grain of choice because it cooks so well. This is one of those splendid recipes in which you can substitute ingredients to suit the contents of your pantry.

SERVES 10

scant ½ cup/1¾oz/50g navy (haricot) beans, and
scant ¾ cup/2¾oz/75g chickpeas, and
scant ½ cup/1¾oz/50g kidney beans, and
generous 2 cups/8oz/225g pot barley or pearl
    barley, all soaked in water overnight
⅓ cup/2¾oz/75g short grain rice, and
3½oz/100g chopped dried apricots, and
scant ⅓ cup/1¾oz/50g raisins, and
scant ⅓ cup/1¾oz/50g golden raisins, and
scant ⅓ cup/1¾oz/50g currants, and
¼ cup/1¾oz/50g dried chopped figs, all
    soaked in water for 30 minutes

generous ½ cup/1¾oz/50g blanched,
    chopped almonds
½ cup/1¾oz/50g chopped walnuts
2¼ cups/1lb/450g sugar
1 tablespoon cornstarch
scant ½ cup/3½fl oz/100ml rose water

TO DECORATE:

2 tablespoons fresh pomegranate
1 tablespoon pine nuts
1 tablespoon chopped pistachios
5–6 dried apricots, sliced real pretty

Cook the beans and chickpeas (about 45 minutes should do it), then drain them. Place the barley together with the water in which it has been soaking into a big pan, and bring to a boil. After 15 minutes, add the rice. After a further 15 minutes, add the cooked beans/peas, and the chopped fruit and nuts. Allow to cook for another 15 minutes, then add the sugar. Then blend a little of the hot barley water with the cornstarch and add this to the pudding, mixing well. Finally stir in the rose water and, if it is looking too thick, dilute with more water or a splash of milk. Let it cook through for a few minutes more, then take off the heat.

This is traditionally served cold, but I rather like it hot with a when-no-one's-looking-dash of cream. Anyway, to be authentic, pour the *aşure* into a bowl, sprinkle with the garnish, and pop it in the fridge to chill.

# Siwayan

# NOODLEY PUDDING

Do you dream in food? There are certain memorable dishes, meals, and taste sensations that stick with you, I find. This is one of those. Creamy, custardy, spiced: oh yes. When I make this it is mine-all-mine.

It is actually from the Eastern limits of Veggiestan: Pakistan. But it was introduced to me by one of my Kashmiri customers. While Pakistani cuisine strongly resembles Indian food, the Kashmiri kitchen owes more to its position on the Silk Road, with elements of Afghan and Persian spicing and a huge range of possibly-not-entirely-indigenous ingredients. Which also probably explains why my Kashmiri greengrocer, Mr Imtiaz, is so knowledgeable about the world's weirder vegetables and what to do with them. It would have been hard to write this tome without him.

SERVES 4

4½oz/125g vermicelli/rice noodles (crumbled vermicelli nests will do in a pinch)

knob of butter/ghee

½ teaspoon turmeric

½ teaspoon ground cardamom

4 cups/33fl oz/1 liter whole milk

1 tablespoon custard powder

1 cup/9fl oz/250ml condensed milk

scant ⅔ cups/3½oz/100g raisins, soaked in water for 15 minutes

⅓ cup/1¾oz/50g chopped almonds/pistachios

⅓ cup/1¾oz/50g roughly chopped cashews

Ok, so you break the noodles roughly and fry them in the butter, turning them regularly. After a few minutes, add the spices. Pour the milk into a heavy-bottomed pan, add the spiced, browned noodles and bring it all to a gentle simmer. After about 15 minutes, the noodles should be soft/cooked. Take a little of the milk and mix it with the custard powder, then stir it back in to the pan along with the condensed milk. Cook through for another 5 minutes, stirring well; if it looks a bit thick, add some water or more milk. Finally stir in the raisins and most of the nuts, retaining a few of the pistachios/almonds to decorate.

Serve hot or cold.

# Basbousa

# ARABIC SEMOLINA CAKE

Semolina cake. Hmm. This just so doesn't do this utterly divine confection justice. It's soft and nutty and syrupy with a surprisingly floral yet sharp finish—and is incredibly rich.

It is made across the Arab world (where is it also variously known as *Namoura* and *Shamali*), and crossed to Africa in the same convoy as Islam. It is a great favorite during Ramadan—the sugar rush it gives is just what those breaking fast are looking for. But it's too good to limit to one month a year. And it is really really easy to make.

Try it still warm from the oven with a drizzle of cream, crème fraîche, or ice cream.

MAKES 24–30 SQUARES
FOR THE SYRUP:
¾ cup/6fl oz/175ml water
9oz/250g sugar
juice of ½ lemon
1 teaspoon orange blossom water (traditional), or 2 teaspoons rose water

FOR THE CAKE:
scant 1½ cups/5½oz/150g unsalted butter

generous 2 cups/14oz/400g semolina
1 teaspoon baking soda
generous 1 cup/3½oz/100g shredded coconut
generous 1 cup/3½oz/100g ground almonds
generous ⅓ cup/2¾oz/75g superfine sugar
¼ cup/2fl oz/50ml orange blossom (or ⅓ cup rose) water
⅔ cup/5fl oz/150ml plain yogurt
a handful of blanched almonds, to decorate

Firstly make the syrup. Boil the water with the sugar, lemon juice, and flower water: simmer for around 15 minutes until it turns, well, syrupy. Set aside.

Preheat the oven to 350°F/180°C.

Next melt the butter gently in a pan, stir in the semolina followed by the other dry ingredients and finally the blossom water and the yogurt.

Grease an oven dish (a springform pan is ideal), and then press the cake mixture into it. Bake in the oven for about 15 minutes, then remove from the oven and cut into squares, decorating each with a blanched almond. Pop back in the oven for another 10 minutes, or until the cake is a pleasant shade of golden brown. Carefully drizzle the syrup over the *basbousa* while it is still warm and allow it to soak in. Great with strong dark coffee, or you can serve it as a dessert. What diet?

# DESSERT COUSCOUS
## WITH DATE "TAGINE"

It is not uncommon in North Africa to eat couscous as dessert. Strange though the idea seems. Fluffed with sweet butter, steamed with rose water, and stirred through with fruit and nuts, this is an almost healthy dessert. Especially if you use whole grains. And it makes for a fabulous breakfast.

While I am all for cheating with savory couscous, this is quite a delicate dish, and so I usually improvise a couscousier using a sturdy sieve, a saucepan, some muslin, and a very clean dish towel.

SERVES 4

1 ⅔ cups/9oz/250g whole-wheat (or white, if you must) couscous

generous ¾ cup/7fl oz/200ml water

2 tablespoons rose water

scant ½ cup/3½oz/100g unsalted butter or ghee

7oz/200g soft dates, pitted

3½oz/100g raisins, pre-soaked for 30 minutes

⅔ cup/3½oz/100g chopped pistachios and almonds

⅔ cup/3½oz/100g pine nuts

½ teaspoon ground cardamom

½ teaspoon ground ginger

4 tablespoons confectioner's sugar

Firstly, place the couscous in a shallow dish and pour the water over it, mixing it well and breaking up any lumps. Set aside to soak for around 15 minutes, during which time the grains should absorb all of the liquid.

Bring around 4 cups/1 liter of water to a boil in the bottom of a saucepan (or a couscousier if you happen to own one), and then find a sieve or colander that fits snugly across the top of the pan above the level of the water. Line the sieve with muslin and spoon the soaked couscous into it. Wrap the lid of the saucepan in a clean dish towel, and leave to steam for around 20 minutes. At this point empty the couscous into a bowl, fluff it with a fork and sprinkle it with the rose water, then return it to the pan to steam for another 20 minutes.

Meanwhile, melt about half of the butter in a frying pan and stir in the dates and raisins. Add the nuts, cardamom, and ginger. Cook for 5 minutes, and then turn off the heat, cover the pan and leave the fruit to sweat.

Next melt the rest of the butter. Place the steamed couscous in a bowl, and pour the butter over it, stirring well with a fork so that each grain gets coated. Sprinkle all over with the confectioner's sugar, then make a well in the center and spoon the date tagine into it. If you indulge in this as a dessert, try serving it with ice cream or cream: if this is breakfast fare, add thick plain yogurt.

# Abrayshum Kabaub

## SILK KEBAB

This Afghan sweet is fascinating. Although the finished product looks like edible graffiti or guerilla knitting, it can actually be quite fiddly (albeit fun) to make. It is very delicate and sweet, so it should come as no surprise to learn that it is prepared mostly for special occasions. Beaten egg is streaked like silk into hot oil, bathed in spiced syrup, and then rolled into tubes to cool. These are usually cut into bite-sized pieces, but you can serve them whole filled with spiced fromage frais or frozen yogurt as a naughty-but-nice dessert.

This is largely based on Helen Saberi's recipe.

### Veggiestan Spiced Frozen Yogurt

This is great stuff: really versatile. Experiment: try replacing the cardamom with cinnamon, or adding different nuts and seeds to it. Anyway, this is especially delicious stuffed gloopily into the middle of a silk kebab.

3 cups/25fl oz/750ml thick,
    Greek style yogurt
generous ⅓ cup/2¾oz/75g sugar
½ level teaspoon ground saffron,
    steeped in a dash of
    boiling water
½ teaspoon ground ginger
½ teaspoon ground cardamom
generous ½ cup/2¾oz/75g
    chopped almonds or
    pistachios

Mix the ingredients thoroughly together, and put in a freezer-safe container. Freeze for 1 hour, mix it again and then pop it back in the freezer for at least 1 hour.

SERVES 3–4
1 cup/9fl oz/250ml water
2¼ cups/9oz/250g sugar
zest and juice of ½ lemon
¼ teaspoon ground saffron
½ teaspoon ground cardamom

splash of rose water
6 eggs
pinch salt
scant ½ cup–generous ¾ cup oil/3½–
    7fl oz/100–200ml, for frying
generous ⅓ cup/1¾oz/50g chopped pistachios

Firstly the syrup: put the water in a pan, add the sugar, lemon juice, and zest, and bring to a boil. Simmer gently for around 10 minutes, or until the mixture is syrupy. Add the saffron to a little boiling water in the base of a saucer, and then stir it into the syrup together with the cardamom and rose water. After a few minutes more, take the syrup off the heat and set to one side to cool.

Beat the eggs with a pinch of salt until they are well homogenized but not foaming. Pour the oil into a 8–10in (20–25cm) frying pan: there should be enough to cover the base to a depth of around ¾–1¼in (2–3cm). Heat it for a couple of minutes on high, and then turn it down fractionally. You want it real hot but not smoking. Next comes the tricky bit. You need to dip one hand, palm up, into the egg mix. As you withdraw it, slide it over the hot oil, and turn it so that it is now palm down. The egg will start to drizzle into the oil: as it does so, move your hand in striped patterns, creating a sort of hash-brown effect circular mesh (of around 8in/20cm in diameter) in the process. Repeat swiftly two to three times, so that the holes in the omelet are largely but not entirely filled in. Then, using a pallet knife (or two skewers), lift the part cooked "kebab" and turn it so that it is face down. Give it 30 seconds, and then lift the whole thing out, holding it above the pan to drain briefly before plunging it into the syrup for a few moments. Finally lift it on to a plate and roll it while it is still warm and malleable, preferably with the side that was cooked first facing inwards. Sprinkle the "kebab" with the chopped pistachios.

Repeat the exercise with the remaining egg—you should get 8–10 rolls altogether. Either slice each one into 3–4 pieces (nice with tea), or fill them with Veggiestan Spiced Frozen Yogurt (see left).

# AT THE VEGGIESTAN PANCAKE HOUSE

*Ataif* are pretty much ubiquitous in Arabistan. Somewhat resembling an American pancake, they are fat syrupy pancakes, which are often served sandwiched with *kishta* (or *ushta*), which is buffalo milk clotted cream.

You can make them flat, sculpt them into gateaux, or fold them around nuts and cream and then deep fry them (Elvis where are you now?).

MAKES 14–16
FOR THE PANCAKES:
1 x ¼oz/7g envelope active dry yeast
1 teaspoon sugar
about 1¾ cups/14fl oz/400ml tepid water
approx 2½ cups/9oz/250g all-purpose flour

FOR THE *ATAR*, OR SYRUP:
2½ cups/1lb 2 oz/500g sugar
1 cup/9fl oz/250ml water
1 lemon
2 tablespoons orange blossom water

All you do is sprinkle the yeast and the sugar on to about one-quarter of the water and set aside for around 10 minutes. Then sift the flour into a bowl, make a well in the middle, and pour in the yeast together with the rest of the water, mixing well with a wooden spoon. Cover the bowl with a clean cloth, and leave it somewhere warm for 1 hour so that the yeast can do that thing that it does.

In the meantime, prepare the syrup exactly as for *Kunafa Jibni* (see opposite): when it is done pop it in the fridge to chill.

After 1 hour, the batter should have swollen, and have a gloopy, primordial texture to it. Grease a frying pan with a little ghee or oil, and set on a medium heat. Once it is hot, pour in about 2 tablespoons of the batter, tipping the pan slightly so that the mixture spreads. It will not travel far—you are aiming for roughly 2¾in/7cm in diameter. When the first side is cooked (after about 1 minute), turn it over with a spatula and cook the other side. Repeat the exercise with the rest of the batter.

Dip the still warm pancakes in syrup and enjoy. Or let them cool, then dip them in syrup, and build into a pyramid sandwiched together with clotted cream and decorated with nibbed pistachios. Or stuff them …

Stuffed pancakes:
Prepare the *ataif* as above, but cook only one side of the pancake. Fill the cooked side with either chopped nuts mixed with sugar and cinnamon, or cinnamon-spiced ricotta, then pinch the edges together and deep-fry.

# Kunafa Jibni

## CHEESE PASTRIES

This is waistline-evil incarnate: we're talking pastry and cheese and syrup. And I'd even suggest making things even worse by having it with cream or ice cream. Like a lot of sweetmeats in the Middle East, it is most enjoyed during Ramadan.

It uses *kataifi* pastry: *kataif* is the stringy, Dougal-esque *baklava* that is usually filled with nuts, although this version is filled with ricotta. The pastry itself is incredibly messy to make (part-baked dough is finely shredded and then quick fried), so I happily cheat and buy ready-made frozen stuff—this is now thankfully available in Middle Eastern stores and even some supermarkets.

There are two very good reasons to make *kunafa jibna*, apart from its intrinsic deliciousness: it is ridiculously easy (assuming you have bought ready-made pastry), and it costs silly amounts of money to buy at patisseries.

SERVES 6–8
FOR THE *ATAR*, OR SYRUP:
1 cup/9fl oz/250ml water
2½ cups/1lb 2oz/500g sugar
1 lemon
2 tablespoons orange blossom water

FOR THE REST:
1lb 2oz/500g *kataifi* pastry, defrosted
2¼ sticks/9oz/250g unsalted butter, melted
2¼ cups/1lb 2oz/500g soft ricotta cheese

Firstly make the syrup: boil the water and sugar together until the mixture thickens (about 15 minutes). Pare the zest from the lemon and then juice it: the zest we will need later on, but the juice you should now add to the syrup, together with the orange blossom water. Mix well and set aside.

Preheat the oven to 350°F/180°C.

Stretch out the pastry in a shallow dish, and pour the melted butter over it. Turn the pastry over carefully, massaging the butter all over it with your fingers.

Next beat the cheese with the lemon zest.

Place about half of the pastry in a lightly greased oven dish or baking tray (1½in/4cm deep and 14 x 8in/35 x 20cm), spread the cheese mixture over it, and then top with the rest of the pastry.

Bake it in the oven for 45 minutes, or until the pastry is a pale golden brown. Once it is cooked, drench it with the *atar* while it is still hot. Allow to cool, then cut it into squares—though this is also good served hot with cream or ice cream. It keeps well for 4–5 days in the fridge, but store it wrapped up to prevent it from drying out.

# POMEGRANATE ETON MESS

Now I'm a bit angry about this dish. 'Cause I sort of invented it. And then a friend of mine in Australia said she'd read a similar recipe in the *Melbourne Times* or some such. And then the divine Nigella Lawson came out with another version of it.

Anyway, this is my recipe. Completely inauthentic but drawing upon the very finest ingredients of the Middle East. And the perfect conclusion to a Middle Eastern feast.

Eton Mess, a traditional English dessert, has to be the easiest sweet in the world to prepare. And, as this recipe shows, it is so easy to dress up.

Rose syrup is easy to find in Greek stores—ask for "*triandafilou.*"

SERVES 4

2 egg whites
½ cup/3½oz/100g superfine sugar
¼ teaspoon baking powder
(or replace the above 3 ingredients with
    4–5 store-bought meringue nests)

2 medium pomegranates
1 cup/9fl oz/250ml heavy whipping cream
2 tablespoons rose syrup
handful of rose petals (optional decoration)

*On pomegranates*

Never choose a pom because it will look good in your fruit bowl; generally speaking the ones with the tauter, drier skins and the slightly angular shape are best. Size is immaterial—the smaller ones are often the sweetest.

Ideally you should do as the above recipe suggests: pummel the fruit gently, make a hole in the flesh, and either stick a straw straight in or drain the juice into a glass. Then open up the rest of the fruit and, using your thumbs, carefully break the rest of the seeds into a bowl. Pick out any bits of pith as you go: it is very good for you, and made into a tea in the Middle East, but it is really incredibly bitter. Chill the seeds and eat with a spoon. Or use them in one of the range of pomegranate-flavored recipes in this tome.

Meringues first. Preheat your oven to 325°F/160°C. Whip the egg whites until they start to peak, and then fold in the sugar little by little, followed by the baking powder. Line a baking tray with parchment paper, and then spoon the mixture on to it in random blobs—the finished product is to be broken up anyway, and so appearance and uniformity are irrelevant.

Turn the oven down to 250°F/120°C, and pop the tray in there for 2 hours. If you have time on your side, and the luxury of a warm, dry linen cupboard at home, take the meringues out of the oven a little earlier, cover them lightly with a cloth, and leave them in the linen cupboard overnight—this will get you the perfect, light finish.

Next to the pomegranates. Take one in both hands and gently knead it all around with your thumbs: you will be able to feel the seeds inside popping as you go. Do not do this too vigorously, as you may burst the skin, which will at the very least splatter you with largely indelible red juice. After a couple of minutes, make a small incision in the skin of the pomegranate, and invert it over a glass: you should now be able to squeeze out the juice from all the seeds you have burst. Now that the tension in the skin has been eased, it will be easy to pry the fruit open, and you will be able to crumble all the intact seeds into a bowl. Repeat this exercise with the other pomegranate.

Next, whip the cream together with the rose syrup and the pomegranate juice. Such a pretty pink, no?

Assembly time. Don't do this until just before you want to serve—the whole thing will sink slowly if you do it too early. Break the meringue roughly into the rose cream, and then stir in most of the pomegranate seeds. Arrange a few rose petals around your chosen serving dish, pile the Eton Mess into the center, and strew with the reserved pom seeds.

# Halwah

## CARROT AND RICOTTA *HALVA*

*Halwah* is a very confusing concept. You probably think of it as that nice sesame stuff that you get on good nights at the Greek restaurant, right? The word actually just means "sweetmeat" in Arabic, and is applied to a whole range of gooey substances, not all of them especially yummy. Iranian *halva*, for example, is barely more than a sweetened roux. Quite yucky.

Carrot *halwah/halva* crops up a lot in the more easterly parts of the Middle East: our version owes a little to Indian sweet-making, but this recipe is nine tenths Afghan.

This is far too rich to have as a dessert, actually. But it makes for a terrific and unusual *petit four*. And it is incredibly wholesome. I have served it as a tart by piling it into a pie crust: just serve some crème fraîche on the side …

We have already met Mullah Nasruddin, aka Juha or Hoja, the clown philosopher of Veggiestan. The story goes that he wasn't too successful at making *halwah*, although he was very partial to the carrot variety above. When his friends asked him how come he had never made it, even though it was so easy, he replied that he simply had trouble getting all the ingredients together.

"When there are carrots in the house, I can't find the ricotta," he cried. "And when there is ricotta in the fridge we're all out of carrots. The only time that they're ever in the house together seems to be when I'm out and thus unable to make it …"

SERVES 6, OR *PETIT FOURS*
FOR 20
6 large carrots (about 1lb 2 oz/500g), peeled
    and then topped and tailed
scant ½ cup/3½fl oz/100ml milk
1oz/30g sour orange peel, blanched in hot
    water for 5 minutes (optional)
2¾oz/75g vegetable ghee (or butter)

¼ teaspoon cardamom powder
1¾ cups/12oz/350g sugar
1½ cups/12oz/350g ricotta
1 cup/3½oz/100g powdered milk
⅓ cup/1¾oz/50g chopped almonds
1¾oz/50g chopped pistachios
scant ⅓ cup/1¾oz/50g raisins, soaked in cold
    water for 20 minutes and drained

Simple stuff, this. The carrots are traditionally grated, but I prefer to lob them in the blender along with the milk and the blanched orange peel to get a smoother finish.

Melt the ghee/butter in a heavy-bottomed pan, and tip the carroty mixture in, along with the cardamom, sweating it on a low heat until the carrots are cooked through (20–25 minutes should do the trick). Stir in the sugar and cook a little more until the sugar has dissolved.

In the meantime, blend the ricotta with the powdered milk, and beat this into the hot carrot mix. Cook gently until the mixture is thick and creamy, then stir in most of the nuts and raisins.

This can be enjoyed hot, or pressed into a shallow dish, chilled and served cold. Use the remaining nuts as a garnish.

# Vişne Şerbet

## SOUR CHERRY SORBET
## WITH PISTACHIO WAFERS

Sour cherries are really big in Iran (where they are called *albaloo*) and Turkey (where they are known as *visne*). They are nearly the same thing as morello cherries.

The sour cherry season (mid-summer) lasts about five minutes, and so in Iran every household goes into a frenzy of domestic goddessness, pickling and salting, juicing and conserving. The cherries are sour enough to be a tart accompaniment to many savory dishes, as well as making great syrup and jam. Persian taste buds are kinda weird—they also enjoy the fruit semi-dried with salt. Buy fresh when you see them as they freeze beautifully. If you can't get Turkish or Iranian sour cherries, buy the morello variety.

SERVES 6
FOR THE SORBET:
1lb 2oz/500g sour cherries
½ cup/3½oz/100g superfine sugar
zest and juice of 1 lemon
2 egg whites

AND FOR THE "WAFERS":
2 egg whites
½ cup/3½oz/100g superfine sugar
⅓ cup /1¾oz/50g all-purpose flour
3½ tablespoons/1¾oz/50g cool melted butter
few drops almond essence (optional)
scant ¾ cup/2¾oz/75g chopped pistachios

Sour cherries first: Wash and sort through them, removing the stones and any stalks. Put them in a pan with 1 cup/9fl oz/250ml water and the sugar and cook gently for 20 minutes. Then take off the heat and press the mixture through a sieve. Add the lemon rind and juice, and bring to a boil for a further 5 minutes, then pour into a freezer-safe container. Allow the mixture to cool, then place the container in the freezer. After 1 hour, whisk the egg whites until they peak, and then fold them into the semi-frozen sorbet, mixing well. Put back in the freezer for at least another 3 hours.

Next the wafers. This recipe will give you about 25—if you just want enough for your sorbet, halve the ingredients. But they are great with coffee, so I recommend making extra…

Whisk the egg whites (but not too vigorously), and then sift and beat in the sugar and flour followed by the butter and essence. Mix well, then dollop spoonfuls of the mixture on to a greased baking tray. Smooth and shape the dollops into 2–2½in (5–6cm) diameter rounds, and scatter the pistachios on top. Bake at 350°F/180°C for 8 minutes, or until they are a pale golden brown (but still soft in the middle), and then cool them on a wire rack. If you have the time and the inclination, you can drape the still warm wafers over a rolling pin or clean bottle: they will thus assume a pretty curved shape. (You can then call these "tuiles" and everyone will be frightfully impressed.)

The wafers will keep for a couple of weeks in an airtight container.

# Budza bil Halwah

## *HALVA* ICE CREAM WITH CHOCOLATE SPICE SAUCE

The *halva* in this recipe is the kind to which we are most accustomed in the West: the sesame stuff. It is a rich confection, to the extent that it is impossible to eat more than a few mouthfuls. (No, that wasn't a challenge; please don't—you'll make yourself sick.) But chunk it into this ice cream and suddenly it becomes far more manageable. Add the warm spiced sauce and we are talking dessert battlefield, as in you really won't want to share.

Use any sort of *halva*: vanilla, pistachio, or chocolate, Greek or Turkish or Arabic.

SERVES 6

FOR THE ICE CREAM:

9oz/250g *halva*

½ cup/4fl oz/125ml whole milk

½ cup/3½oz/100g sugar

generous 2 cups/17fl oz/500ml heavy whipping cream

FOR THE SAUCE:

1 cup/9fl oz/250ml water

scant 1 cup/6oz/175g superfine sugar

2 cinnamon sticks

2 cloves

1 teaspoon chopped fresh ginger

3 star anise

6 peppercorns (or chili flakes, if you're feeling really adventurous)

9 squares/9oz/250g good quality dark chocolate

2 tablespoons/1 oz/30g butter

First the ice cream. Cut half the *halva* into small cubes, wrap in plastic wrap and freeze. Put the rest of the *halva* in a blender, give it a quick pulse, and then add the milk and sugar, mixing gently for about 2 minutes, then add the cream. Blend so that the mixture is thick without becoming clotted in appearance.

Pour into a freezer safe container, cover, and freeze for 1 hour. After this period is up, mix in the *halva* chunks and place it back in the freezer.

Next the sauce. Put the water and the sugar in a pan, and bring to a boil. Set to simmer, and lob in the spices. Bubble gently for 15 minutes, or until the liquid is quite syrupy. Then turn off the heat and allow to sit for at least 30 minutes: this gives the spices a better opportunity to mingle and get to know each other. Next strain the syrup into another pan and put back on the heat. Crumble the chocolate into it, and when this has dissolved whisk in the butter.

Either serve this hot over the ice cream (oh my!), or pop the ice cream in the fridge for 20 minutes, then serve and top it with cool sauce (the logical and decorous option).

# PECKHAM DELIGHT

This is of course really Turkish Delight—*lokum*. But for some reason, the Turks have failed to seek or gain PGI—Protected Geographical Indication (only the humorless, sexless, senseless, soul-less European Union could come up with such dry nomenclature). This means that any Mehmet, Mahmoud, or Malcolm can, and does, make the stuff. The Cypriots, on the other hand, have patented Cyprus Delight. And the Iranians call their Persian Delight by an entirely different name—*baslogh*—and indeed make it using a somewhat different method.

Anyway, to me one of the biggest delights about this most famous of confections is that it is actually vegan. The second is that in its most basic incarnation it is very simple to make. The third has been in convincing wide-eyed children that, as a vendor of Turkish Delight through my store in Peckham, I am in fact the White Witch in disguise.

So this is our recipe. Just five ingredients. Brilliant.

MAKES A TRAYFUL

2½ cups/500g 1lb 2oz sugar
2½ cups/16fl oz/600ml water
1 cup /3½oz/100g confectioner's sugar
generous ⅔ cup/3½oz/100g cornstarch

scant ½ cup /3½fl oz/100ml rose water
few drops of pink food coloring, or
      1 tablespoon rose syrup or grenadine
      (optional)

Place the sugar and water in a pan, and bring to a boil. Set to simmer for around 15 minutes, stirring regularly.

In the meantime, prepare a shallow tray (¾in/2cm deep and 8 x 8in/20 x 20cm as a rough guide): line it with wax paper, and then liberally dust the paper with about half the confectioner's sugar and a quarter of the cornstarch.

Mix around 1¾oz/50g of the remaining cornstarch with a little water, and then tip a little of the hot syrup into it. Stir well, and then pour the whole thing back into the syrup pan along with the rose water and the coloring, if using. Continue to stir until the mixture is pleasantly gloopy: you can tell when it is ready by dropping a tiny bit into cold water—it should form a ball.

Take it off the heat and allow it to cool a little, then pour it into the prepared tray. Cover with a clean cloth/piece of paper towel and allow to cool completely. Finally sift the rest of the confectioner's sugar and cornstarch together on a tray. Turn the set *lokum* out upside down on to the tray, and cut it into cubes. Roll the pieces gently in the sugary flour, and then store in a dry, airtight container.

Enjoy with Turkish coffee. And lean forward when you eat it: otherwise, you will end up with a telltale trail of confectioner's sugar across your cleavage/paunch.

*Variations on the theme:*

Replace the rose water with the juice and zest of 1 lemon for lemon *lokum*.

Or stir in chopped pistachios, chopped hazelnuts, or walnut pieces for nutty delights.

# IN AN ARABIC CANDY STORE

An awful lot of confectionery today is held together with gelatin: the hidden enemy of the vegetarian. As gelatin is not for the most part *halal* either, Middle Eastern sweets are often a viable alternative for the vegetarian with a sugar habit.

They have the thrifty custom of puréeing and drying all fruit bi-products into fruit leather, which is the world's healthiest treat for children. In Iran this is known as *lavashak*, and comes in a huge variety of flavors. The Arabs make *amardine*, which is a squidgy apricot paste: it can be used to make apricot tart, or as a counterpoint with rich savory dishes, but it is used most often as a snack, or dissolved in water to make a creamy fruity drink.

It is easy to make your own fruit paste: wash your fruit, and remove the less ingestible parts (seeds, stalks, and the peel of anything tougher than a peach). Boil it with a splash of water (a ratio of about eight parts fruit to one of water is good), sugar to taste (easy on this), a squeeze of lemon juice, and, if you like, some cinnamon or nutmeg. After about 20 minutes, or when the fruit is well cooked, blend the contents. Line a baking tray with parchment paper and pour the purée on to it in a very thin layer. Place it in the oven on the lowest setting for 1 hour or so, and then leave it somewhere warm to dry out overnight.

The other trick is to use mastic or gum Arabic to inject chewiness. I get confused customers asking for both, so I outline below what I have learned thus far.

GUM ARABIC is one of the world's most extensively used hidden ingredients. It is a resin and thus entirely natural. It is in greatest demand in the printing trade, but it is also to be found in cosmetics and pharmaceuticals. In the food industry it is prized for its ability to stabilize other ingredients, ensuring that they remain suspended in fluid and preventing crystallization. While it appears a lot in packaged food, it is hard to find in stores: if you find a recipe that calls for it, I'd be inclined to cheat.

MASTIC, on the other hand, is widely available in Middle Eastern stores. This is the original chewing gum, and has a strong, curiously antiseptic flavor. It is used as a thickener in ice creams and sauces, and a flavoring in plain *lokum* and some cheeses and bread. In the Maghreb, it is even used to flavor water: a pitcher is inverted over a slow-burning fire into which a handful of mastic has been tossed. After 30 minutes, the vessel will be infused with resinous scent, to the extent that it flavors any water set to chill in it thereafter. To use mastic in the kitchen, it is best to grind it to a powder.

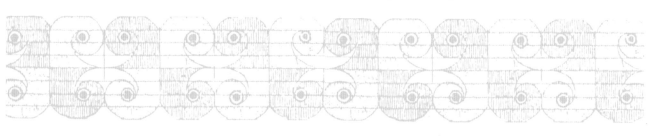

# Ma'amoul

## DATE PASTRIES WITH FIGGY ICE CREAM

*Ma'amoul* are the Arab World's "other" dessert—well, I mean, everybody knows *baklava*, but these little datey, nutty pastries are not perhaps quite as familiar. In my ignorance, I used to regard *ma'amoul* as the ugly sister, mousy and uninteresting, something to be left on the shelf. Well, like many of the more restrained, classier things in life, the subtle butteriness of *ma'amoul* is actually infinitely more appealing than the floozy-ish, syrupy sweetness of *baklava*. The pastry melts in the mouth like shortbread, and the filling is oh-so-tasty. And when they are served just a tad warm with our sensuous fig ice cream, well, what can I say? It's the sort of dessert for the love of which a girl might just skip the main course.

The basic recipe for this is from Dina Foods, our Lebanese bakers, but I have interfered with it a bit. Fresh Iranian dates will make your life easier—they are good and soft. I should also recommend unsalted butter, but I like salted in this context.

SERVES 6
FOR THE PASTRY:
3⅓ cups/1 lb 2oz/500g all-purpose flour
generous 1 cup/7oz/200g semolina
½ teaspoon ground cardamom
1 teaspoon ground allspice
3 sticks/12oz/350g butter
3–4 tablespoons of rose water or orange
    blossom water

3–4 tablespoons milk or water
confectioner's sugar, for sifting

FOR THE FILLING:
2½ cups/1 lb 2 oz/500g pitted chopped dates
7oz/200g finely chopped your-nut-of-choice
    (I do walnuts)
1 teaspoon ground cinnamon

Sift the flour into a bowl, mix in the semolina and the spices, and then chop the butter into the mix and rub it through with the tips of your fingers. Add the flower water, and then beat in enough milk to make the dough cling together in a soft, tactile ball. Cover with a clean dish towel and leave to sit for about 30 minutes.

Meanwhile, make the filling: to be honest, I just squidge it all together with my hands. Handy hint: if you are using dried dates, you can make them more malleable by putting them in a small pan, sploshing them with 1–2 tablespoons water, and bringing them to a simmer for 10 minutes.

To form the *ma'amoul*: they should look rather like baby, ridged traffic cones, so break off a little piece of the dough, cup it in your hand, and then use a finger to create a well in it. Press a little of the filling into the middle of each, and then close the pastry around it, flattening it off so that you can turn it upside down and sit it on a baking tray. To get that authentic, ridged look, run a fork gently down the sides of the cone. (If you like this recipe, it is worth investing in a *ma'amoul* mold—you'll not only save yourself time, but you'll also gain one of those kitchen thingamabobs that any avid cook likes to collect.)

*(continues overleaf)*

Bake the *ma'amoul* at 325°F/160°C for about 20 minutes, or until they acquire just the faintest golden hue: it is important not to overcook them, or they will be awfully hard and dry once they cool. Let them cool a little and then dredge them with confectioner's sugar before serving with the ice cream.

FOR THE ICE CREAM:
2lb 4 oz/1 kg fresh figs (16–20)
zest and juice of 1 (unwaxed) lemon

¾ cup/5½oz/150g sugar
1 cup/9fl oz/250ml extra-heavy (or heavy whipping) cream

Remove the knobbly bits from the figs, and quarter them. Pop them into a saucepan with ⅔ cup/5fl oz/150ml water and the lemon zest, cover and cook gently, stirring occasionally, for 8–10 minutes, or until the figs look lovely and soft and inviting.

Next add the sugar, bring the liquid up to bubbling, and cook until the mixture becomes jammy. Allow to cool, then beat together with the cream and lemon juice to taste. Pour into a freezer safe container and freeze for 1 hour. After this time, churn it up again, and then pop it back into the freezer. Remove it from the freezer 10 minutes before serving.

# AFGHAN ANGEL DELIGHT

This fragrant moussey stuff really is comfort food, enjoyed in Iran and Afghanistan (where it is called *firnee*). Another version of it, *ke kül*, is made in Turkey. It is often made for *iftar*, breaking-fast, during Ramadan, but it is patently a childhood favorite.

Iranians enjoy this warm and a little runny, while Afghans go for set and chilled. This is a cross-border recipe, which, *inshallah*, draws upon the best of both.

SERVES 6–8
3 cups/24fl oz/750ml milk
2 tablespoons rose water
½ cup/2¾oz/75g rice flour or cornstarch

⅓ teaspoon ground saffron
1 level teaspoon ground cardamom
generous ⅓ cup/2¾oz/75g sugar
sprinkling of chopped pistachios and almonds

Splosh about ¼ cup/2fl oz/50ml of the milk into a bowl and set aside. Put the rest on to warm gently in a pan together with the rose water. Blend the rice flour into the reserved milk, add a little of the warm milk from the pan, and then tip all of the contents of the bowl back into the pan, stirring well.

Pour a little boiling water on to a saucer, and sprinkle the saffron over it: add this plus the cardamom and the sugar to the milky concoction, and continue to stir like you mean it. After about 5 minutes, it should start to look pleasantly gloopy and thick. Take it off the stove, pour into pretty dishes and sprinkle with the nuts. You can enjoy it warm, or chill it.

We like it with some sharp stewed berry fruits, hot in winter or chilled in summer.

# ON TEA AND COFFEE

Seems the Arabs gave us coffee. Who knew?

The first beans to be harvested came out of East Africa: Ethiopia, to be precise. A visiting *Shadhiliyya Sufi sheikh*, Abu'l Hasan 'Ali ibn Umar, recognized its ability to promote wakefulness, and took the product home with him to Yemen in the middle of the fifteenth century, where it became known as *qahwah*. From there it spread to Saudi Arabia, Persia, and Turkey, and to Egypt, and thence to Italy and Europe. It reached the Americas only when demand became so high that more land was needed to cultivate the beans.

It has enjoyed a checkered career: having taken the Middle East by storm and spawned a thousand and one coffee houses (not to mention many of the sweetmeat accompaniments described in this chapter), it got itself a reputation for fostering rebellion and decadence. The coffee houses became so popular that they doubled as social centers and dens of apparent political iniquity, while in Iran and the Levant they became an important part of the culture, hosting story-telling and theatrical events. Not to mention smoking.

Anyway, the ruling bodies weren't happy and so they declared the *kahveh khaneh* (coffee house) taboo. In most countries this had little permanent effect, but in Iran the door was thrown open to a new invader from the northeast: tea. Coffee never fully recovered.

Tea culture is, of course, far older, but reached the Middle East via Russia only in the nineteenth century. Green tea was already consumed in the region, but black tea was virtually unknown. It quickly took hold in Iran, both in the hearts of the people and along the shores of the Caspian, where it is still grown to this day. And it spread across to Turkey and other countries. As trade routes increased and diversified, the popularity of green tea also spread: it ended up in Morocco in the eighteenth century, and the country remains possibly the world's biggest consumer of the commodity.

What follows is but a guide to the region's choicest beverages: there are endless permutations of spicing and ritual.

# ARABIC COFFEE

An acquired taste, but this is how coffee has been enjoyed for centuries in Arabic lands. *Qahwah* is traditionally served in baby cups without handles (*finjaan*), and involves much ceremony. Honored guests always go first, and coffee is poured with the left hand and proffered with the right.

SERVES 6–8
3 (standard tea-size) cups of water
   (3 x ⅔ cup/5fl oz/150ml )

2 tablespoons ground Arabic coffee
2 tablespoons ground cardamom
¼ teaspoon saffron strands (optional)

Boil the water in a pan, and then stir in the coffee. Bring back to a boil, and simmer for around 15 minutes. Put to one side, and allow to settle for a few minutes. Put the cardamom in a metal coffee pot (or another pan), and then pour the coffee carefully over it, ensuring that the grounds remain in the first pan (or you could just strain it). Finally add the saffron, bring gently back to a boil, and serve.

# TURKISH (OR GREEK) COFFEE

Now this is a very different proposition. Turkish or Greek coffee can only be made in the manner described below. You will need a Turkish coffee pot, which is like a one-or-two-cup sized saucepan with a tiny base, tall sides and a long handle; a very small regular pan would do at a pinch. If you do not have baby coffee cups, just use a normal teacup, and half-fill it.

1 (small, Turkish style) coffee cup of water
   (¼ –scant ⅓ cup/2–2½fl oz/50–75ml)

heaped teaspoon ground Greek or Turkish coffee
sugar, as required

Measure 1 cup of cold water per person into a Greek coffee pot. Add 1 teaspoon coffee per person. Plain coffee obviously requires nothing further, but if you like your coffee sweet, add 1 teaspoon sugar per person; if you like it very sweet, add 2 teaspoons per person. You will either have to agree on the degree of sweetness required, or repeat the exercise separately for each person. Mix the water, coffee, and sugar gently with a long-handled teaspoon, and then put it on the stove—the flame shouldn't be too high, but it should just lick the outside of the pot (if you are using electric, just put it on a very hot ring). It doesn't need constant stirring, but do not leave it unattended. If the coffee is allowed to boil over, or boils, subsides and then boils again, it will not be palatable. It takes just a few minutes to cook; the coffee will froth up the side of the pan; just as it reaches the rim, take it off the stove and pour into warmed cups. Serve the coffee with a glass of un-iced water on the side.

# BLACK TEA (PERSIAN STYLE)

Iranians drink tea all day, every day. Hard core—as in black, straight up. Tea is the language of hospitality and the currency of business. The Kurds and the Iraqis run a pretty close second in terms of tea consumption.

Nearly all households have a samovar, in which water is heated in a large boiler. Tea is made in a pot, which is rested on top of the samovar—the rising steam keeps it hot; a little thick, strong brew is poured from the pot into an *estekhan*, or tea glass, which is then topped up with water from the samovar, resulting in a mellow golden color. Water levels are topped up from time to time, and fresh tea leaves occasionally replace the stewed ones; the samovar can thus be kept running all day.

There are, of course, lots of different blends; apart from the homegrown variety, which is insufficient to cover home consumption, the favored tea is from Sri Lanka (Ceylon tea). It is either consumed plain, or flavored with Earl Grey or cardamom. There are variations—sometimes jasmine, cinnamon, or mint are mixed with the tea leaves, or more popularly saffron (said to make you laugh: I believe it works).

You will need 1 heaped teaspoon of your tea leaves of choice per 2 tea drinkers. Put the tea in your pot (a teapot with a built-in strainer/tea receptacle is ideal), and then pour boiling water over the leaves. Try and keep the pot hot—in Iran, a patent tea-stand with a candle underneath it is often used. Steep for around 5 minutes, and then half-fill the relevant number of tea glasses with the brew, then top them up with boiling water. Serve.* If you are offering a second round, top the pot up with some more boiling water. As the tea gets more stewed, you will need to add more and more water, and thus less and less black tea.

 Serve with *nabat* (rock candy or rock sugar) or Persian sugar polyhedrons, which are strangely resistant to instant melting, although they are water-soluble: sugar is rarely added to the tea, but rather held on the tongue and the tea then drunk through it.
Tea can also be served with fresh dates, *noghl* (sugar-coated nuts), or your choice of sweets.

# GREEN TEA

Afghans drink green tea by the bucketful. It is, of course, up there with blueberries and red wine on the antioxidant scale of goodness, and is a very refreshing drink.

To make it, you need to boil the leaves in water, 1 spoonful per person: use either a proper old-fashioned stove kettle or a metal teapot. Ginger is often added for extra winter warmth.

*Note*
On special occasions, green tea is enjoyed with *qaymaq*, which is thick and gloopy and very similar to clotted cream.

# MINT TEA

The Moroccans are noted for mint tea, which is green tea with mint in it. Great stuff after a heavy meal.

Once again green tea is boiled (in one of those fancy tea pots with a heavy flat bottom), and then fresh mint is shredded into the pot and it is taken off the heat. Sugar is spooned into individual glasses and the tea is poured over it, quite often from a great height.

# index

# further reading

This is rather more than a run-of-the-mill bibliography. During the evolution of this cookbook some of these books have been indispensable, others I have but lightly dipped into. Some I have simply read and enjoyed. But they are all highly recommended for anyone wishing to know more about the region and its cuisine.

## FOOD

Claudia Roden, *A New Book of Middle Eastern Food* (London, Penguin Books, 1968)—the undisputed doyenne of Middle Eastern food writers

Helen Saberi, *Noshe Djan* (London, Prospect Books, 1986)—remains unsurpassed on the subject of Afghan cooking

Margaret Shaida, *The Legendary Cuisine of Persia* (Interlink Books, 1992)—the first lady to write a Persian cookbook in English

Arto de Haruotunian, *Vegetarian Dishes from the Middle East* (Century Publishing Co, 1983)—respect for what was probably the first Middle Eastern vegetarian cookbook

Anissa Helou, *Modern Mezze* (London, Quadrille Publishing Ltd, 2007)—brilliant

Nevin Halici, *Sufi Cuisine* (London, Saqi, 2005)

Rodinson, Arberry and Perry, *Medieval Arab Cookery* (London, Prospect Books, 2001)—the most complete medieval work of reference on Arabic cuisine

Sally Butcher, *Persia in Peckham* (Prospect Books, 2007)—more of the same as this, with added meat and a lot more Iran thrown in

*Petits Propos Culinaires*, various authors (London, Prospect Books)—the collected papers of the Oxford Symposium, an incredibly useful source of food info (in the context of this book I specifically referred to issues 14 and 55 and the articles on *trahanas* by Charles Perry)

## TRAVEL

Daniel Metcalfe, *Out of Steppe* (Hutchinson, 2009)—delightfully eccentric and energetic English chap takes a warm and humorous look at vanishing lifestyles across Transoxiania

Michael Wood, *In the Footsteps of Alexander the Great* (London, BBC, 1997)

And all or any of the Bradt and Lonely Planet Guides: I sell and stock both and they both do the job.

## AFGHANISTAN

Jason Elliott, *An Unexpected Light*, (London, Picador, 1999)

Angelo Rasanayagam, *Afghanistan, A Modern History* (London, I.B. Tauris, 2003)

## IRAN

Jason Elliott, *Mirrors of the Unseen* (London, Picador, 2006)—a beautiful, lyrical look at this largely unknowable land

Michael Axworthy, *Iran, Empire of the Mind* (London, Penguin Books, 2007)—an amazing amount of historical stuff in one compact volume

John Simpson and Tira Shubart, *Lifting the Veil, Life in Revolutionary Iran* (London, Coronet Books, 1995)—a really, really well-written intro to Iran

Iraj Pezeshkzad, *My Uncle Napoleon* (New York, Modern Library Paperbacks, 2006—translated by Dick Davis, originally written in Farsi in the 1970s). Very funny.

## IRAQ

Barbara Nimri Aziz, *Swimming up the Tigris, Real Life Encounters with Iraq* (Florida University Press, 2007)

## TURKEY

Louis de Bernieres, *Birds Without Wings* (London, Vintage, 2005)

Jeremy Seal, *A Fez of the Heart* (London, Picador, 1996)

## EGYPT

Alaa Al Aswany, *The Yacoubian Building* (Cairo, The American University in Cairo Press, 2002)—what an ace read...

## KURDISTAN

Susan Meiselas, *Kurdistan, In the Shadow of History* (Chicago, University of Chicago Press, 1997)—very big, but beautiful

## LEBANON

*Lebanon Through Writers' Eyes*, ed. T. J. Gorton and A. Feghali Gorton (London, Eland Publishing, 2009)—a beautiful anthology

## THE MAGHREB

Paul Bowles, *Morocco* (Abrams, 1993)

Hisham Matar, *In the Country of Men* (London, Penguin, 2007)

## SYRIA

Fred H. Lawson, ed., *Demystifying Syria* SOAS Middle East Issues Series (London, Saqi Books, 2010)

## SAUDI ARABIA AND THE GULF STATES

Ham, Gordon, and Maxwell, *Arabian Peninsula* (London, Lonely Planet, 2004)—the whole kit and caboodle in one handy volume. Probably the most useful of the Lonely Planet series.

## CENTRAL ASIA

Peter Hopkirk, *The Great Game—the Struggle for Empire in Central Asia* (Kodansha Globe, 1990)

## RELIGION

*The Holy Qur'an*, translated by Abdullah Yusuf Ali (London, Wordsworth Editions, 2000)

Paul Kriwaczek, *In Search of Zarathustra, The First Prophet and the Ideas that Changed the World* (London, Orion, 2002)

Sir James Frazer, *The Golden Bough* (London, Wordsworth Edition (printed 1993), originally written 1922)

## LITERATURE

Peter Washington, ed., *Persian Poems* (London, Everyman, 2000)

Ferdowsi, *The Shahnameh* (London, Penguin, 2007—translated by Dick Davis, originally written a thousand years ago)

Stephen Mitchell, transl., *Gilgamesh* (London, Profile Books Ltd., 2004)

Kahlil Gibran, *The Prophet* (Arcturus Edition, 2007)

*Penguin Anthology of Classical Arabic Literature*, ed. Robert Irwin (London, Penguin, 2006)

## LANGUAGE

Any or all of the Lonely Planet phrasebooks as a starting point—they are unusual in offering phonetic assistance, meaning that you do not have to learn the alphabet in order to use them.

Follow up with any or all of the *Teach Yourself* guides (published by Hodder and Stoughton)—I taught myself to read and write Farsi using these and can vouch for them.

## MEDICINE AND HERBAL LORE

Dr. Sohrab Khoshbin, *Giahan Mojezegar (Miraculous Herbs)*(Tehran, Nashreh Salez, 2005)—this volume is in Farsi; the book is reputedly now available in English from the good doctor's Canadian website: www.drkhoshbin.com

V. Mozaffarian, Dictionary of *Iranian Plant Names: Latin, English, Persian* (Tehran, Farhang Moaser, 1996)

www.pfaf.org is the best online resource I have found with reference to plants and their uses

## GENERAL

*Saudi Aramco World Magazine*—check out their online resources at www.saudiaramcoworld.com.

And any or all of the Culture Shock guides.

## BLOGS

I rarely visit food-blogs but there are a couple I wholeheartedly recommend:

http://www.anissas.com/blog1/ —wherein Anissa Helou recounts her culinary exploits.

http://helengraves.co.uk/—which has little to do with Middle Eastern food and everything to do with Peckham food.

You can also visit the Veggiestan "tourist board" online at: www.veggiestan.com. You will find a lot of extra material there: outtakes, bloopers, quizzes, recipes, and trivia galore.

# acknowledgements

A book is but the product of a lifetime of encounters, culinary and otherwise, and thus the credits are potentially endless. But I will have a go.

Firstly some profound and very specific thank yous: to Emily Preece-Morrison, my editor, for her warm and informal approach, and to Anna, Rebecca, and the rest of the team at Anova. I am in awe of the photoshoot team: Valerie, who cooked it; Wei, who styled it; Yuki, who shot it; and Georgie, who tweaked it. You rock, ladies.

I owe a very big and heartfelt thank you to my agent, Veronique, for her faith and patience.

I must also acknowledge the input of all of my customers: the ones who like to talk about ingredients, the ones who like to test recipes, and the ones who just like to eat food. Trust me—you're all in here, one way or another. Having an emporium in multicultural Peckham, and having married into the Middle East, has opened up new vegetable vistas for me. Being a shopkeeper is the key to lots of doors, and that counter between you and the customer operates surprisingly frequently as a confessional. I have spent many a happy hour quizzing my customers on their dinner arrangements, and comparing recipes. I have similarly worn the local greengrocer down with incessant questions about some of his weirder ingredients.

And as for our wholesale customers ... Our chief business, run by my very business-like husband, is import and distribution, and we have customers from Syria, Palestine, Iraq, Afghanistan, Uzbekistan, Kashmir, Georgia, Turkey, Egypt, and Lebanon. I have been poking around in restaurant kitchens, quizzing startled customers in other shops, and talking to other (amused and bemused) shopkeepers. Fortunately, food is an international currency, and even the shyest housewife can usually be persuaded to lift the veil on her kitchen.

For my love of vegetables I believe I need to thank Great Uncle Don via my mother: it's amazing what a few well placed words over a plate of rutabaga can do for a nipper.

I probably ought to thank the people who taught me how to cook: my mother and grandmother, and then later Reg, Kim, the late Big Mike Koutas. And the lovely Jilly in Devon. Not forgetting my mother-in-law, who gave me a unique insight into the Persian kitchen.

Finally, I would like to thank all of my friends for their belief and support: not only the ones who tried out recipes and ate my food, but also the ones that were simply there. This includes my best friend (and husband) Jamshid: as he is a committed carnivore, this book has indeed been a trial for him.

Sally Butcher,
Peckham, 2012

First American edition published in 2012 by

INTERLINK BOOKS
An imprint of Interlink
Publishing Group, Inc.
46 Crosby Street
Northampton, Massachusetts 01060
www.interlinkbooks.com

Text © Sally Butcher, 2012
Design/Layout © Anova Books, 2012
Photography © Yuki Sugiura, 2012
Americanized text © Interlink
Publishing, 2012

*Commissioning editor:*
Emily Preece-Morrison
*Design concept:* Georgina Hewitt
*Cover design:* Julian D. Ramirez
*Photographer:* Yuki Sugiura
*Prop stylist:* Wei Tang
*Home economist:* Valerie Berry
*Layout:* Miranda Harvey
*Copy editor:* Caroline Curtis
*American edition editors:*
Leyla Moushabeck and Sara Rauch

ISBN: 978-1-56656-883-8

Library of Congress Cataloging-in-Publication data available

10 9 8 7 6 5 4 3 2 1

Printed and bound in China